Stewards of Grace

Eugene and Phyllis Grams

Rollin S. Grams

Stewards of Grace

A Reflective, Mission Biography
of Eugene and Phyllis Grams
in South Africa, 1951–1962

ROLLIN G. GRAMS

WIPF & STOCK · Eugene, Oregon

Wipf & Stock
An Imprint of Wipf and Stock Publishers
199 W. 8th Ave., Suite 3
Eugene, OR 97401
www.wipfandstock.com

ISBN 13: 978-1-60899-552-3

Manufactured in the U.S.A.

All scripture quotations in this book have been translated by the author (unless otherwise noted) from the Hebrew or Greek, using Biblia Hebraica Stuttgartensia, 4th ed. (Stuttgart: Deutsche Bibelgesellschaft, 1990) and Novum Testamentum Graece, Nestle-Aland 27th ed. (Stuttgart: Deutsch Bibelgesellschaft 1993).

For the supporters of mission work:
faithful in prayer,
joyful in giving,
and eager to hear the good report,
"Your God reigns!"
Second Corinthians 9.12–15

And for the grandchildren of
Eugene and Phyllis Grams:
Victoria, Brandon, and Michael;
David, James, and Rachel
Deuteronomy 4.7–9

Contents

Foreword

THE STORY TOLD HERE, about Eugene and Phyllis Grams, is a story of missions in the mid-twentieth century. It is a partial biography of their lives, from their childhood in the United States of America through the first decade of six that they spent in ministry in South Africa. It is also a reflective biography in the sense that, at several points throughout the story, I explore related matters a little more deeply in capsules, with an eye towards the historical context and a theology of mission and Christian discipleship. Readers only interested in the Grams' story will find it possible to skip these capsules, while readers interested in exploring the history and practice of missions, mission theology, and discipleship through their story can begin with the brief reflections that I have offered. Mostly, however, I have simply told this part of my parents' story.

The biography of Eugene and Phyllis Grams is also about third generation Pentecostalism, largely in the Assemblies of God. As presented here, their story is a negotiation of the strengths and weaknesses of this tradition, to which they were wholly committed but critically engaged. I myself avoid much critical comment on the issues raised.

While Pentecostalism is an essential part of the story, my hope is that all Christian readers, not only Pentecostals, will find this book useful for reflection and encouraging for Christian discipleship. Most Christians in Africa, no matter what their church affiliation, have to deal with what in the West is more often compartmentalized as Pentecostal. In my view, however, the Christianity of Africa and many other parts of the world will find the issues raised here very relevant.

Gene and Phyllis Grams obediently followed calls from God to ministry in Africa that they received while still children. Their work in South Africa began in the early 1950s when they were but twenty and twenty-one years old and continues to the time of the writing of this book. Together, they were involved with numerous ministries over the years: evangelism, church planting, children's ministry, women's ministry, men's ministry, denominational administration, healing, deliverance, advocating justice, befriending the poor, formal and informal education, establishing Bible schools, pastoring churches, and living the Christian life against the grain of society and despite the obstacles that they faced. Readers interested in such ministries, in baptistic,[1] Pentecostal, and/or Assemblies of God ministry, and in South Africa should find this story exciting, interesting, challenging, and inspiring.

The story of Eugene and Phyllis Grams is a story of one way to live justly amidst the social injustices of apartheid—the policy and practice of racial separation and inequality in South Africa. It is one way to live missionally before the needs of the world. It is one way to affirm Jesus' lordship in territories held by demonic power and witchcraft. It is one way to hold on to hope in a suffering world. It is one way to live faithfully to a call to ministry when circumstances and human authorities and institutions make obedience difficult. It is one way of living in the purpose and power of God.

My parents' lives as missionaries in South Africa are deeply etched into my own theology, ministry, and life. As a Biblical scholar, I find that my reading of Scripture is all the clearer for the faith that they have lived. As an Anabaptist,[2] I find that my Pentecostal upbringing has taught me

---

1. By "baptistic" I mean that church tradition that holds to the notion that the church is a gathered community of believers. They are not born into Christian faith by virtue of their parents' faith or geographical context. They determine by their own conviction to attach themselves to Christian community and seek to follow Jesus in radical discipleship. Thus baptistic churches practice believers' baptism, emphasize missions, and reject the idea of a state church. Free churches, Baptists, Mennonites, Amish, Pentecostals, Brethren, and a number of others may be described with this broad term.

2. Anabaptists (Radical Reformers) formed one of the three wings of the Protestant Reformation in the sixteenth-century. It was baptistic, in the sense explained in footnote one, and some of the early adherents to the movement experienced charismatic phenomena. As Stuart Murray, *Biblical Interpretation*, states, "Grebel, Mantz, and Blaurock were all reported to have had visions. Hans Hut relied strongly on prophetic dreams and visions, as did Thurinian Anabaptists generally. Among the more extreme was a group of about forty imprisoned Anabaptists in Thurinia who spent their time singing, dancing, and experiencing visions, before confronting their judges with joy and peace and going to execution 'as if in a trance' . . . . Jacob Hutter claimed a miraculous dimension to his ministry as an authentication of his calling . . . . There were prophetic processions and prophetic utterances" (133). George Williams refers to an area in Germany where some, "excited by mass hysteria, experience healings, glossolalia [speaking in tongues], contortions and other manifestations of a camp-meeting revival" (quoted in Murray,

well what it means to live in the tradition of the Radical Reformation. As a seminary professor, I realize from my life as a "missionary kid" that theology should not be abstracted from the contexts in which it is formed (and performed) or from the purposes that it should serve. As a missionary in my own right, I have been challenged by their lives to live faithfully before the Lord. As a disciple of Jesus Christ, I have learned from my parents' ministry that the empowering presence of the Spirit is as much a part of life in Christ as right belief and righteous living. And as a minister of the Gospel I have realized from them that ministry is not about being leaders but about being stewards of God's grace.

For me, the theme that emerges from their lives is one of the keys to a theology of mission—perhaps the key. This key can be found in Paul's first chapter of Ephesians: the mission of God is "for the praise of his glory and grace." I offer in this biography a story that illustrates what it means to be stewards of God's grace that leads to the praise of his glory. My hope in telling part of their testimony of God's glory and grace in the rural villages and squalid townships of apartheid South Africa is that readers anywhere will begin to comprehend what is the breadth and length and height and depth of God's glory and grace.

I am grateful to my parents, who helped immensely in writing this book. Their story simply had to be told, even if only in part. They are truly stewards of God's grace who have lived for the praise of God's glory. This book could not have been written without their discussion of the events recorded or their newsletters from 1951 through 1962. Readers should know that my father's precise memory of dates and particular details often provided fun in the family as we tried to find a day many years in the past about which he could not remember some detail. Without his razor sharp memory, some details would have had to be omitted from this work.

Also, I could not have written this book as it stands without the help that I found in the archives of the Pentecostal movement made

---

p. 134). 'The *Anonymous Biography of David Joris* refers to speaking in tongues (134). Pilgrim Marpeck testifies to some people who were raised from the dead after being killed. He states that some were still alive to give their testimony (134). Murray further avers: "That the Anabaptists' descendants have tended to err on the side of literalism and to denigrate the role of the Holy Spirit, in both their own experience and their understanding of their heritage, is a result of the move towards literalism and away from reliance on the Spirit which occurred in the movement's second and third generations (a familiar pattern in revival movements)" (136).

available on-line by the Flower Pentecostal Heritage Center.[3] I have also consulted with several others who have known about these events, and I have relied on my own memory of South Africa and my own work as a researcher and Biblical scholar.

My wife, Wendy, helped tremendously in the editing process. I would like to thank her and our children for the sacrifice that they made while I devoted time to my writing at their expense. I offer the work back to them as a reminder of our rich heritage and an encouragement to pursue their own calling to be radical disciples of our Lord, Jesus Christ. I also wish to thank friends for their encouragement as I wrote, including Ian Randall, Bob Roberts, and Reid Satterfield, who read early drafts of the manuscript.

Rollin G. Grams

3. See http://ifphc.org/.

1

Under the Thorn Tree

The LORD will keep your going out and your coming in from
now on and forevermore. (Psalm 121.8)[1]

THE CHILDREN WERE OVERJOYED at the thought of a picnic away
from their squalid township with its little cement block houses, their
corrugated tin roofs baking in the African sun, bits of rubbish blowing
along the dirt roads, and the uncertainties of life that poverty daily deliv-
ers. "What is a picnic?" they had asked. This was a new idea to them. Ed
Louton and his older sister Phyllis had grown up taking picnics on Belle
Isle near East Detroit, Michigan in the United States of America. They
told the children that they were going to go to the countryside, and there
would be lots of interesting food, places to run, singing, and games.

Ed, Phyllis and their new African friend, Clifford Dammie, trans-
ported thirty children to the picnic site a few miles outside Mokopane,
the African township that lay beside the white town of Potgietersrus.
Most of the children had never driven in a car before, and Ed had only
recently learned how to drive his father's car. The Louton family had
settled in this small town just a few months earlier as first-time missionaries to South Africa. The year was 1951. Potgietersrus was about
one hundred and seventy miles north of Johannesburg on the road to
Rhodesia and just thirty-six miles to the south of the larger town of
Pietersburg,[2] which was situated at 4,035 feet above sea level and 1,000

---

1. Scripture passages in this book have been translated by the author (except
for the reference to the King James Version) from the Hebrew or Greek, using *Biblia
Hebraica Stuttgartensia*, 4th ed. (Stuttgart: Deutsche Bibelgesellschaft, 1990) and *Novum
Testamentum Graece*, Nestle-Aland 27th ed. (Stuttgart: Deutsch Bibelgesellschaft 1993).

2. Mokopane is pronounced "Ma-ko-pah-nee." The town of Potgietersrus is now
also called Mokopane. Pietersburg is now called "Polokwane" ("Po-lo-kwah-nee"),

feet higher than Potgietersrus. Both of these northern Transvaal towns are dry and dusty. The hot climate of this region of South Africa does, however, give way to luscious, green, forested areas as the elevation changes to still higher heights not far from Pietersburg. Still, the sights, sounds, and smells of their new home in Africa were completely different from the large, American city that the Loutons had so recently left behind.

The Mokopane location was named for the people of the area. The name "location" or "township" was given to areas set aside for non-white residents that sprang up around white settlement areas. The largest of these in South Africa was "Soweto" ("*South Western Townships*") on the West Rand near Johannesburg. These townships sprang up as service communities to the white towns and cities.

Ed and Phyllis had initiated a ministry to children and youth in the Mokopane location. On Friday nights, they would begin to sing and walk through the streets of the location. Children playing in the streets and young people about their own ages would hear them, leave what they were doing and follow them to the church building, where they would hold a service.

Their parents, Albert and Louise, also had a ministry in the surrounding villages. The whole Louton family, including little, two year old Joy, would drive out on a Saturday or Sunday to a nearby village and begin to sing under the trees until people gathered, and then they would hold an open air service. The Africans loved to sing, to move with the music, to wave their hands. They could sing the same song repeatedly, and they could continue singing for a full hour. In this regard, church meetings were quite different from many Western services, with their liturgies, recited prayers, hymnal singing, and so forth. Such worship was formal, even logical, but all too subdued for a continent of people who sang as much with their bodies as with their voices, were by and large an oral culture, and did not concern itself with form. As Pentecostals, however, the Loutons had little concern for formal worship too, and they saw extended times of worship as the mark of spiritual fervor. Pentecostal worship, itself influenced by the black church in America, was a natural fit for Africa.

On Sundays, the Loutons would again go out to the villages to transport whoever wished to the church service in the Mokopane location.

Johannesburg is now "Gauteng," and the country of Rhodesia is now "Zimbabwe."

These were in many ways happy days. The missionaries were appreciated and well received, and they in turn enjoyed the people in the villages and locations. The people in these more remote areas had not yet fully felt the bite of apartheid as it was taking hold, law by law, of the country.

As Ed ferried the Sunday School children in his father's Suburban to the picnic, he was just beginning a lifetime of ministry in this country. He was all of eighteen years old, adaptable, exuberant, and, most of all, he loved the people. He quickly learned the language of Sepedi, came to understand the culture, and would, many years later, become an instructor in missions at the Africa School of Missions in Nelspruit.

The picnic that day was highly unusual, if not illegal. Since 1948, South Africa was settling into the social and political cement of apartheid (meaning "separateness"). The government was industriously passing laws for racial separation in intricate detail. The children might not have been aware of any such laws, but an immense wall of legislative acts was dividing the country into color zones. Beaches, parks, benches, drinking fountains, toilets, places to live, who could marry whom, schools, busses, trains—the list was endless to establish "separateness" between the races. The British had practiced such separation throughout their Empire, including in the Union of South Africa, but the Afrikaner government in the country turned apartheid into a fine art—and legal system. These were now the days in South Africa when the Nationalist Party was in power. Some three years before the Loutons arrived in the country, the Nationalist leader Daniel F. Malan had led his party to victory in the national elections.

CAPSULE: APARTHEID

In the Afrikaans Dutch Reformed Church, apartheid was law and even doctrine. In 1857, the General Synod ruled that blacks should worship separately from whites on account of the church's weaker brethren's wishes. Over time, the Bible was used to back up this view. God had separated the races that had attempted unity at the time of the Tower of Babel: what God had set apart, let no man bring together. As the Afrikaners trekked inland in the 1800s, they saw themselves as the Israelites entering the promised land. The Israelites long ago had confronted the Canaanite inhabitants in battle for the land; now the Afrikaners met the African tribes in battle. Were the Canaanites not descendants of Ham, who had been cursed by his father, Noah? The victories of these new

Israelites settling Canaan only confirmed that they were God's chosen people to dwell in this land. Just as God had warned the Israelites to remain separate from the Canaanites, so God's people in Africa should remain separate too.

Since the Nationalist Party took charge of the government in 1948, several laws had been enacted to establish apartheid in the country. In 1949, the Mixed Marriage Act made marriage between whites and blacks illegal. That year also saw passage of the Population Registration Act, which classified the races of South Africa into three groups. English speakers were grouped with the Afrikaners by virtue of their European ancestry, while the various African tribes were grouped together as natives or Africans. Another major group under apartheid was the so-called Coloured race, a mixture of races. It at first included Indians and other Asians, but they would later be distinguished as a separate group.

The largest grouping by far was the "Bantu," or native Africans, who belonged to a number of different tribes. While different areas of the country would have different percentages of these "races"—more Indians and Zulus in Natal, more Coloureds in the Cape, more Basotho in the Orange Free State, more Xhosas in the Eastern Cape, for example—each larger racial group was well represented almost everywhere, including in the northern Transvaal. However, another law, the Group Areas Act, permitted the government to designate certain areas of the country as regions restricted for use by a given race. The Illegal Squatters Act of 1951 permitted the government to relocate people from urban areas. And the Abolition of Passes Act, despite its title, required blacks to carry identity books—passes—at all times. In 1951, the government began to create "homelands" for each tribal group that were intended eventually to separate African tribes from each other and remove them completely from white-ruled South Africa.

Potgietersrus bore a name that told the story of apartheid itself. It symbolized the separation of races and the domination of the races by the white settlers. The town had been named for Hendrikus Potgieter, a commandant who was killed in the region in 1854 when his forces engaged an Ndebele chief by the name of Mokopane. His forces had been ambushed, and so they pursued Mokopane's warriors, laying siege to them in a cave. Most of the three thousand warriors died of thirst, and the rest were killed when they tried to break free.

Nobody in 1951 could have guessed that apartheid would one day be overturned. The Afrikaners were still advancing against the Bantu, no longer with their weapons but now with their laws. Yet just forty-two years later, in 1994, Nelson Mandela would become South Africa's president, and Potgietersrus would be renamed Mokopane.

In 1951, Mandela was already working towards that end as one of the key leaders in the African National Congress. The ANC had been organized in 1912 by various African leaders in order to protect the rights and freedoms of all Africans. In 1950, Mandela was elected to the ANC's National Executive Committee, which was reshaping the ANC into a more aggressive form of opposition to the Nationalist Party's apartheid agenda. In response to the Nationalist Party's victory in 1948, the ANC in the following year called for full citizenship of all South Africans over against separate development. They called for voting privileges, land re-distribution, trade unions, and free education for all. To attain this, they advocated strikes, boycotts, non-co-operation, and civil disobedience. In 1952, Mandela became the Volunteer-in-Chief to travel the country and organize people into a mass civil disobedience to defy the injustice of the apartheid laws.

But what would the picnicking children have known that day in 1951 about all this separation of the races? Neither did Ed, Clifford, or Phyllis have politics on their minds. They had simply planned a picnic outside the African township, outside white Potgietersrus: two white American adults, one African adult, and some thirty African children. The air was full of excitement, with the joyful singing of the children as they travelled into the countryside. Some of the children sang songs learned in their Sunday School classes in their native Ndebele and Sepedi tongues, and Phyllis and Ed joined in as best they could. Both of them had lovely voices, and the exuberant singing of the children was irresistible.

After leaving the first group of children and Phyllis at the picnic site, Ed and Clifford returned to Potgietersrus to bring the food and the rest of the children from the township in the Suburban. The children ran higgledy-piggledy along the riverbank, climbing rocks, and trying to kick over the two or three foot high anthills that dotted the landscape. The picnic already seemed a success, but Phyllis suddenly felt the great responsibility she had as the only adult present with these children. There seemed to be no danger from the river, which was at this time of year more of a riverbed with a little stream running in it. However, she had already heard of the flash floods that would suddenly swell these African rivers downstream without a cloud in the sky and sweep people away to their deaths. Or perhaps one of the little ones might slip and slide down the rocky embankment and injure herself. As Phyllis surveyed the timeless kopjes (hills) that emerged like little heads popping up through the veldt (grassland), she remembered a story about the leopards and poisonous snakes that were there. She had not yet become familiar with the beat of life on this strangely wonderful continent. In truth, they were fairly safe, since most of the truly dangerous African animals had retreated to more remote areas and thrived only in the game parks—except for the snakes. There were a variety of deadly adders and cobras, as well as mambas and boomslangs. Phyllis shuddered at the thought.

Just then, she noticed that the children were chasing what seemed to her to be butterflies. They were actually ants that emerged from the anthills with wings at this time each year to fly away and begin a new colony. The children caught them, plucked off their wings, pinched off their heads, and popped them into their mouths. Phyllis was aghast. She had never seen anything like this, and she did not know that eating flying ants was a time-honored tradition all over Africa that was not at all dangerous. They were tasteless: eating flying ants is all about texture— bush popcorn, without the salt and butter, and a little wigglier.

Phyllis decided that she had best restore some semblance of order. She called to the children and had them sit in the shade of a large acacia tree. "Let's sing," she said. After a few songs, Ed and his friend had not yet arrived, and so Phyllis told the children a Bible story. She was just finishing when the rest arrived, and the prepared food was set out. After the picnic, the children chased the flying ants once again while the adults sat in the shade of the large acacia tree and watched them at play.

This part of South Africa, with its warm, sunny climate, grows some very different foliage from what the Loutons had known back in Detroit, Michigan. It is a good climate for planting bougainvillea and poinsettias, and these, along with the beautiful jacaranda trees, give delightful color and scent to the town. But these were not indigenous plants. Here in the countryside, the indigenous plants of the northern Transvaal dotted the veldt. Potgietersrus is warm enough and far enough to the north, very near the tropic of Capricorn, for marula and baobab trees to be seen in the veldt. The marula tree's overripe fruit is the wild animals' beer, and they love it. A staggering elephant that had had its fill of marula nuts once sat on a car! The swollen trunk and root-like branches of the baobab tree, seldom in leaf, give it the appearance of being stuck into the ground upside down. But the most common tree is the fever tree, also known as the thorn tree or acacia, whose wood had once been used by the Israelites to build the ark of the covenant during their wanderings in the Sinai. The acacia is said to be a symbol of refuge, since its branches extend far out from its trunk and form an inviting umbrella in the African sun. Its little leaves help it to survive very dry conditions; a larger leaf would quickly dry out and wilt. The acacia offers more than refuge from the sun, however; it is capable of providing food for animals, birds, and insects, and yet its long thorns give it protection from some animals.

Ed and Phyllis noticed a plaque on the thorn tree under which they were sitting. They stood up and walked over to the trunk, being careful to avoid a low-hanging branch with its three-inch thorns. "David Livingstone slept here," Ed read out loud. Dr. Livingstone, the famous African explorer and missionary, had begun his ministry in South Africa. He had arrived at Kuruman in the northern Cape Province in 1841 to join the mission work begun by Dr. Peter Moffat. Not long afterwards, Livingstone married Moffat's daughter, Mary. His explorations drove him ever onwards into the heart of Africa, gaining him worldwide fame. What lay ahead for these young missionaries in South Africa who had arrived 110 years later?

Phyllis remembered her own call to mission work in Africa thirteen years earlier, when she was only seven years old. She had been sick with the chicken pox and, feeling truly miserable, she asked her mother to pray for her. Louise was a woman of prayer, but at that moment she was busy with housework. She looked at her little girl, thought a moment, and then said, "Phyllis, you are old enough to pray for yourself. Why don't you pray this time and ask God to help you." So she did, and while praying she had a vision of herself teaching black children under a tree of a sort that she had never seen in Detroit—a tree that spread its thorny branches out wide across a dry, grassy plain.

While on the picnic, Phyllis realized that she was experiencing the vision she had had when a little girl. This was a calling she would never doubt, even if the cost seemed beyond bearing at times. She had already left her fiancé, Eugene Grams, in America. The notion of "great cost" and mission work went together, and not yet one year into her new life in missions she had felt it deeply. Gene was at that time training for ministry at Central Bible Institute (CBI)[3] in Springfield, Missouri. He and Phyllis had talked of mission work some day, but the route seemed far too winding to Phyllis. Gene still had one year of education at CBI, and then he would have to pastor a church for several years to gain ministerial experience before he could be appointed for mission work with the Assemblies of God. If he were appointed as a missionary, he would then need to travel around the Midwest to raise mission support. Phyllis had seen her parents go through the lengthy and agonizing process of raising funds and noted that it had taken them over three years. They had come to South Africa without appointment by a mission board as, in those days, the Foreign Mission Board of the Assemblies of God was not taking any applicants over the age of thirty-five. For Phyllis, the long process towards mission appointment with Gene was too long, and so she departed for Africa with her parents and her younger brother and sister.

Just before embarking on the Queen Mary in New York harbor, Phyllis wrote an agonizingly painful letter to Gene. She loved him very much, she said, but she could not wait for him to become a missionary. Her opportunity had come to go to South Africa, and she was going to take it whatever the cost. She felt God's call to Africa could not be delayed and so, she concluded, she was leaving with her parents on the ship that very day. Her last words were the most painful: she would not hold Gene to their engagement and would return the ring he had worked most of the summer to buy two years earlier. With tears in her eyes, she posted the letter and resolutely made her way on board.

While still en route to England, Phyllis celebrated her 20th birthday on the 17th of April, 1951. In England, the Loutons saw that the country was still struggling to recover from the Second World War, which had ended nearly six years earlier. They did not realize at the time that the British Empire, weakened by the war, was losing control of and influence in its colonies. Despite its success against the Afrikaans in the second Boer War in 1899–1902, the United Kingdom was now watching the Afrikaans Nationalist Party take control, and in 1961 South Africa would withdraw from the British Commonwealth. The Loutons' move to the northern Transvaal would place them squarely in one of the more Afrikaans sections of South Africa, but they could still get along quite

3. Central Bible Institute is now called Central Bible College.

well with their English. Most Afrikaners were bilingual, and a number of the Africans knew some English. People, especially the Africans, were accustomed to learning a little in different languages and to listening to someone translate. But as English speakers, and as Americans, the Loutons were not seen as "allies" to the Afrikaner vision for South Africa, and as missionaries to the Africans they were understood to be helping the Africans rather than supporting the Afrikaner cause.

After about a week in England, the Louton family took a Union Castle passenger ship to Cape Town, South Africa. On board, they were amazed to find that they were travelling with some other missionaries, the John Richards family, who were headed not only to South Africa but to the very same region. The two missionary families arrived in Cape Town on the 10th of May, 1951.

"Yes," thought Phyllis, sitting under the acacia tree near Potgietersrus a few months after her arrival in the country, "I am where God has called me. And I will give my life to serving Him on this continent." She would, too, in a ministry devoted mostly to children and women in the Transvaal, Orange Free State, and Cape Province. Her last trip to South Africa would be fifty-seven years later.

Phyllis's parents' desire to become missionaries in South Africa was just that—a deep desire to serve God in missions. There were no voices from God and no visions, just a heartfelt certainty that this was the right thing to do. Albert Louton had pastored an independent Pentecostal church in East Detroit (today East Pointe) for several years. Prior to that, he had been involved with two of his brothers-in-law in starting another Pentecostal church in Detroit, now known as Christian Trinity Assembly of God. Christian Trinity would be the main supporting church for the Loutons over the years to come in South Africa. Albert and Louise were part of a Pentecostal movement that saw missions as the purpose and priority of the church in the remaining days before Jesus returned. God's pouring out His Spirit in "these last days" was not simply for deeper spiritual experiences but also—indeed, more so—for empowering the church to fulfill the great commission. Either one went as a missionary or one worked to support missionaries. They wanted to go.

Phyllis's maternal grandmother, Theresa (Oster) Rettinger, had often spoken of an unfulfilled call to Africa that she believed lay upon her life when she was a young woman in the Slavonian region of Austria-

Hungary (now in Croatia). Her Lutheran pastor in the village of Selište,[4] Slavonia, must have spoken about missions to Africa too, for he too felt such a call. Sadly, Theresa believed that the grief her family faced so many times was the result of her not obeying this call.

Theresa's husband, Jakob Rettinger, had been the co-owner of a food store in Slavonski Brod after the family had moved there and before he escaped the region to avoid being called back into military service: war was brewing in the Balkans in 1913. He had served in the Austro-Hungarian army, even as a guard at the palace in Vienna for a time, but he had no interest in being called back into military service. As it happened, he left just in time: the First World War erupted when Archduke Franz Ferdinand and his wife, Sophie, were assassinated in Bosnia on the 28th of June, 1914. Many other German families from the region had left for America over the previous years, and so Jakob determined to do so as well. Leaving, however, was not easy, as by this time men were already being conscripted. He could not travel with his family, but once he had left, the authorities would be glad for his family to leave rather than have no provider for them in the country. So he left on his own one autumn day as though he were simply on one of his business trips. He boarded a train headed to the coast with nothing but his briefcase. Nobody stopped him to ask where he was going, and he kept travelling until he arrived in Detroit, Michigan.

Jakob's first job in Detroit was in a cheese factory. After sharing his Slavonian recipes for cheese, he was promptly fired by the unscrupulous owners. Even so, he managed to save up enough money to send for his family. Theresa and her children Adam, Louise, Theresa, and Jack arrived at Ellis Island, New York on the 14 January, 1914.

In addition to his military service in the Engineers Corp. of the Austrian Army and his attempts at business, Jakob Rettinger had been active in Christian service. He was much better suited for ministry than business. As a young man, he travelled to various villages as a colporteur

---

4. The village is now called "Velimirovac" (pronounced Veli-meer-o-vats) and is located on the outskirts of the lovely Slavonian town of Našice (pronounced Na-she-tsa) in Croatia. The pastor was Karl Friedrich Büsse, and this story of his desire to go to Africa comes from an on-line history: Barwich, *Welimirowatz*. The history states that Büsse "dreamt of going to Africa to witness for Christ." His dates in the village are not clear, but he would have been there in the 1890s when the Oster and Rettinger families were part of the same Lutheran church. See http://www.hrastovac.net/Slavonia/Welemirowatz2.htm (accesses 19 September, 2009).

for the British and Foreign Bible Society, selling Bibles to any who were interested in purchasing them at affordable prices. Catholicism at the time was not favorably disposed to Bibles being made available to any but the clergy, and in one village he was actually run out of town while being pelted with stones.

As a businessman, he had nothing but trouble. He had taken over his father-in-law's business in the village. Adam Oster had built up a good village store in of Selište. But his son-in-law was in the habit of extending credit to families who could not pay for the food and household items that the shop stocked. When the store burnt down in a fire that also destroyed the barn and a number of their farm animals, the Rettingers moved to Slavonski Brod to start life again, leaving family, friends, and two little graves behind. Slavonski Brod was on the Sava River, where Croatia and Bosnia met. In this larger city, Jakob joined with a Jewish partner to have another try at running a store. But after just a few years in Brod, with war brewing, the Rettingers left for America.

The family continued to struggle in their new homeland. Apart from losing his employment at the cheese factory, the Rettinger's oldest son, Adam, was killed when a small airplane flew too low over their fishing boat on the Detroit River. The young man and his friend were killed, and Jakob could only recognize his son's body by one of his toes.

As the Lutheran church where they lived proved to be quite different from what they had known in Europe, the Rettingers joined a German Baptist church in East Detroit. Jakob was appointed an elder. But one day, while praying, he began to speak in tongues in a language he did not know, whether some human speech or that of angels.[5] When

---

5. Scriptural passages used to interpret such experiences include: "And they were all filled with the Holy Spirit and began to speak with different tongues as the Spirit was enabling them to do so" (Acts 2.4); "And the believers from the circumcision group who had come with Peter were amazed, for the gift of the Holy Spirit had been poured out even over the Gentiles, for they were hearing them speaking with tongues and exalting God" (Acts 10.45–46); "And when Paul laid hands on them, the Holy Spirit came upon them, and they were speaking with tongues and prophesying" (Acts 19.6); "But you are yourselves the body of Christ and members of its parts that God placed in the church: first apostles, second prophets, third teachers, then those exercising power, then those with gifts of healing, those helping, those administering, then those speaking in various tongues" (1 Cor 12.27–28); "Do all have gifts of healing? Do all speak in tongues? Do all interpret?" (1 Cor 12.30); "If I speak in the tongues of men and of angels, but I do not have love, I have become ringing bronze or a clanging cymbal" (1 Cor. 13.1); "Love never fails; but should there be prophecies, they shall pass away; or tongues, they shall cease; or knowledge, it shall pass away" (1 Cor 13.8); "Now I want you all to speak in

he shared his spiritual experience with others at the church, he was excommunicated. That is how the Rettinger family became Pentecostals.

Phyllis remembered her grandfather as one of the kindest men she had ever known, and she often spent time with him and with her grandmother, Theresa, who lived downstairs in the same house while she was growing up.

Phyllis's grandparents were a calm and stable presence in the midst of a sometimes tumultuous Louton home. Louise had a nervous breakdown when Phyllis and Ed were still young. But the happiness Phyllis knew with her grandparents was partly shattered when Jakob slipped on ice while trying to catch a tram. He hit his head on the ground and, while he lived for a number of years afterwards, the injury that he suffered to his brain left him somewhat demented and with a changed personality.

If the Rettinger family was just the sort that one might expect to produce a missionary somewhere in the family tree, the Louton family was not. When Louise Rettinger met Albert Louton sometime in the mid-1920s, she was working for his older brother, Floyd. Louise kept the financial books for Floyd's dry-cleaning business in Detroit. Albert and Floyd were two of fourteen children that had been born to William Bleven ("Blev") and Willie Ann (Rucker) Louton on a farm near Pearcy, Arkansas. The Loutons were poor cotton farmers with a family history of moving west, generation by generation, from South Carolina to Alabama to Mississippi to Arkansas during the 1800s. Albert was a twin in the middle of fourteen children. He remembered having to wear his sister's clothes until he was about seven years old because the family was so poor. Once he received a sore bottom after riding a horse bareback too long in a dress! When he reached sixteen years of age, he and an-

---

tongues, yet preferably to prophesy: the one who prophecies is greater than the one speaking with tongues, unless someone interprets, so that the church might be edified. But now, brothers, if I came to you speaking with tongues, how will I benefit you unless I speak to you with a revelation or with knowledge or with a prophecy or with a teaching?" (1 Cor 14.5–6); "I give thanks to God: I speak in tongues more than all of you" (1 Cor 14.8); "In the Law it is written, 'By foreign tongues and by the lips of others will I speak to this people, and they will not even listen to me in this way,' says the Lord. Tongues, then, are a sign not for those who believe but for those who do not believe, while prophecy is not for those who disbelieve but for those who do believe. If, then, the whole church has come together and everybody speaks in tongues, and were those who have no experience or belief to enter, will they not say that you are insane?" (1 Cor 14.21); "So then, my brothers, be zealous to prophesy and do not forbid speaking in tongues" (1 Cor 14.39).

other brother hopped a train headed for Oklahoma, where they worked on a ranch as cowboys for about two years. Then Albert followed his brother, Floyd, to Michigan. And that is how a poor, Southern, cowboy-turned-dry-cleaner met a cultured, German girl from the Croatian part of Austria-Hungary.

And that is also how a rough, tough, nominal Christian young man met a gentle, cultured, strongly Christian young woman. When Albert showed an interest in Louise, she told him that she would not have anything to do with him unless he became a Christian. Albert had some exposure to a Methodist church in his early years. His mother was probably a believer. Albert's ties to the Christian faith were not at first very strong, not even after a decision to follow Christ in a Christian and Missionary Alliance Church in Detroit. A few years later, when he worked as a milkman delivering milk from door to door with a horse-drawn van, a woman on his route encouraged him to attend Bethesda Missionary Temple, a Pentecostal church in Detroit that was pastored by Mrs. Myrtle Beall.

Twenty years later, in the late 1940s, this church would become involved in an aberrant Pentecostal teaching called the "Latter Rain Revival."[6] Practices associated with this teaching involved passing out spiritual gifts and direction for life—even marriage—to people who came from far and wide. Stenographers would write out the prophecies as they were delivered by the church's prophets and then give them to the expectant people. One person even changed his fiancé simply because someone prophesied that he should marry an unknown woman in the worship service. Others claimed to have the gift of casting out demons believed to be beleaguering Christians. A common demon that was cast out was the so-called demon of smoking. It was at this time that the church left the Assemblies of God and followed its own path, remaining independent to this day. The Assemblies of God came to denounce the teaching that Christians could be possessed by demons, although such a teaching has persisted in certain charismatic contexts. But the Loutons left Bethesda before the church took this direction and never themselves held to such a teaching on the basis that Scripture says nothing of the sort.

---

6. See James 5:7–8 in the *King James Version* for this language. The Latter Rain movement was officially opposed by the Assemblies of God General Council of 1949 (resolution #7).

For Louise, being a Christian had nothing to do with merely going to church; to be a Christian meant committing one's life wholeheartedly to Jesus Christ, walking in step with the Spirit, and serving God to the utmost all one's days. While this would come to be Albert's commitment also, he was decidedly not fully signed up when he and Louise were married on the 19ᵗʰ of October, 1929.

Albert's embrace of Christianity—and eventually Pentecostalism—did not smooth out his rough edges completely, and he remained an interesting mixture of seemingly impossible alternatives the rest of his life. A Southerner born and bred, he lived in Michigan to the far north and then in South Africa; a person in whom was ingrained the conviction that black people were inferior, whose ancestors had fought for the South in the Civil War, but who, incredibly, became a missionary to black Africa; a nominal Christian who became a holy roller; and a Christian in the holiness tradition whose temper kept almost everyone on edge around him much of the time, while his laugh could be infectious. At his funeral in Pietersburg in 1985, many Africans and Coloureds rose to speak of his kindness and love for them through his thirty-four years of service in the northern Transvaal, and it was all true. But there, in the Pietersburg cemetery, lay a cowboy who owned a pistol, a missionary who loved the blacks with whom he worked but who could at times treat them very roughly, a Christian who once poured a gallon of milk on the dairy floor because it was sour and nobody would exchange it, a minister of the Gospel who once threatened to fight another missionary who had done him a great wrong, a tough talking man who preached the Gospel of God's grace—and on and on the amazing stories of Albert Louton go.

So it was that Theresa Rettinger's hope of being a missionary to Africa—a hope that flickered in her heart while she was still in a small, German village in Croatia around 1900—came to fruition in her daughter's and grandchildren's lives in 1951. Here, sitting under a thorn tree where the renowned missionary David Livingstone had once stopped, Ed and Phyllis were ministering to African children.

Phyllis and Ed began to clear up from the picnic while the African children continued to play. Phyllis looked at her younger brother. "You love it here, don't you?" "Yes," he replied, "this is my calling too." At seventeen, he was not in Africa simply because his parents were missionaries. He had himself come as a missionary in his own right, and he is there to this day.

Apart from Phyllis's direct call to Africa at a very young age, she also had several spiritual experiences that helped deepen her faith. When she was about nine years old, she suffered a long bout of pneumonia. During this time, God gave her a vision that encouraged and comforted her. The family was praying, and suddenly Phyllis understood herself to be in heaven, rather like Paul's experience of not knowing whether he was in or out of the body.[7] Her vision of heaven was simply of its beauty and awesome wonder. She grew up with a sense of calling to be a missionary and a sense of God's closeness and comfort.

For Ed, Africa was just right. When he was about eight years old, the Loutons moved from Detroit to Pearcy, Arkansas. Albert wanted to return to his family home and start a Pentecostal church. The family packed their old car with a few household items and set off from Detroit. The car was so old that, during a rainstorm, an umbrella had to be opened inside the car.

The church that Albert started in Pearcy had a brush-arbor structure and was located in a cow pasture. Phyllis, who was by then ten years old, waited by the church structure with her mother one evening while her father took various members home in the family car. Before he returned for them, a herd of cows came through the field and chased after them. Apparently, a neighboring farmer was driving the cows at night through the area to try to destroy the makeshift church building. Louise and Phyllis ran for their lives, they thought, until they managed to jump a ravine to safety.

Phyllis deplored this rural, backward region of America, with its strange people and their way of life. She refused to go to school, saying that she could not understand whatever language the people were speaking and that she in any case knew more than they did. One might say her attitude was all wrong, but she may have been correct in her assessment of the school. Her own grandfather, Blev, never said a word to her. He spent much of the day sitting on the front porch and spitting tobacco juice into a spittoon. She did like her grandmother, Willie Ann, but was glad after four

---

7. Paul, speaking of himself in the third person, says, "And I know that this person, whether in the body or outside the body I do know (God knows), was caught up to paradise and heard inexpressible words that are not permissible for a man to speak" (2 Cor 12.4).

months when her Uncle Roland and Aunt Tessie Ernst came for a visit and took her back to Detroit with them. There would be no more boys riding horses around the outhouse while she was inside, no more snakes coming up through the floorboards that her father would shoot right in the living room, and no more of an impossibly strange culture—not, at least, until she found herself in Africa ten years later!

Ed, however, thrived in Arkansas. It was a boy's dream in many ways: guns, horses, creeks, snakes, and the great outdoors. He wanted to fit in with the local children as fast as possible. On the first day of school in Pearcy, Ed walked off in the morning with no shoes on his feet, just like the other boys. At the end of the day, his new friends delivered him home on their shoulders: the road had become too hot for his tender feet. Still, the challenges of a new culture fascinated him—an interest that would serve him well all his days, not least when he taught cross-cultural missions many years later.

The Loutons stayed only one year in Arkansas. They returned to Michigan, and Albert pastored a Pentecostal church back in Detroit. Phyllis was reunited with her family.

All that had taken place ten years earlier. Now, Ed and Phyllis were faced with a whole new cross-cultural challenge. This time, brother and sister alike were happy in their new home. For Phyllis, the Sunday School picnic confirmed the visionary call to Africa that she had received thirteen years earlier. Where would this adventure in God's service lead in the years to come?

2

An Outpouring of the Spirit

... I will pour out my Spirit on all flesh, and your sons and your daughters will prophesy, and your young men will see visions . . . .
(Acts 2.17)

IN APRIL, 1948, EUGENE Edgar Grams fell instantly and forever in love with Evelyn Phyllis Louton at the sight of her picture. He declared to himself, "That is the girl I intend to marry." He was seventeen years old, and it was the month of her seventeenth birthday.

Albert Louton, Phyllis's father, had come for a mission service to the small town of Athens in middle Wisconsin, where the Assemblies of God church was pastored by William Frederick Grams, Gene's father. Albert, at forty-six years old, was at the beginning of what would take three years to raise funds for his family to go to South Africa as independent missionaries. He had been invited to speak at the church in Athens by Gene's mother, Martha (Zietz) Grams, who had gained Albert's acquaintance while she was recovering from cancer at one of the "faith homes" in Zion City, Illinois. Zion City was forty miles outside Chicago on the way to Milwaukee, and Martha had come here after attending a healing service in Elgin, Illinois that was conducted by William Branham, since the trip home was too far for someone so weak.

CAPSULE: FAITH HEALING AND PENTECOSTALISM

Faith healing ministries and faith homes were fairly well known by the time of faith healer William Branham, especially in Pentecostal circles. Faith homes were places for the sick to come for healing. One of Branham's predecessors was John Alexander Dowie, who drew up plans for Zion City in 1900, while he was ministering in Chicago. His ministry not only filtered into early American Pentecostalism but also had a major impact on South African Pentecostalism.

Born in Scotland in 1847, Dowie moved to Australia with his parents and, over time, ministered first in New Zealand, then Australia, and eventually in the United States of America. While in New Zealand in 1885, Dowie was greatly frustrated during a fever epidemic that claimed many lives in his congregation. Beside the bed of a suffering girl, he found the courage to pray for healing, and the girl and her two siblings quickly recovered. From this time on, Dowie's faith was strengthened to pray for the sick. Towards the end of the nineteenth-century, in Chicago, he would pray for some seventy thousand each year.[1]

Dowie's healing ministry was not the only foretaste of the Pentecostal movement to come. There were also other holiness religious centers that emphasized healing. Charles Parham established the Beth-el Healing Home in Topeka, Kansas, in 1898. Elizabeth Baker established the Elim Faith Home in New York in 1895. Here, the sick could wait while their faith in God's healing built up until they were healed. The same idea stood behind the faith homes that Dowie established. There were also other faith healers at the turn of the century, such as Maria Woodworth-Etter, Robert Kelso Carter, and Carrie Judd-Montgomery.[2]

Pentecostalism built upon the holiness and faith healing movements.[3] It especially emphasized speaking in tongues, which, for many Pentecostals, was believed to be the initial evidence of a second act of grace after salvation: being baptized by or filled with the Holy Spirit. Pentecostalism was, moreover, a missionary movement: the Spirit of Pentecost was given to the church for worldwide missions. This "outpouring" of the Holy Spirit was viewed as an outpouring in the last days, and so Pentecostalism also maintained that the world was now entering the end of history. All this provided the energy, empowerment, excitement, and urgency that characterized Pentecostals. Acts 1–2 (with its

1. Lindsay, *John Alexander Dowie.*

2. See the discussion in Newberry, "Pentecostal Missions."

3. While the initial focus of Zion City was on healing and pre-dated Pentecostalism, Pentecostal teaching came early to the ministry. See "A Pentecostal Revival in Zion City, USA," 79. John G. Lake, a missionary from Zion City to South Africa, speaks of "praying for the baptism" in his meetings in Johannesburg in 1908 ("Latest News from Africa," 2. Lake's experience is discussed below. According to Vinson Synon, Charles Fox Parham visited Zion City in 1906, recruiting many to Pentecostalism while "failing in his attempt to take over Dowie's faltering movement." Synan, *Tradition,* 102.

fulfillment of Joel 2.28–29) captured the association of a baptism with the Holy Spirit, speaking in tongues, courage in ministry, missions to other nations, and a belief that these were the last days. What happened on the day of Pentecost to the early disciples of Jesus was happening again in the last days.

As a movement, Pentecostalism is often dated to 1906, the time of the Azusa Street revival. Worldwide, however, several revivals can be cited that involved experiences of the Spirit just prior to this date, including the Welsh Revival of 1904 to 1905 and two revivals in India in the Khasi Hills (northeast India) and at Pandita Ramabai's Mukti Mission in Kedgaon for widows and orphans in 1905.[4] The Azusa revival was an extension of a 1901 outpouring of the Spirit with the gift of speaking in tongues that began with Charles Fox Parham. Parham and his students at Bethel Bible School in Topeka, Kansas had become convinced (cf. Acts 10.46) that the baptism of the Holy Spirit was evidenced by speaking in tongues. While seeking this gift, about a dozen of them, including Parham, began to speak in tongues.[5]

However, already in April, 1897, Dowie had stated from the pulpit:[6]

> Well, I do not know, I think some of you are getting a new tongue. You are getting a tongue that gives praise to the Lord, for a new blessing that has come into your homes, and He is giving us new tongues. We have not everything yet, that is true, but He gives the Word of Wisdom, and the Word of Knowledge, and Faith, and Gifts of Healing, and Workings of Miracles, and Prophecy and Discernings of Spirits, and He will give us in due time Tongues and Interpretation of Tongues. He will. That is coming in its right time.

In 1901, Dowie spoke to crowds of twelve and a half thousand at the Chicago Coliseum. A remarkable healing ministry in the area had led up to such large crowds. One celebrated healing was that of a Miss Amanda Hicks of Clinton, Kentucky, who was president of Clinton College (1873–1913) and a cousin of President Abraham Lincoln. In 1894, she was brought on a stretcher to Chicago to see Dowie. Her doctors had

---

4. Anderson, "Compass."

5. For a more detailed description of these events, see chapter 5, "The American Jerusalem—Azusa Street," in Synan, *Tradition.*

6. As quoted in the movement's "Leaves of Healing" magazine (see Jennings, "John Alexander Dowie").

given up treating her for a cancerous tumor that had burst in the alimentary canal. She was expected to die shortly, and her difficult trip to Chicago to see Dowie was her last hope. After arriving at Dowie's home, she was prayed for and instantaneously healed. A few days later, large amounts of the cancerous material passed from her body.[7]

To be sure, Dowie's story is complicated by other stories that might be told of him, not least the conviction he held from 1901 until his death in 1907 that he was Elijah returning at the end of time. Excesses of some sort seem to go hand in hand with revival and healing movements, to the point that Christians are almost forced to choose between wild fire or no fire at all. This is not an easy choice, but for those within such movements, there is always an internal critique that is seldom noticed by those outside.

The church in Zion, Illinois was known for healing miracles that had taken place there. Mementoes, such as crutches, lined the walls of the church as a testimony to healings that had taken place. The whole town of Zion was planned as a Christian town—even smokers would be fined when passing through. Also not permitted were theaters, alcohol, gambling, dancing, secret lodges—and doctors. One of the elders of the church, known as "Elder Brooks" (Eugene Brooks), established the faith homes in Zion. These were places of refuge for people with various needs, whether physical or material, and they were known never to have turned anyone away. God miraculously provided for the needs of these homes; on several occasions, it was said, someone would show up with food for people staying at the homes just before mealtime. Such stories only increased the faith of many that God would provide their every need. What was a key to the faith home teaching was the idea of "waiting on the Lord" until God provided whatever was needed.

Out of the ministry in Zion, Illinois also came that of the Canadian, John Graham Lake. Lake became connected with Dowie when he sought healing for his sister and wife in 1898 as they faced death. After both were healed, Lake moved to Zion to learn from Dowie. In 1907, the year that Dowie died, Lake received what he referred to as the baptism in the Holy Spirit. His description of what this meant for him personally entailed an awareness of God's presence in a bright light, a cleansing from sin as a voice reminded him of his past faults, and an experience

---

7. Lindsay, *John Alexander Dowie*, referencing the *Clinton Democrat*, March 8, 1894.

of various spiritual gifts such as speaking in tongues, knowledge of person's illnesses, and a tremendous power to heal.[8] In 1908, he traveled to South Africa, and for the next four years he was known for services of healing around the country. He was also a founder, along with Thomas Hezmalhalch, of the Apostolic Faith Mission of South Africa, which was officially established in 1913.

At the end of the 1940s, one of the major faith healers in the United States was William Branham. Branham was a visionary healer, holding large crusades all over the United States and in other countries. His healing ministry began in 1946. The following year, two of America's great healing revivalists, Smith Wigglesworth and Charles S. Price, died. Branham was also associated with South Africa: the year before Gene Grams arrived in South Africa as a missionary, Branham held a famous campaign in Durban, and to this day there are Branham churches there that continue his teachings and practices.[9]

Like Dowie, Branham's ministry is also clouded by some of his Biblically unfounded notions. He was certainly willing to fill out uncertainties in a theology of healing with his own experiences and assumptions. And he later endorsed a "Oneness" or "Jesus Only" doctrine—no doubt because his ever so literal and experiential approach to theology could not appreciate the mystery of the Trinity. Branham was also known to prophesy over people; in fact, his ministry began with seven supposed revelations about the future.

His simple understanding of the Bible, and perhaps his need for a complete practical theology of healing even when the Bible offered no teaching, led him to some simplistic views: God had promised healing to the person who believed, and so God had to heal a believer who prayed for healing in faith; demonic spirits were responsible for sickness and sin; one only had to have enough faith to be healed; faith was often tested in healing since it did not come immediately; recourse to medicine may indicate a lack of faith; and if a person's faith wavered, the healing could be lost.

---

8. Lindsay, *John G. Lake.*

9. See the study by Weaver, *William Marion Branham.* There is a Branham website for the ministry that he started. See the interview in which he tells of his own calling to ministry at http://www.williambranham.com (accessed 1 May, 2009).

∾ ∾ ∾

Elder Eugene Brooks, who established the faith homes of Zion City, Illinois, travelled to various areas of the country to hold meetings, and this is how he and Zion City first became known to William Grams and Martha Zietz in the 1920s. They asked him to perform their marriage on the 17th of December, 1927 and named their first son after him.

Another connection that the Grams had with Zion, Illinois was Zion Bible Institute (ZBI). Eventually, this training institute for ministers would merge with Central Bible Institute. Before it did, however, William Grams studied there in preparation for pastoral ministry in the 1930s. ZBI had no connection with the faith homes—the general thought was that the faith home folk were, in a word, crazy. The president of ZBI was Finis Dake, whose study Bible was used for decades by many preachers in the Assemblies of God, despite the fact that Dake was dismissed for certain indiscretions and despite the work's lack of scholarly insight.

In the 1930s, the William Grams family held to a theology of faith healing similar to what Alexander Dowie taught in the early 1900s. They later came to appreciate doctors, as did the famous faith healer, William Branham, in the 1940s. But when Gene broke his arm at the age of four in 1934 after slipping on ice on the family farm, they would not take him to the doctor. Even with his radius protruding through the skin at the wrist, his parents would not take him to the doctor. William Grams made a cast from a wooden shingle and strips of a bed sheet, which he wrapped around Gene's little arm after pulling the bone into place. His grandmother protested vociferously. The family, however, not only had its understanding of faith to keep them from doctors; it was also very poor. Not everyone could afford doctors.

This theology at some point always falters: people get sick and die in this present world of sin, suffering, and death. Yet alternative theologies that make excuses for God's absence where people have needs are essentially faithless and rationalist. Evangelicalism itself strangely encompasses the extremes of "Cessationism," the notion that no miracles (or prophecy or speaking in tongues) take place today, and of the "Prosperity Gospel," the notion that one will be in good health and do well in life if only one has enough faith. Finding the right balance between these extremes can be difficult, but it seems to begin with an understanding of faith that both expects God's answer to prayer and trusts in God even when things do not get better. Faith is of both kinds. And, it must be added, any theology that sets itself over God's sovereignty is an affront to God. To "name and claim" promises in Scripture in an effort to make God fulfill His Word is not unlike the child who tries to manipulate her parents rather than interact in a relationship of love.

Separating out what is a truly bad "Prosperity Gospel" from what is in fact real faith in God is sometimes difficult. When Gene's arm did not heal properly, it seemed as though God had failed to answer the prayers of faith uttered out of great love for a child with expectancy and trust in God. When the crude bandages and splint were removed six weeks later, Gene's hand was crippled. It had healed at such an angle that his fingers were touching his wrist. Gene's grandmother was angry at his parents for not going to the doctor, but his father said simply, in his thick German accent, "If God can heal his hand crooked, He can also heal it straight." So the family prayed some more.

The next morning, as Gene came downstairs from his bedroom, his father was entering the house after milking the cows. "Sonny," he said, "how's that arm?" The little boy looked at his arm and, for the first time that day, noticed that it was different. He moved his hand around and showed everybody that he had been completely healed.

One might say that God permitted this to test Gene's own and his parents' faith, only to show that he is indeed faithful to hear and answer our prayers. While this may be true, it is equally possible that God healed a child's crooked arm out of compassion despite the parents' inappropriate care. That it is not wrong to seek help where help is to be found—including in the medical profession—is the practice that the family eventually adopted. This family did not lack faith. They knew that God often healed the sick. But they came to understand in time that medicine is one of God's gifts to all people—a common grace—and that brains to make use of medicine are equally so. They also encountered times when no healing came despite the same faith and prayer from the same people, as when Gene's younger sister, Arlene, died from a weak, rheumatic heart.

While Branham was yet to move into even greater theological error, and while the Grams were still coming out of some of theirs on these matters, Martha Grams grew increasingly sick. During much of Gene's childhood, his mother was in very poor health. She apparently suffered from malnutrition as a child. Just two years after Martha's birth in Russia, her family moved to Wisconsin. Five years later, Martha's father, Andrew Zietz, died when a train hit his sleigh drawn by a team of horses in a snowstorm. He had waited until a train passed before moving across the tracks, but a second train coming in the opposite direction and hidden by the first train hit his sleigh squarely, killing him instantly. The bereft family remained in poverty for a number of years, and young Martha's liver was apparently damaged at this time: she had a yellowish color to her skin throughout her life. When she died on the 29th of November, 1967, it was discovered that she had lived with a very poorly functioning liver due to cirrhosis. Gene, being the oldest child, had to grow up quickly, helping inside and outside the home more than most children, even farm children, do.

Martha Grams nearly died from a different health concern, a kidney condition, in 1945, three years before she was healed of cancer. She was expected to die at any time and lay bedridden. William sat by her side one day, supposing it to be her last. She could barely speak, but managed to ask for prayer. As the family prayed, she was heard to repeat the name of Jesus. Her voice grew stronger, and soon she was shouting "Jesus." After this, she rose, washed, and went to church in the evening— to everyone's great surprise and amazement. She had been healed.

Then, in 1948, Martha Grams was again at death's door with cancer. Doctors were by this time involved in the family's life, and it was known that she had a gastrointestinal cancer. Once again, she was not expected to live. William and Gene drove Martha to William Branham's meetings in Elgin. Gene, now seventeen years old, listened as Branham told the congregation to close their eyes while he prayed for healing, because demons were also being cast out and, he informed his audience, they entered the body through the eyes! Branham spoke to William and Martha Grams when it was their time in the long queue for those seeking healing. By this time, Martha could hardly stand up for exhaustion. The cancer had already reduced her to ninety pounds. "You are a minister," he said to William, whom he had never met and with whom he had never spoken. "And you," he said to Martha, "have a cancer that is about to take your life." He simply told them what was the case: they had given him none of this information. Branham claimed that his ministry involved listening to what an angel told or showed him. "But God will add years to your life," he continued, "and in five days you will pass this cancer."

Elgin, Illinois was about two hundred and fifty miles away from the Grams' home in Athens, Wisconsin, and so William took Martha to the faith home in Zion City, Illinois to recover. Five days later, Martha did pass the cancer.

While Martha was recuperating at the faith home, Albert Louton arrived in Zion. When Martha invited Albert to stay with the Grams in Wisconsin and speak in their church, William Grams was rather perturbed: "What if he's a crook?" He did, however, host Albert and permit him to speak.

As Albert showed the Grams the picture he had of his family, Gene's eye fell on Phyllis. She was a slender sixteen-year-old with a lovely smile and a beautiful face. Her straight, dark hair curled up on the sides and touched her shoulders. It was parted in the middle, and she had bangs falling onto her forehead. Gene became determined to visit the Louton family one way or another. He managed to get himself invited to Detroit to see the automobile factories, but his ulterior motive was to meet Albert's lovely daughter, Phyllis.

In June, 1948, two months after seeing Phyllis's picture, Albert was still travelling in Wisconsin. He visited Gene, who was working at his Uncle Paul Grams' farm for $50.00 a month. They arranged to let Gene leave the farm in order to visit Detroit. Since Albert had sold his car in Wisconsin, he and Gene travelled together by Greyhound bus to Detroit.

On the second day of his visit with the Loutons, Gene was discouraged to learn that Phyllis was leaving home to stay with her cousins, Carol and Dave Ernst. The forward young man that her father had picked up from a farm town in the middle of Wisconsin was not the knight in shining armor about whom she had dreamt. But Gene just stayed on in the Louton home, waiting for Phyllis's return. He and Phyllis's brother, Ed, enjoyed each other's company while Phyllis waited at her cousin's home for Gene to leave her's. After several days, Louise Louton telephoned her daughter to say, "If you don't return, he will never go home!" So Phyllis returned to her home in order to get Gene to leave the Loutons alone. Louise further counseled Phyllis, "He will probably ask to write to you, and you should say that you will. There is no harm in writing." He did, and so did she.

With his mission partially accomplished, Gene returned to Wisconsin.

3

A Clear Calling

And I heard the voice of the Lord saying to me, "Whom shall I send, and who will go for us?" And I said, "Behold, send me!" (Isaiah 6.8)

THAT AUTUMN, 1948, GENE went to Bob Jones University in Greenville, South Carolina. Although Bob Jones was not Pentecostal, it was a Fundamentalist university, affirming certain fundamentals of the faith that placed it squarely in orthodox Christianity and over against liberal teachings. Pentecostals were also Fundamentalists, and it did not seem too great a stretch to Gene to study there. One of the popular songs that summer was "You Can't Be True, Dear." That was exactly how Gene felt about Phyllis as he boarded the bus in Wisconsin. While most maps would not place Detroit on the path from Wisconsin to South Carolina, the logic of love placed it directly en-route.

This time, things went better in Detroit. During the visit, Gene, Ed, and a friend went to the beach on Belle Isle. Gene had his glasses off when he dove head first off a long pier that stretched far into the water. When he did not surface, Ed ran after him to see what had happened. Gene was floating in the water, unconscious. Ed could see that the water was quite shallow, but Gene had assumed that it was deeper. He had knocked himself out when his head hit the sand. Perhaps anybody else would have broken a neck, but Gene seemed to have been built providentially for just such mishaps, his head sitting squarely on his shoulders with only the suggestion of a neck between them.

Ed and his friend dragged Gene out of the water and laid him on the pier until he came around. They returned to the house, and Gene lay on the sofa in considerable agony. This was probably the first time

Phyllis saw him in a different light, not as his usual steamroller self but as someone who also had vulnerabilities and needs, someone who could be cared for. Looking down at him, she felt compassion, a compassion that was the seed of love. A few days later, Albert drove Gene to the bus station for his long journey to Bob Jones University in Greenville, South Carolina. Phyllis and Gene rode together in the back seat, and she did not resist his hand on the way.

Despite its draconian system of demerits for any and every infraction of an interminable list of rules, Gene enjoyed his year at Bob Jones. He particularly enjoyed his demanding English literature course. Yet finances dictated another approach to college. Gene, whose high school grades were exceptional, particularly in mathematics, had actually turned down the offer of a scholarship to study engineering at the University of Wisconsin. He was headed into ministry, and a Bible College education was needed.

Gene saw Phyllis again on his Christmas break in 1948, and Phyllis graduated from East Commerce High School the next month. When the couple saw each other again, it was June, 1949. Gene was returning from Bob Jones University. Albert Louton caught them having their first kiss on a hill in the evening after a picnic—a truly romantic moment. The couple could hear him saying, "It looks like there is some kissing going on up there." On a Sunday afternoon, at the age of eighteen, Gene asked Phyllis, also eighteen, to marry him. Her initial response was, "No, I don't think so," but by Friday night, her answer had changed.

It was one thing to become engaged at eighteen and quite another to be ready for marriage. Gene and Phyllis went to tell William and Martha Grams. Gene's parents had recently moved to Detroit, where William became the pastor of Tabor Tabernacle, an Assemblies of God church in the German Branch. William and Martha moved from rural Wisconsin to one of the largest, American cities, and their ministerial compensation increased dramatically as well, to $60.00 per week. Gene's parents were delighted with news of the engagement, and they immediately arranged a celebration.

Although Phyllis's parents had not stood in the way of courtship, they now raised understandable objections to the young couple's intentions. Albert's question cut to the heart of a father's first concern, "What source of income do you have?" This was not a question so much as a statement: he thought that Gene had better mature a little before he presume to ask for his daughter's hand in marriage again. Yet Gene and Phyllis resolved to marry, no matter what obstacles might need to be overcome in the interim. They would become missionaries to Africa together, and the intertwining of their lives was assuredly God's doing.

That summer, Gene worked at Bud Wheel, inspecting wheels in order to buy an engagement ring. The unpleasant work was eased as Gene let his thoughts soar. He and Phyllis talked about being missionaries someday together in Africa, remembering their remarkable visions as children that God had given to each of them.

Gene's call into missions when he was thirteen years old could not have been clearer, nor could it have come at a more tender moment. His beloved sister, Arlene, had died shortly before her twelfth birthday of heart failure due to rheumatic fever on a Sunday, the 6th of August, 1944. As it happened, this was the same day that Allied forces began their invasion of Normandy. Arlene had suffered from rheumatic fever several times in her life until her heart could no longer function. Gene's call into missions came the Sunday after she died. Some might wonder what psychology was at play for a young boy to think that God had spoken directly to him at such a time. But the thought never occurred to Gene, nor should it have. Pentecostals are not suspicious of emotions, and in severe trials they expect to hear from God. Yet what happened was truly wonderful: a clear, direct call to missions.

CAPSULE: *HEARING* GOD

Most calls into missions are not so clear in the sense of an audible voice and vision. Often people put together Jesus' general mandate to the church to go into all the world to proclaim the Gospel with circumstances in their lives, an awareness of their own giftedness, and an inward desire and peace. These added together can constitute a call to ministry. A look at calling to certain ministries in the book of Acts suggests that God's direct, audible, or visionary call comes when one does not know what to do or is moving in the wrong direction. Such a calling is typically a redirection. Even so, a direct call to one ministry or place of ministry may actually last only a short while. This was so for Paul when he received the call to leave Asia and minister in Macedonia. His ministry in Macedonia lasted only a few weeks, whereas his subsequent ministry in Corinth lasted one and a half years.

The baptistic practice of going forward after a service was expanded in Pentecostal churches to become an extended time for further ministry and worship. It primarily involved people praying together or on their own while others sang songs that an organist or pianist played. In this worshipful atmosphere, the pastor and others would lay hands on people, praying for them to accept Christ into their lives, to be baptized in the Holy Spirit (thought to be indicated by speaking in tongues), to be healed, or to have some need met. It was a time to meet God, and possibly to hear from him. Thus the altar service was not simply a conclusion to the worship service but a service in its own right. It was a mini-"tarrying" service.

Tarrying services were part of the warp and woof of the Pentecostal revival campaigns conducted by persons such as Aimee Semple McPherson. The services followed the actual revival services, as people spent long hours—sometimes all night over several days—tarrying for the infilling of the Holy Spirit. Such an end to services in these Pentecostal churches left people with the understanding that they were all in need in one way or another and that nobody could supply their needs other than God alone. Pentecostal congregations would later be rocked with a theology of health and wealth that directly challenged this humble demeanor, as though God's children should have no needs and, if they did, they had something wrong with their faith. But in these earlier years, the movement was represented not by spiritual triumphalism but by more of an earnest seeking of God out of great need and a grateful thanksgiving for His tender mercies. The whole movement could be summed up as a seeking for more of God—a "tarrying."

Gene's call was a life's calling to mission work in Africa, and it was similar to Paul's calling to be an apostle to the Gentiles. He went to the church's altar at the conclusion of the Sunday service to pray. He primarily went forward because he was grieving for his beloved sister. He wept and wept. After awhile, becoming self-conscious, he lifted his head to look around. When he did, he had a vision of a living map of Africa on the front wall of the church building. The topography was amazing, with hills, plains, and waterfalls in three-dimensional color. He saw many people of various colors coming out of the map. The people he saw surprised him greatly, since what he knew of Africa at the time suggested that all the faces should be black. Some of those faces were etched in his memory to the point that, years later, he remembered seeing them in this vision, even remembering the clothing they wore. As he watched the living map of Africa, he heard God ask, "Will you go?" The voice was loud enough that Gene thought everyone would have heard, and he looked around. But only he heard the voice.

This divine call was tied into Arlene's death not just because of timing but also because Arlene wanted to be a missionary to Africa. She had often told this to her family. Even two days before her death, she spoke with Gene about her desire to be a missionary. Gene, however, had to this point never entertained the thought for himself. He was thirteen at the time and had determined that he did not want to follow his Grams relatives in farming or ministry. His grandfather, Gottlieb Grams,[1] was not a true believer when he, his wife Augusta, and his first two sons, William and Ralph, came from Volhynia in Russia (now Ukraine) to Milwaukee, Wisconsin in 1907. Shortly afterwards, he bought a Bible and began to read it, looking for meaning in his life. He became a Christian, along with his family, and would later pastor Assemblies of God churches in the German Branch in Wisconsin and Michigan. Seven of Gottlieb's nine sons became ministers with the Assemblies of God, and two of their three daughters married Pentecostal ministers. Others from the third and fourth generations would also enter the ministry, mostly in the Assemblies of God. But at thirteen, Gene had no intention of pastoral or mission work, and even after his call to missions he still toyed with the idea of becoming an engineer or even joining the navy.

The time was right, therefore, for God to redirect this youth's focus. God spoke a second time, "Will you go?" Again, Gene gave no answer. The third time that God asked if he would go to Africa as a missionary, Gene replied "Yes."

After his year at Bob Jones University, Gene transferred to the Assemblies of God Bible college in Springfield, Missouri. Bob Jones was no longer affordable, and Central Bible Institute permitted Gene to be trained in the context of his future ministry. At CBI, Gene studied with godly men whom he regarded as giants of the still-young Pentecostal movement: Stanley Horton, Cordas C. Burnett, Ernest S. Williams, J. R.

---

1. See the tribute to Gottlieb Grams by his youngest son and missionary to South America, Monroe Grams, "Dad's Faith," 8–9.

Flower, and Robert Cummings. Each impressed on Gene that ministry was a sacred matter, not to be taken lightly.

Some of Gene's closest friends at CBI were Elmer Kirsch, Bill Menzies, Dave Krist, Dave Irwin and Bob Colombo. Another close friend was his own cousin, Melvin Grams, who, later in life, would become a missionary in Africa and Europe. He, his brother Jim, and Gene Grams would all serve as Assemblies of God missionaries in South Africa. Mel's uncle, Andrew Liebelt, visited Azusa Street in California, where one of the major early Pentecostal revivals gave birth to the movement in the United States. Liebelt took the message of Pentecostalism back to Wisconsin, and he, along with the Grams and several others, helped to establish the Fond-du-Lac Gospel Tabernacle (now Lighthouse Christian Church) in 1924. Liebelt pastored this church until 1956, and Mel briefly became its interim minister after having been a missionary in Liberia for several years.

Gene and some of his college friends enjoyed visiting a Pentecostal church on Sunday evenings. The young men visited the church purely for entertainment. Not all Pentecostals are the same, and this church provided something entirely new. Some Pentecostal churches are heretical on the doctrine of the Trinity, and some have handled snakes to prove their faith in God. The full spectrum of the movement should be remembered, especially as it continues to grow worldwide. The Bible School students were forming their own views on all this, and their lively discussions involved a tremendous amount of humor about what someone had seen or heard from some "off-the-wall" ministry as well as serious concern for Biblical truth and for pleasing God.

The services on these Sunday evenings would typically go past CBI's curfew, and so the young men would have to leave before everyone else. One Sunday night, the minister announced that they would drive the demon of stubbornness from a certain woman in the congregation. The woman immediately knew that the minister was speaking about her, and she shouted, "Oh, no!" "Oh, yes!" the minister insisted, and he added, "and we have some young men from CBI here tonight that I am going to ask to help us pray the demon out." The young men timidly eased from their seats and went forward. The minister asked Gene to begin to pray, but he only managed a few sentences before the minister interrupted him. "There ain't no demon nowhere that's ever gonna leave if you just pray like that!" he said. He began to pray with shouts and to pound the poor woman on the back with his fists at the same time. "Are you ready to go?" he would ask, and she would reply, "No!" This went on for about fifteen minutes until the woman screamed in pain, "Yes!" Then the minister turned to the young men from the Bible college and said, "Now, that's the way you deliver people from demons!" The young men thought the whole event was great fun and returned to the services as often as they could. Gene, however, did not at this time realize that he would one day encounter people really possessed by demons—a completely different affair from the charade they had just witnessed.

Gene was preparing for ministry at an Assemblies of God Bible college. His father was a Pentecostal pastor. So were some of his uncles. His grandfather was a Pentecostal minister. To be ordained in the Assemblies of God one has to be "baptized in the Holy Spirit," the sign of which is said to be the Spiritual gifting of speaking in tongues.[2] But Gene did not speak in tongues, and so he earnestly sought this gift. During one prayer time, a fellow student was particularly energetic in praying for Gene. He pounded his hand with his fist, repeatedly praying, "Lord, fill him tonight; Lord, fill Gene tonight." He was, in the earnestness of prayer, truly beating his fist into his other hand. But on one occasion, his fist missed his hand, and it landed squarely on Gene's head, knocking him out cold for several minutes. Once Gene came around, he wobbled to his room and lay on his bed, groaning. He would receive this gift at another time. However, useless for study that evening, Gene turned the radio on

---

2. Not all Pentecostal groups hold to the same theology of a baptism of the Holy Spirit and the gift of speaking in tongues. The Assemblies of God states its views in articles seven and eight of their sixteen "fundamental truths." Article seven states: "All believers are entitled to and should ardently expect and earnestly seek the promise of the Father, the baptism in the Holy Spirit and fire, according to the command of our Lord Jesus Christ. This was the normal experience of all in the early Christian Church. With it comes the enduement of power for life and service, the bestowment of the gifts and their uses in the work of the ministry . . . . This experience is distinct from and subsequent to the experience of the new birth . . . . With the baptism in the Holy Spirit come such experiences as: an overflowing fullness of the Spirit, a deepened reverence for God, an intensified consecration to God and dedication to His work, and a more active love for Christ, for His Word and for the lost." Scripture passages are given to support this article. Article eight reads: "The baptism of believers in the Holy Spirit is witnessed by the initial physical sign of speaking with other tongues as the Spirit of God gives them utterance.... The speaking in tongues in this instance is the same in essence as the gift of tongues, but is different in purpose and use . . . ." See http://www.ag.org/top/Beliefs/Statement_of_Fundamental_Truths/sft_full.cfm#7 (accessed 3 June, 2009).

and was surprised to hear the broadcast of a world title heavyweight-boxing match with Joe Lewis. Gene listened with great empathy as Lewis pummeled his opponent.

CAPSULE: THE SPIRIT'S WORK
AND THE HUMAN RESPONSE

There is indeed a humorous side to spirituality—a very human side—but this does not discount a very real encounter with God. Humans may respond in all sorts of ways, not always appropriate and often culturally determined, to the moving of God in their midst. From the frenzied displays and (at least sometimes) confused prophesies of the Montanists in the second-century church to the falling, jerking, dancing, barking, laughing and running of pioneers on the American frontier in the 1800s, there have always been some Christians displaying strange, human behaviors as their response to the moving of the Spirit of God in their midst.

The problem these ever so human responses pose is to be able to appreciate and distinguish a real move of God in people's lives from human, cultural responses. This is further complicated by some Pentecostals thinking that the more peculiar the behavior the more beneficially humbling the experience. In this way, people are thought to be prepared to become ready to let God do whatever he will in their lives. Yet all this may just as easily be human inadequacies rather than something that pleases God: only God knows the heart. Ministers often have to discern between what is from God and what is merely human, fine enough, perhaps, for what it was, but not definitive for all. The early revivals of the Assemblies of God, for example, are full of impressive stories of the move of God among gatherings of worshipers as well as some remarkably strange, human responses.[3]

While in the second semester of his third year of college, in 1951, Gene received a letter from Phyllis. Her grandfather, Jakob Rettinger, had died just days before the Loutons were to board ship for South Africa. Since she was engaged to be married to Gene, Phyllis did not plan to travel with her parents, her brother Ed, and their little sister Joy to South

3. Stories of the early years of the Assemblies of God may be found in Menzies, *Anointed To Serve.*

Africa. However, during the funeral, Phyllis decided to accompany her family to South Africa. Just before embarking on the boat, she wrote her agonizing letter to Gene to tell him that she was leaving the country and would not hold him to their engagement.

The letter destroyed Gene. He was in such agony that one of his friends, Bill Menzies, took him into the woods beside CBI to pray. Gene somehow completed his studies that year, but then left college a year before graduation. Instead of following the long path to becoming a missionary with the Assemblies of God, a path that would include successful pastoring over several years, getting Foreign Mission Board approval, and a year or more of fund-raising—he decided to head to South Africa as fast as he could. William Grams set up meetings with churches in Wisconsin and Michigan that he knew, and Gene laid his heart for missions before the members. Some churches pledged $1.00 per month, others as much as $5.00. Between June, 1951 and March, 1952, Gene raised the funds he thought he needed to start life in South Africa with a wife: $105.00 a month.

Gene almost did not survive the four-week voyage to Cape Town aboard a freighter. After a two-day layover in Trinidad, where the freighter was loaded with tar, the ship ran into several terrible winter storms. As the ship tossed on the waves, he became severely sea sick for many days. With just one engine working, the captain sent out a distress signal. He called the crew and the ship's two passengers together to tell them that they very possibly might not make it to shore. But the storm abated and the ship limped along towards Cape Town.

On one of the days before landing, Gene discussed the monarchy with two British sailors when they received the news that King George VI had died. His daughter, Elizabeth, was on a visit to Kenya when she learned of her accession to the crown on the 6th February, 1952. In the excited discussion among the British crew, Gene volunteered that this might actually be a good time to do away with the monarchy altogether. There was a momentary, awkward pause, and then two of the sailors picked the young missionary up and dragged him to the side of the ship. Holding him irreverently overboard, they demanded, "Say 'God bless the Queen.'" Gene, staring at the ocean far below him, was terrified and quickly shouted, "God bless the Queen, and anything else!" The sailors hauled him back on board and suggested that he be more careful in future. Some measure of cultural sensitivity was a lesson well worth learning before arriving in Africa.

The ship sailed into Cape Town harbor one week late on the 26th of February, 1952. Three hundred years earlier, on April 6th, 1652, Jan van Riebeeck established a Dutch colony here for the Dutch East India Company's ships en-route to the spice islands of South East Asia. Gene had lost considerable weight on his eventful voyage, but he was on the mend and full of excitement when he peered out of his porthole. He saw the lights of South Africa's glorious city of Cape Town as the ship came into harbor at night. The majestic Table Mountain and Devil's Peak came into clearer view, dark shadows rising behind the city. The romantic setting was perfect for a young man arriving at the place to which he had been called some eight years earlier and arriving to meet his fiancé just three weeks before their wedding day.

When Gene arrived, he observed the busy hands at the dock. He was bemused to see many of the white men of the city sporting long beards: they were participating in a contest to grow a long, full beard like that of Jan van Riebeeck himself.[4] He also saw black Africans from various tribes, Coloureds (people of mixed race), and some Indians—African faces of different colors, just like his vision and call to Africa at the age of thirteen.

Phyllis was there waiting for Gene. She had travelled the 1,200 miles from Potgietersrus with her father, but they had to wait a week for the delayed ship. She had checked at the docks every day to see if there was any news of his ship's whereabouts. When Gene came down the gangway, Phyllis threw her arms around him. It had been nearly three years since they were engaged and nearly a year since the Loutons had arrived in South Africa, and now they were together again and to be married. All their discussions over the years about life together in South Africa and serving God in missions were finally about to begin.

---

4. Oddly enough, many portraits of Jan van Riebeeck, including those on coins, paper bills, and stamps, show him without a beard.

4

The First Wedding

The man who finds a wife finds what is good; he gains favor from
the LORD. (Proverbs 18.22)

IN SOUTH AFRICA AT that time, banns of marriage had to be proclaimed over three weeks in a public gathering, usually a church,
before a marriage could take place. Phyllis asked the Afrikaans minister
in Potgietersrus in the Apostolic Faith Mission church where she and
Gene were to be married to announce the union. In exchange for these
announcements and the use of the church building, Gene had to preach
the Sunday before his wedding to a congregation of white Afrikaners
through an interpreter. He had preached several times already in an
African church in Mokopane. He literally dove right into ministry.

Although between Gene's arrival in South Africa and his wedding
there were just twenty-three days, his honeymoon with Africa itself had
already begun. His first experiences on this new continent were powerful, and he felt affirmed in his calling. He wrote his first missionary
newsletter on the 11th of March, 1952:

> . . . I cannot begin to tell you of the joy in my soul as I sat in
> the first African service. My heart just went out to the people
> as I realized in a better way their need of Jesus. They were so
> happy to have me minister to them, and many gave me welcome
> speeches through an interpreter. There is such joy in minister-
> ing to these people because they are so hungry for the Word of
> God. They sit through a whole service and hardly move a muscle
> because they just seem to want to drink in every word that is
> said. When I heard them sing our old familiar hymns in their
> African language, it was just like a little glimpse of heaven when
> some from every tribe, tongue, and nation shall sing the song of

the redeemed around the throne of God. This mission is a light in a dark place, and I thank the Lord for the freedom through the Spirit to minister His Word. The Christians' faces beam forth the radiance of the love that Christ has put in their hearts. Many unsaved heathen come to the services also, and there is such a difference as they appear to be in such spiritual darkness until they receive Christ as their Savior.

Africans are generally most hospitable and gracious. They make a visitor feel honored, welcome, and needed. This is part of the shared culture from tribe to tribe all over the continent. Many a first-time visitor mistakes this natural hospitality on the part of Africans for their own worth, as though they were just what the people needed. Only time can tell whether foreigners might contribute something to this continent, which pulses with its own heartbeat. Gene rightly understood the welcome that he was given as a reception of a minister of the Gospel rather than that he was in himself some sort of blessing. Still, he was in his element, about to be married and doing what he knew was God's bidding. Forty-eight years later, reflecting in a chapel service on his years of service together with Phyllis in South Africa, he stated that neither of them had ever felt out of God's will for their lives, not even for one day.

Gene also mentioned other ministry with the Loutons that he had immediately undertaken rather than wait around for his wedding day. He continued:

> Out in the villages, the darkness even appears to be much greater, and one must really be filled with the Holy Spirit to be able to sow the seed effectively. Last Thursday night, we had the privilege of ministering at an asbestos mine where there are many men who are hungry for the Gospel, some of whom have never heard the story of salvation before. It was so impressive to see the people sitting on the ground, underneath the stars, listening to the Gospel message after their long day's work. They were so appreciative of our coming that they brought out some chairs and stools for us to sit on. It is through your sacrifices that these needy souls can be reached.

The main event, however, was the impending wedding. Gene and Phyllis were married on a warm, sunny Thursday on the 20th of March, 1952. Perhaps every wedding has a story around the central event, but theirs had several. For one thing, they had two weddings on the same day. Gene's parents had had a double wedding, but Gene and Phyllis were themselves married twice on the same day. As this was the era of apartheid, they were first married in a white church in the white town of Potgietersrus, but then they travelled out of town to the African township for a second wedding. But their wedding ordeal began on the previous night.

Gene and Ed stayed together in the Grand Hotel in Potgietersrus because the wedding guests took up all the available accommodation in the Louton home. Ed kept Gene awake around the question "How does one know that one is marrying the right person?" The question was somewhat disconcerting for Gene, who had spent most of the last year fighting the odds to get to this point and the past two and half years dreaming about it. Coming from his future brother-in-law and best man, the question seemed a little shy of supportive, but Ed was wondering about finding a wife some day for himself.

Phyllis spent the evening before the wedding and the early hours of the next morning preparing food for the luncheon. As the time of the wedding drew near—10:00 a.m.—Louise left for the church building and unthinkingly left Phyllis alone at the home without helping her into her wedding dress. This was not a little problematic because the dress had numerous buttons down the back. Thankfully, one of the wedding guests, Helen Guthrie, stopped by and saved the day.

The wedding itself was fairly simple. Phyllis wore a dress of ivory brocaded satin, a headpiece of seed pearls, and her finger-tip veil and blusher was made in France of French lace and veiling. Her bouquet was a collection of African flowers, and her little sister, Joy, was the flower girl. What nobody in attendance noticed was that she also wore slippers instead of shoes so as not to appear taller than the groom, who was less than an inch taller at five feet six inches. Gene wore his best suit, which hung loosely on his frame as he had not yet regained his weight from the stormy voyage to South Africa.

The wedding was not a matter of family and friends through the years coming to show their support and to join in the celebrations. The couple was too new to the country for this. Several missionaries had travelled for the marriage ceremony, and Gene met some of them for the first time. These missionaries were in some ways interdependent, with their mutual Pentecostal[1] distinctives, missionary concerns, and

---

1. Of course, there is considerable variation as to what it means to be a Pentecostal. One should note that many in South Africa think of "Pentecostal" as a "Jesus-

work in the same region of South Africa. But they were also very independent, a quality that could make them stay the course under difficult circumstances even as it also entailed idiosyncrasies and, at times, disharmony.

The Loutons had been introduced by John and Mabel Richards to the African church in Mokopane where Gene and Phyllis were married, and the Richards were also present at the wedding. They were Assemblies of God missionaries from America who had been in South Africa since the early 1920s. John's parents had also been missionaries in South Africa: he was one of the links to the earliest years of Pentecostal missions in the country. Although he lived in Johannesburg, he travelled all about South Africa holding tent meetings. This was the missionary couple that the Loutons had met on the boat while en-route to South Africa.

Albert and Louise Louton, however, remained independent Pentecostal missionaries throughout their lives. Their ministry was focused in the northern Transvaal, what is today called the Limpopo Province, and they lived most of their years in Pietersburg. Louise had sixteen years of ministry in the region, working mostly with African women. She would hold meetings for the women and children in the afternoons during the week, and at times she would also preach in services. She and Albert not only worked with established churches but also held tent campaigns in the more remote regions of the northern Transvaal. They would stay in a tent or caravan while holding meetings.

They had sixteen and a half years of ministry together in South Africa. Louise died suddenly at the young age of 63, on the 27th October, 1967, from heart failure. Albert lived on to 83 years, dying in November, 1985 en-route from Pietersburg to Johannesburg when a tractor pulled out into the path of the car in which he was travelling. He had married a second time, to Dorrel Healy, one of the South African single missionaries in the area. After six years of marriage, Dorrel died—also from a weakened heart. All three were buried in a cemetery in Pietersburg.

In the surrounding area, there were a number of mission stations. These outposts provided a connection with the African people in traditional villages that mission work from towns and cities could not provide. Many of the missionaries at these stations were single women, and several of them had established mission stations. Laura Waite, for example,

only"—non-Trinitarian—group, with which the Assemblies of God is decidedly not in agreement.

established Bethesda Mission Station near Tzaneen, about one hundred miles northeast of Pietersburg. She was a missionary sent out from Zion, Illinois. An early co-worker of hers from the United States was Ada Reitz, who supervised a government school for children.[2]   Another mission station was at Zebediela, which was located about thirty miles southeast of Potgietersrus in what was reputed to be the largest orange grove in the world. This station was established by a Canadian missionary, Ruth Williamson. Laura Waite and Ruth Williamson had at one point worked together at a third mission station, Lebaka Mission Station, northeast of Pietersburg. There were several other Pentecostal mission stations in the northern Transvaal and other single women Pentecostal missionaries, such as Jenny Fremmersvick (Norwegian) and Ruth Monroe. Ruth was from Phyllis's home church, Christian Trinity in East Detroit.

CAPSULE: WOMEN IN MINISTRY

A defining mark of early Pentecostalism was an openness to women in ministry.[3]   This openness had little to do with the movement towards women's ordination that developed later in the mainline Western denominations, which originated more out of changes in culture than in a study of Scripture and reflection on ministry. The 1960s version of freedom in Western culture could claim liberation themes in Scripture, but the lens for viewing these themes was crafted in the workshop of the Enlightenment. Freedom "in Christ" in an individualistic culture that was freeing itself from tradition and devoting itself to human reason could easily be translated into freedom "for me."   Intermingled in America with voting and civil rights for women and Blacks, including the anti-slavery movement often led by Evangelicals, were other expressions of freedom. Darker freedoms in America's history were the manifest

---

2. Reitz, "South Africa Work Prospering," 9.

3. Influential women in the early history of the Assemblies of God included "Zelma Argue, Marie Burgess Brown, Etta Calhoun, Alice Reynolds Flower, Hattie Hammond, Chonita Howard, Alice E. Luce, Aimee Semple McPherson (in the Assemblies of God from 1919 to 1922), Carrie Judd Montgomery, Louise Nankivell, Florence Steidel, Lillian Trasher, Louise Jeter Walker, Alta Washburn, and Mildred Whitney." Women were initially ordained only as evangelists and missionaries, but from 1935 they were also ordained to pastoral ministry. Over 1,000 women were ordained before 1950, although the numbers declined in the second half of the 20th century. From "The Assemblies of God: Our Heritage in Perspective," on the Flowers Pentecostal Heritage Center's website, http://ifphc.org/index.cfm?fuseaction=history.main (accessed 6 March, 2010).

destiny of white settlers to conquer new lands and the native Americans who lived on them, easy divorce, sexual freedom, the right of women to choose abortion, and the freedom of homosexual "marriages."

However, the pre-1960s impetus towards women's roles in ministry was rather motivated out of an understanding of God's sovereignty to call whomever He wished—often the most unlikely of sorts, such as the apostle Paul himself (cf. 1 Cor 15.8–9; 1 Tim 1.12–14). While women had been socially active, such as in opposing slavery and the use of alcohol, and active in healing ministries, the early Pentecostal women could add a powerful verse to their understanding of why they were preaching, teaching, healing and prophesying: Joel 2.28–29—the foundational verse for the early church's ministry quoted in (Acts 2.17–18):

> "Now it will be in the last days," says God, "that I will pour out my Spirit on all flesh, and your sons and your daughters will prophesy, and your young men will see visions, and your old men will dream dreams. I will also pour out my Spirit in those days on my male and my female servants, and they will prophesy."

This verse also gave legitimacy to women's ministries in light of the end-time urgency of God's mission in the world. The sense of urgency was palpable, as many involved in missions worked under the conviction that their ministry was taking place in the last days. Under such conditions, the argument for the role of women in ministry did not stem from a sense of equality or even ability but from a sense that whomever God would empower for ministry was a worthy vessel for His mission in the world in these last days.[4] Thus, related to the sense of divine call and the urgency of the mission was an awareness that ministry did not stem from human desires, efforts, and wisdom. Ministry was rather conceived of as the work of the Holy Spirit through God's people, and proof of this was frequently seen in how the missionaries were divinely assisted despite circumstances. One such circumstance was being a woman, not

---

4. Debates among Evangelicals today about the role and status of women in ministry are often framed in terms of the egalitarian (equal roles for both genders) and complementarian (different roles for different genders) camps. But these both miss the point for Pentecostals. The cross is neither an image for equality nor for hierarchy but for sacrifice. Spiritual gifts are not about natural abilities but the Spirit's indwelling, enabling, transcending power. The present age is not about how things might be done decently and in order but about the in-breaking rule of God in desperate times, about the end of the age when God pours out his spirit on all flesh.

only in the West, where women were gaining increasing rights, but even more so in Africa, where women could still be viewed as property.

Consequently, not much attention was paid to 1 Timothy 2.11–12, where women were, as some interpreted the passage, commanded to be silent and not teach. That sort of command made perfect sense from a human perspective in certain cultures and in circumstances such as that which Timothy was facing in the church in Ephesus, where women were a part of the problem of false teaching.[5] But from a divine calling perspective, God not only could but often did use the least of the least to be His stewards of divine grace. Were not Peter and John all the more amazing as ministers for being uneducated and untrained men (Acts 4.13)? Did not Paul's understanding of his own ministry entail being chosen despite who he was? He knew himself to be a blasphemer, persecutor of the church, and a man of violence (1 Tim 1.13; 1 Cor 15.9). To call persons to ministry who were not in themselves qualified to minister made perfect sense. To choose the educated, rich, and powerful would mean to try to transport a message of grace in vessels of beauty and perfection, that is, in vessels that could draw attention to their own merits. Did Paul not say that his word and preaching were not in persuasive words of wisdom but in a demonstration of the Spirit and of power (1 Cor 2.4)? So, from a Pentecostal perspective, on the one hand, it made perfect sense to tell uneducated women of the first-century—or today in certain areas of the world—not to teach. And it made perfect sense to tell women involved in a false teaching not to teach lest they fall into Eve's error of leading others astray. And it made perfect sense to tell women not to usurp authority by placing themselves above either their husbands

5. 1 Tim 2.11–12 is best understood in light of the generally subordinate roles of women in the first century and the problem with false teaching in the church that involved women (1 Tim 4.3, 7; 5.11–15; 2 Tim 3.6–7). In 1 Tim 2.11–12, the injunction for women not to hold undue power (the Greek word, *authentein*, is stronger than "authority" and suggests an abuse of power) over men is based on Adam's being formed before Eve. The injunction for women not to teach is based not on God's intent for women in creation but on Eve's being deceived by the serpent. Thus the injunction for women to be "silent" or "quiet" needs to be understood, like 1 Tim 2.2's use of the same word ("in order that we might lead a peaceful and *quiet* life"), as a word appropriate for the cultural context and the false teaching in the church rather than an insistence that women be literally silent. In the same way, the injunction that women bear children speaks to the false teaching that women should not marry, and it is related to Eve's "salvation" through her offspring (Gen. 3.15–16). The use of Genesis in 1 Tim 2.9–15, then, is to offer a narrative parallel (typology) in Genesis 3 for the Ephesian church that Paul is addressing in 1 and 2 Timothy.

or men in the role of teaching. And it made perfect sense to think of ministers as persons needing some skills of communication that could come through training and natural abilities. But, on the other hand, it made even more sense to acknowledge that God's calling often took the most unlikely candidates for ministry and made of them object lessons of grace (1 Tim 1.16) and opportunities to demonstrate that ministry was always and only through God's empowering presence (2 Cor 4.7).

All the single women missionaries at the wedding were Pentecostal. Several of these women had bought into a peculiar teaching. Instead of cherishing careful interpretation of Scripture, fresh words from the Spirit were sought out. So, as Gene and Phyllis were soon to discover, for a number of these women meetings entailed gathering together and waiting on the Lord by sitting for long periods of time, moaning. They would then read supposedly prophetic utterances of a Brother Andrews, who was an elder in the Zion, Illinois church. Another missionary, Earl Pottinger, had come from this "faith homes" movement and introduced Andrews' prophecies to these women. After a period of moaning and waiting, the women claimed to see visions and receive words of knowledge. Pentecostals on the fringe of the movement but fully in the spirit of the movement will at times depart from a strong emphasis on the Scripture and give attention to some new prophecies or experiences. There is, of course, no reason to contrast a strong emphasis on careful Biblical study on the one hand and listening to prophetic words on the other, but in this case there was a clear preference for the prophet over the teacher, of spoken words over the written Word.

This always causes tension in the camp, as it did among the Pentecostals of the northern Transvaal. Albert Louton vehemently opposed the teachings of Andrews and the women's approach to meeting together, and he was no supporter of Pottinger either. In the early years of the Assemblies of God, Pentecostals had insisted that visions and alleged inspirations by the Holy Spirit needed to be "plumb-lined by the Word" and "placed on the square of God's Word."[6] And William J.

---

6. As quoted by Wacker, *Heaven Below*, 70. Wacker's sources are two news magazines for early Pentecostals: *Midnight Cry* (Glad Tidings Hall Apostolic Faith Mission in New York), March-April, 1911, p. 4 and *Apostolic Faith* (Azusa Mission, California), February-March, 1907, p. 1.

Seymour, the major leader at the Azusa Street revival in 1906, had said, "Stay within the lids of God's word."[7] Once, after Gene and Phyllis were married, several of these women and the Pottingers visited them in their home and proceeded to hold one of their meetings on the Grams' porch. As they moaned and tarried for spiritual knowledge and visions, they also read from quotes of Andrews's own prophetic utterances. Gene and Phyllis were shocked, and Gene told them that they were never to have such a meeting at their house again.

The number of Pentecostal missionaries in this remote region of South Africa at the time is remarkable, particularly because the Pentecostal movement had only started in the early 1900s. Pentecostal missionaries in the northern Transvaal came not only from America but also from Canada, Great Britain, Ireland, Sweden, Finland, and Switzerland. These missionaries and their various works in South Africa came together in 1912, two years before the American Assemblies of God formed formally in Hot Springs, Arkansas. At some point, these South African Pentecostals adopted the name "Assemblies of God" as well, with direct involvement by the American denomination of the same name. It was a loose federation of independent church bodies. But this was a unity that eventually broke up in 1964 as the extreme differences amongst them became increasingly awkward.[8] One "Pentecostal" group actually did not believe in the continuation of miracles. Some were opposed to theological education, and others held differing views about worship, particularly the Lord's Table. Thus in 1964, the Americans withdrew to form the International Assemblies of God. It was a painful separation, and one the Grams would seek to bridge when they founded the Cape College of Theology in Cape Town in the 1980s.

One of the Pentecostal couples at the wedding was the Masons, who were also from Detroit. He went by the name "Dr." Mason. While he had studied medicine for a while, he never completed his degree. Dr. and Mrs. Mason were the first people to tell the Loutons about ministry in South Africa and encouraged them to become missionaries. Dr. Mason

7. Grant Wacker, *Heaven Below*, 71, quoting from *Apostolic Faith* (California), January 1908, p. 3.

8. A personalized story of the Assemblies of God in South Africa, as well as the division of the American group from others in 1964, is available online at http://www.nu-paradigm.co.za/Bond%20Book/H.%20C.%20Phillips.html (accessed 3 March, 2010). Here John Bond, one of the leaders of the Assemblies of God during the time that the American, International Assemblies of God broke away, tells the history.

wanted Gene and Phyllis to live at their mission station in Saaiplaats, a tin mine northwest of Potgietersrus with villages in the surrounding area. The Grams' house was to be a mud floor rondavel near the mine. As far as the Masons were concerned, all this was settled.

At the wedding, Gene's best man was his brother-in-law, Ed Louton, and Phyllis had only one maid of honor, Eunice Richards. Rev. John Guthrie, a missionary with the International Pentecostal Holiness Church who was born to missionary parents in South Africa in 1915, performed the wedding.

John and Helen Guthrie were Pentecostal Holiness Missionaries from Georgia, in the United States of America. John, however, was born in Zululand, South Africa, where his parents had been missionaries with another denomination. Phyllis met them before Gene arrived in South Africa and arranged for John Guthrie to perform their wedding. They were delightful people and seasoned missionaries who loved and respected the Africans. They opposed a patriarchal or colonial attitude towards the people, and they saw African colleagues as fellow laborers rather than inferior in any respect. This seemed to be a minority view-point among missionaries at the time—at least those with whom the Grams first associated. It is sometimes said that new missionaries should avoid contact with other missionaries so as not to learn their prejudices. But it might equally be said that finding the right mentors in ministry is crucial to success in missions. The Grams, at any rate, were grateful for the Guthrie family in their early years of ministry in South Africa. As it happened, the Guthries lived two blocks away in Pietersburg on Burger Street during the Grams' first term of ministry.

5

The Second Wedding, and a Honeymoon

For what does it matter? As long as in every place, whether by false or true motives, Christ is proclaimed. Indeed, I rejoice in this. (Philippians 1.18)

AFTER THE FIRST WEDDING, Gene and Phyllis went to the magistrate to register their place of residence as a married couple. This was required of all foreigners dwelling in the country. Phyllis stayed in the car while Gene went into the police station to begin the paperwork. The police sergeant was an Afrikaner and apparently required English speaking South Africans, who typically knew Afrikaans, to dialogue with him in his own, and surely God's own, language. Afrikaans is a Dutch dialect, and Gene had some start on the language for knowing a little German. But this was not sufficient on this occasion. In any event, the sergeant took pleasure in humiliating this American unlucky enough not to know Afrikaans. When Gene tried to pronounce "Magazyn Straat," where they were to live in Pietersburg, the magistrate doubled over in laughter. The "g" was supposed to be guttural, the "-zyn" had a clipped sound, the "r" had to be rolled, and the double "a" was pronounced "ah." The magistrate enjoyed listening to Gene try to get all this right over and over again while Phyllis waited an eternity in the hot car.

Phyllis had no idea why things were taking so long. She had not wanted to go into the building in her wedding dress, but she had to find out what was happening. When she was ushered into the magistrate's office still dressed for the wedding, he finally realized that he was pressing things a bit too far. The papers were signed, and the couple returned to the luncheon being served in the Louton's garden.

During this time, Dr. Mason discovered that the newlywed couple had made plans to live in Pietersburg. As he had intended for them to join him in Saaiplaats, he was shocked to learn of this turn of events. The prospect of living in a mud hut with round walls and a thatched roof in the bush did not appeal to the young couple as much as living in a town. Phyllis thought that she and Gene should move to Naboomspruit, some 35 miles south of Potgietersrus: she had even located an available house that they could move into after their wedding. But the couple had decided shortly before their wedding day to live in Pietersburg on the advice of Ruth Williamson and Laura Waite, who told them of the possibility of developing a church in the Black township of New Pietersburg. The District of Pietersburg had about 300,000 Africans, and there were about 6,000 in New Pietersburg itself. While there were other missionaries working in the area, Gene and Phyllis saw that there was much pioneer work to be done that would not infringe on anyone else's work. At this point, they particularly believed that they were to focus on the great needs of the township itself, although they would soon find themselves involved in village ministry.

Dr. Mason became very angry once he learned of their decision to minister in New Pietersburg: his plans for his mission station had been thwarted. Besides, he had guaranteed to the South African government Gene's intended ministry, and on this basis Gene was granted a visa. Gene correctly understood this only to mean that Mason had vouched for Gene and said that he would be engaged in mission work, not that he would have to do specific work in a specific area. However, this was not the best day to make an issue of anything pertaining to the bride and groom. The father of the bride never struggled with social finesse; he simply never exercised it. So the situation reached boiling point when missionary Mason announced that he would have Gene deported. Missionary Louton, rising to his new role as a father-in-law as much as stepping back into his old role as a cowboy in Oklahoma, announced that, if this were the case, he would proceed to beat missionary Mason up then and there.

Thankfully, Phyllis Grams did not witness this incident with Mason and her father. She had retired for a little rest before the second wedding that evening in the African township. Since the buttons on her wedding dress were a little too much work, Phyllis simply lay down in full attire.

Because there was to be a second event that evening, the wedding reception lingered on at the Louton's home at 66 Bezuidenhout Street in Potgietersrus, long enough for yet another painful encounter. A self-appointed dean among the missionaries told Gene to follow him as he had some important advice to share. In the back garden, the older missionary entered the outhouse to address an additional matter of importance simultaneously. To Gene, the two items of business increasingly coincided.

"I wanted to talk with you about how to relate to the Africans," he began. He, the seasoned missionary, needed to sort out this young man fresh from America before irreparable damage was done. "They are not . . . uh . . . they are not like us, you see. These Africans. I understand the black people. I have been in South Africa for a long time, and my parents were missionaries too . . . . Uh . . . , God made them inferior to us. They do not even spit like white people . . . . You must . . . uh . . . maintain control at all times. The missionary must always remain above the African pastor. Show him that you are in charge . . . . They mustn't eat at the same table as you, for instance . . . . And, uh . . . they should always enter your house through the back door so as not to offend your neighbors." The conversation continued for some time. Gene reflected that, if such thoughts were to be expressed, the venue could not have been better chosen.

Missions—ministry—is a delicate balance between fitting properly into the context, being contextually sensitive, and being able to change the context, being a steward of transforming grace. Listening to the voices of context can help the new missionary avoid many mistakes, but, as in this case, it can be a way to neutralize any new energy to bring justice, righteousness, and grace to an old situation. This little talk with the senior missionary on his wedding day was most helpful to Gene: he determined to be an agent of transformation in his future ministry in South Africa.

As evening drew near, many of those attending the first wedding proceeded to Mokopane for the African wedding. Who had ever before been married twice to the same person on the same day? And what white couple had ever been married in an African church in apartheid South Africa? The Africans had never had such an event. Some people walked or rode bicycles as far as twenty miles away to attend the wedding. There were so many in attendance that some of the guests had to stand outside the church building. The second ceremony began at 8:00 p.m., and the festivities went on until late that evening. A number of speeches were given, and Gene used the occasion to tell of a future heavenly wedding between Jesus Christ and his people from every tribe and nation. He and Phyllis had not received much in the way of gifts from their missionary guests at the first wedding, but they were deeply moved by the gift of the equivalent of about seventy-five American cents at their second wedding. "It was a real sacrifice for them and we felt so unworthy to accept it," wrote Gene in their first joint newsletter to supporters in the United States.

Gene and Phyllis arrived at the Louton home after 11:00 p.m. As they stepped out of the car to enter the house, they met the man whose job it was to collect the toilet buckets from the outhouses. Collection of excrement took place after hours to avoid unpleasantries. But the poor man whose employment this was nearly dropped the bucket that he was carrying on his shoulder, letting out a startled cry when he encountered Phyllis in her white wedding gown at that dark hour. Sometime around midnight, Phyllis finally took off her wedding dress and changed into something comfortable.

However, the night was not over—not by any means. Perhaps every wedding night has a story or two around the central event, but the first three nights of Gene's and Phyllis's marriage took comedy to a new level. The plan was to travel three days from Potgietersrus to East London, some eight hundred miles away, and enjoy a seaside honeymoon.

After Gene put their suitcases in the car, the newlywed couple said farewell to Phyllis's parents and drove away. Despite the late hour, they had no intention of spending their wedding night in Phyllis's parents' home. Gene told Phyllis about his own parents' wedding night. William and Martha were married in the same service as Martha's brother and his wife. Then the two couples drove off on their honeymoon in the same car. They even rented a single room together with only one double bed. This story provided endless laughter for all the relatives for years to come. Gene and Phyllis managed to reverse the story by being one couple with two weddings instead of two couples with a single wedding. Gene drove for about an hour to Nylstrom, on the road to Johannesburg. They had survived their weddings and looked forward to needed rest.

Phyllis washed up and changed into her nightgown, while Gene occupied himself with an unexpected challenge: rats. He noticed a rat dive into a large hole in the floor just as Phyllis slipped into bed. She was so exhausted that she promptly fell asleep.

Gene, however, worked furiously. His first plan of attack was to plug the hole in the floor with a roll of toilet paper. The rats were ever so pleased to receive the contribution to their underground nest. He then attempted to close the hole with the leg of a chair, but after a little while the rats pushed the obstruction out of their way. Exasperated, Gene looked about the room. A large, wooden wardrobe that stood some distance from the hole seemed his only hope. It was extremely heavy; a challenge for two men. He put his shoulder to the wardrobe, grasped it with his two arms, and nudged it inch by inch towards the hole. Sweating and out of breath, his mission accomplished, he collapsed onto the bed beside his sleeping bride. He lay there, listening to Phyllis's peaceful breathing and to the rats gnawing away at the bottom of the wardrobe until he, too, fell asleep, exhausted.

They slept until 10:00 a.m. the next morning. It was past breakfast time in the hotel, and there were no restaurants in any of the towns. So the couple found a cafe selling ice cream and then went on their way.

Their next stop was Johannesburg—the big city begun some sixty-five years earlier around the discovery of a gold reef that ran from west to east in what was called the Witwatersrand. They found a restaurant in Jo'burg, and so they had their first meal together as a married couple in the city that would one day be their home. Then they travelled as far as Kroonstad, another area in which they would one-day work.

Once again arriving at their hotel in the dark, they prepared for bed. "At least this time, there are no rats," Phyllis said, climbing into the bed. Gene hopped in alongside her and almost immediately let out a yell. He threw back the covers to find himself covered in bedbugs. Phyllis began to laugh uncontrollably as Gene faced night number two's challenge. A man in the next room called through the wall for them to be quiet. "Bedbugs!" Gene shouted back, slapping his body and trying to pick off the insects. The neighbor kept quiet, Gene kept vigilant, the bedbugs continued to bite him throughout the night, and Phyllis once again slept peacefully. She suffered not one bite throughout the entire night. No doubt, they much preferred Gene's blood.

The final leg of the journey should have seen a full day of travel and a timely arrival at the beach house by early evening. Complicating this plan was the one hundred mile detour they took in the Transkei due to some prankster's alteration of a road sign to East London. So, once again, the young married couple made their way to that day's destination, Bonza Bay Resort, in the late evening. The resort was about seven miles outside the city, and the road passed along the coast. A dense fog lay all along the beach, and Gene struggled to see the edge of the twisting road.

Suddenly, the road took a sharp turn and, before he could see what was happening, Gene drove off the road and straight into the Indian Ocean. The front wheels of the car were in the water, and the rear wheels spun in the sand. Phyllis would have to take the wheel, and Gene would have to get into the sea and push. The problem with their only plan, however, was that Phyllis did not know how to drive, and she certainly did not know how to work gears and a clutch. Thankfully, she only had to keep the car in reverse and press the accelerator.

Phyllis sat behind the wheel, ready to press the accelerator and ease up on the clutch whenever Gene told her to do so. Gene made sure she was in reverse then walked to the front of the car and into the ocean. At first, he was only ankle deep in the water, but then a wave came along and soaked him well above the knees. First rats, then bedbugs, and now the Indian Ocean, Gene thought as he bent forward to grasp his car. He would overcome all these obstacles and any others too. One of his strongest characteristics was an iron will, a determinedness to accomplish anything that he had set his mind to do.

However, his seriousness did not match Phyllis's reaction to events. Her response was to laugh uncontrollably. The more Gene was determined to meet the odds, the more Phyllis was beside herself. She, like her mother, could get into such a fit of laughter that she could barely breathe. And when Gene found a policeman not long afterwards and asked him for directions to the beach house, Phyllis was still snickering. The policeman was Afrikaans, and he and Gene had difficulty understanding each other's accent even though both were speaking English. Gene's experience with Afrikaners in the past month had not been encouraging. All this was too much for Phyllis, and she burst out laughing once again. Thankfully, the policeman did not haul the two of them into the police station for drunken and disorderly conduct.

About midnight, they found the place, but there was no reception office and no person on duty. Gene walked up onto a verandah and noticed that the top half of a Dutch door was open. He poked his head inside to ask for some assistance. The room, however, was occupied by a woman guest, and, upon seeing a man's head poke into her room in the middle of the night, she let out a scream.

Gene was able to calm her down, and she did eventually find someone who could show them to their accommodations. Their room turned out to be a rondavel—perhaps Dr. Mason would have been pleased about this had he known. They were shown the bedpan under the bed and told that the outhouse was some ways down a path outside. But they had arrived safely after some 800 miles of a most peculiar adventure. Finally, they could swim, rest, and play on the beach for several days before returning to the northern Transvaal.

As it happened, the beach was too cold and rainy for any such thing. They did manage one day on the beach in some sun, but it was too cold to swim. If it were not for driving into the Indian Ocean that first night, they could not have said that they were even in the water during their whole beachside holiday. One day, the couple went into East London and purchased a set of dishes for four pounds.

Upon their return journey, the newlyweds managed to get to Johannesburg before the car's gas meter read "empty." With only a tuppence between them, they still had two hundred and twenty-five miles to go. One solution to this latest challenge was quickly ruled out: they could not call Phyllis's parents. The Loutons did not have a telephone, and besides, they did not have enough money even for a telephone call. So they did the only thing they could think to do: they prayed. They prayed and continued on their journey. They watched the gauge all the rest of the way, and it did not move from empty. This was truly a miraculous trip home.

Upon arriving back in Potgietersrus, Gene and Phyllis Grams discovered that two checks had arrived in the mail totaling $40.00. And so they began their eventful lives together.

6

New Pietersburg and Beyond

When Jesus heard this, he said to them, "The strong have no need for a physician, but the weak do. I have not come to call the righteous but sinners." (Mark 2.17)

T HE NEWLYWED COUPLE MOVED into their house at 40 Magazyn Straat in Pietersburg shortly after returning from their honeymoon. Finding this house had been a miracle. Rental properties in Pietersburg were scarce, and Gene and Phyllis had so meager an income that they could find nothing at all among the few options available.

Before their marriage, however, Gene had had a dream in which he clearly saw a house that could be rented. It was a distinctive home in that it was one of the first houses ever built and still standing in the city.[1] The next day, Gene and Phyllis drove the thirty-six miles from Potgietersrus to Pietersburg and then up and down the streets until Gene saw the house from his dream. There was no sign out front indicating that the house could be rented, but, upon enquiries, they discovered that this would indeed be possible. And, not only could the house be rented, but it was also affordable at 10 guineas ($29.40) per month.

At first, they had hardly any furniture, and so it was the easiest of the many moves the Grams would make over the years to come. One item that they did move into the house was their new bedsprings. It was Phyllis's parents' wedding gift to them. Phyllis had arranged to buy a used mattress from another missionary, but it was only to become available in a month's time. So, for the first month of married life, Gene and Phyllis slept on army cots that were very narrow and sagged in the cen-

---

1. The house is today so altered that it can no longer be recognized as one of the earliest homes in the town.

ter. As beds, these were not very comfortable, but they also had to serve as living room furniture for the time being. They had an old refrigerator that did not work for several months, and they used a primus stove for cooking. Gene made an oven out of a five-gallon kerosene tin that sat upon the stove and had bricks inside. The makeshift oven functioned surprisingly well: they found that they could even bake a cake in it. They lived like this for about a year.

The decision to move to Pietersburg had been made once Gene and Phyllis were introduced to a group of five African women in New Pietersburg who wanted to start a church. They were Mrs. Dammie, Mrs. Konkobe, Mrs. Phashe, Mrs. Motau, and one other. Gene and Phyllis went to the address that they had been given by Ruth Williamson. After they knocked on the door, Mrs. Dammie called "Kena ka khotso" ("Enter in peace"), thinking that a neighbor was stopping by. When the Grams entered the home, they found the five women on their knees, praying for a missionary to come and teach them. As Gene and Phyllis entered the home, the women looked up from their prayers in amazement. They were surprised and overjoyed: here were the missionaries for whom they had been praying standing right in the living room. They stood to their feet and praised God for almost half an hour before they spoke with the Grams. Gene and Phyllis began Bible study classes with the women in a rented store, and soon a few others joined the little gathering, including a number of children. They had begun their first church.

Gene described his first impressions of the African township of New Pietersburg in a letter dated the 25th of April, 1952:

> This is a very needy field, where there is so much spiritual darkness. On Sunday, there is hardly a single person that seems to walk straight. Just about everyone seems to be intoxicated and walking in a dance step in time with the beating of drums. The drums and the dancing hardly ever stop on Sundays, and we sometimes have a difficult time conducting the services because of the noise . . . .

The meetings of which he spoke quickly grew in size. In that same letter, just one month after the wedding, Gene told of how members of the little congregation would walk along the streets and, when they encountered a group of people, they would deliver a brief message of the Gospel of Jesus Christ. Then they would move on, usually with their group swelling to larger and larger sizes. Phyllis and Ed had done this before in Potgietersrus, and it seemed to work just as well in New Pietersburg. As the crowd increased, it followed the Christians to the little church building. Not many weeks later, so many people gathered that they had to leave the store's doors open for those outside to participate.

Gene and Phyllis began studying Sepedi once they had moved to Pietersburg. Sepedi was a northern dialect of Sesotho. The southern dialect was spoken in the Orange Free State province and in a small mountain kingdom surrounded by South Africa that was, at the time, called Basutoland.[2] The Grams went through a succession of teachers in 1952: Mr. John Lebelo, a simple man who was no teacher but whose language it was; Dr. Kriel, an Afrikaner who wrote the first Sepedi grammar book; and Miss Faith Christie, a British Pentecostal missionary. Gene and Phyllis applied themselves somewhat to the language, although they were distracted from their studies by the mission work itself. They were privileged to study with Dr. Kriel, who did not take many students, and they quite enjoyed their lessons with him. Some of the fun they had was that which foreigners have when encountering a different culture. Since Dr. Kriel was Afrikaans, Gene and Phyllis would try their best to wrap their tongues around the sounds of both Sepedi and Afrikaans. At times, Dr. Kriel would call for his two children, Ansie and Jako. The sounds of their names would reduce Phyllis to embarrassing snickers. The missionary couple was, after all, still quite young. Their classes were also not sufficiently intense, being at first only one hour per week. In order to improve this, they had to switch teachers to another missionary, Faith Christie, who offered them two hours per week. Even this, however, was inadequate for serious progress in Sepedi.

In order to get to their lessons with Miss Christie in the town of Munnik, Gene and Phyllis had to drive some thirty-five miles northeast from Pietersburg on a dirt road in the direction of Magoebaskloof. Munnik, like Pietersburg, was hot and dry for much of the year, but the veldt gradually gave way just a little ways to the east to beautiful, green hills, forests, and streams in the area of Magoebaskloof. Just north of Munnik, the road suddenly curved sharply around a large, old tree that had stood right in the path of the road construction but had been spared because the local people believed that their ancestors inhabited it. One

2. Basutoland is today called Lesotho. The pronunciation of "suto" or "sotho" in the various words for the language is "soo-too." The language is Sesotho, the people are Basotho, and the place is Lesotho.

not only had to be careful to avoid the many people and animals but also the ancestors along the roadside.

Near Munnik resided an African pastor with whom the Grams ministered in various towns and villages. One day, Gene was driving a pick-up truck, and this pastor, Rev. Jack Maponya, sat beside him in the passenger seat. A policeman on a motorcycle drew alongside the truck and told Gene to pull over. The policeman parked in front of the truck. The Afrikaans policeman was quite angry at Gene for his infraction of custom. "You must put this native in the back of the truck and not on a seat inside the truck. Only white people ride inside the truck. You must never let a black man sit in the front seat beside you if they must ride in a vehicle with you at all." Gene was not unaware of how things were done in South Africa. Blacks had their own buses, taxis, and even ambulances. If an ambulance for whites happened upon an accident involving black Africans, they would call for a different ambulance rather than provide the help needed. On trains, the back carriages were for blacks and the forward carriages for whites only.

But Gene's indignation towards these sorts of laws and customs was especially heightened on this occasion. Here was Jack, his friend and co-worker, sitting beside him. It was, moreover, raining hard and there was no canopy on the back of the truck. The policeman could not have been more insolent. So Gene replied directly albeit as respectfully as he could. "I am not in your country to question or to break the law. So, I will come with you to the police station and, once you have shown me the law that says this, I will obey it." He suspected that there was no such law. At this, the policeman became furious. Without saying a word, he returned to his motorcycle and gunned the engine, intentionally shooting up stones that nicked the windscreen of the truck. As they pulled away, Jack said, "Moruti, this is South Africa."

Jack Maponya was also present when Gene, Phyllis and her broth-er Ed travelled to an asbestos mine west of Pietersburg to investigate a request to start a school. They were asked to find a teacher for the children and support him, but the building would be supplied by the mining company. As it happened, no teacher could be found, and this opportunity for ministry never materialized. On their first visit out to the mining compound, the missionaries asked the mine manager, Mr. Duff-Grey, for permission to hold a meeting with the miners. They were not sure what sort of response would be given, since they had earlier witnessed him swearing at his African foreman and kicking him. Duff-Grey explained that these Africans were just savages, not worthy of any respect and not much more than animals. He stated this right in front of Jack Maponya. But he agreed to the meeting, and Maponya was so pleased that he extended his hand and said, "God bless you, baas." To everyone's surprise, Duff-Grey replied, "God bless you, my boy." This demeaning response was, in context, positive. That night, they held a service under the stars for about two hundred people, and many signaled a desire to give their lives to Christ. The ministers were pleased to be granted permission to proclaim the Gospel under any circumstances. This was South Africa.

About this time, a young man named Andrias Sebitjo expressed a desire to help in the ministry in Pietersburg. He had finished two years at the African Bible Training Institute in Witbank but had not finished his training for financial reasons. The Grams were delighted to have him assist in the ministry as he was energetic, capable, and helpful in interpreting. Gene was almost the same age as Andrias, and he recalled Paul's words to young Timothy that he should let nobody despise his youth as he ministered among them (1 Tim 4.12). The people called Gene "Moruti," or "teacher," and Phyllis "Ma-Moruti" for "female teacher." These were generous titles of respect in a culture that valued age for teaching. So Gene suggested that the people call Sebitjo "Moruti" as well. After all, he was functioning in this way.[3]

When the elder missionary who had tried to sort Gene out on his wedding day about the inferiority of Africans received word of this, he told the Grams that they were never to go to the church in New Pietersburg again. What they were doing was wholly unsatisfactory. They had lifted up a young African in the eyes of the people. This was the very sort of thing that he had instructed Gene not to do. He himself was an appointed and ordained missionary with the Assemblies of God, and he was, moreover, twice the age of Gene, Phyllis, or Sebitjo. He came down on the Grams with as much authority as he could. However, he actually had no authority over the Grams. He had not had anything to

---

3. Pentecostalism, like any baptistic ecclesiology, involves a strong critique of any form of clericalism, any lifting up of the clergy too far above the congregation. It more readily starts its thinking of ministry from Matthew 23, where Jesus criticizes titles, honors, and hierarchies among his disciples. But Pentecostalism is also often very traditional.

do with the young church in New Pietersburg, and Gene and Phyllis were independent missionaries. During his first term of ministry in South Africa, Gene was sent papers acknowledging his ordination in the South African Assemblies of God—even though he had not asked to be ordained by them! Gene and Phyllis had no official connection with any group: they were responsible only to their supporters. Even so, rather than oppose the seasoned missionary, the Grams accepted the situation: they would leave the work in New Pietersburg.

This situation was the impetus for them to seek ministry in the villages outside Pietersburg in May, 1952. What was a real disappointment among fellow missionaries and an abuse of power by a senior missionary turned out for the good. Thankfully, Gene and Phyllis were quickly able to see it as such, and they called their new ministry in the villages a "privilege," rather than succumbing to sarcasm and anger, which gives the devil a place to work against the unity of the Spirit (Eph 4.27). As always on such occasions, one needs an agent of encouragement and comfort, and the young missionary couple found this in a Mrs. Charlwood. She was from Johannesburg but had some knowledge of the northern Transvaal, and she encouraged them to seek ministry in the surrounding villages. Some time later that year, however, Gene and Phyllis did return to help the little church in New Pietersburg, and the missionary who had told them to leave the township never spoke a word about it.

Over the next couple of years, Gene and Phyllis explored ministry in a variety of villages and townships in the northern Transvaal. One of these opportunities for ministry was in Warmbaths (now Bela Bela), a town between Pietersburg and Johannesburg. At this time, Ed Louton was attending a Bible college in Johannesburg. During a break in the academic year, he and a friend, Paul Watney, began to hold meetings in Warmbaths. A small, African church already existed in the township of people, so the tent meetings were held in order to expand this ministry. Ed and Paul pitched Albert Louton's tent and ministered until they had to return to college. Then Gene and Phyllis continued the tent meetings for another two weeks. They pitched a pup tent for their accommodations in a park on the edge of the African location, since the trip from Pietersburg was too great for daily travel. Women from the church cooked meals for them, and so they were able to devote themselves to the ministry.

People were eager to be prayed over, but Gene thought that they should first clearly understand the message of salvation. So, with the help of his interpreter, he announced that prayer for healing would only be held at the end of the week. But during their first night of ministry, a sixteen-year old girl came running up towards Gene at the front of the tent. She screamed, cursing at him in her own language, Setswana. Gene did not need to know the language to understand the gist of what she was saying, and he did not have to guess that this was a demon-possessed girl. He simply said, "In the name of Jesus, I rebuke you." At this, the girl fell to the ground and began to roll all the way to the back of the tent and then forward again. Her flexibility astounded everyone: she was clearly not in control of her own body. Gene followed her, praying in Jesus' powerful name. Every time Gene spoke the name of "Jesus," the girl would scream. After about half an hour, she quieted down, completely delivered from demon possession.

On the night that people were to come for prayers of healing, the very first man to come forward was crippled. He was carried forward by his son, who was also sick. Gene swallowed hard: this would not be a prayer for healing of some invisible malady. Everyone would see immediately whether the man would be healed or not. Without a sense of great faith, Gene faithfully extended his hand and said, "In the name of Jesus . . . ." Before Gene could say anything further, the man shouted, jumped up, and ran outside and around the tent. He ran around about four times, passing through the tent as well. Gene caught him as he came running inside and asked him, "What are you doing?" The man replied, "If you hadn't walked for nineteen years, you would run too!" He explained that he had been crippled in a shunting accident on the railroad. Everyone in the community knew him as a cripple and now saw that he was healed. The man's son said that he also felt God's power travel through his body when his father was healed. He himself was very thin and sick, but that night was healed of tuberculosis by the same powerful touch of God that had healed his father.

During the same evening, a blind woman came forward for healing. She had been a schoolteacher, but she could no longer distinguish between light and darkness. She had had a disease that had left her blind. As Gene and Phyllis prayed for her, she cried out, "I can see!" Gene picked up a hymnbook, and the woman, weeping, began to read. "It has been eighteen years since I could read anything," she said.

After the Grams returned to Pietersburg, an African minister, Rev. Pheme, continued the ministry in Warmbaths. A few years later, the Grams spoke with another pastor of the church. He told them that the two men were still involved in the church, and he confirmed that they and the woman who had been blind had indeed been healed that evening. The girl who had been delivered from demons had become a youth leader in the church.

In November, 1953, Gene travelled about ninety miles southeast to Sekhukhuneland (named after a Pedi chief in the mid-1880s), an area suggested by Dr. Mason as having much potential for village ministry. Mason took Gene to various village areas in the bush to introduce him to possible ministry. Sekhukhuneland was the very heart of the Sepedi region and a large African reserve. Many in the area had never heard the Gospel. While there, someone brought a communist tract to Gene and explained that it had been released by an airplane over the village. What could villagers make of Marxist ideology presented in a tract dropped from the air?

On the ground in Sekhukhuneland, Gene found a Lutheran missionary from Germany. The Berlin Mission Society, led by Alexander Merensky, had pioneered mission work among the Bapedi during the reign of Sekhukhune in the 1860s.[4] When Gene asked the current Lutheran missionary in the area what sort of success in ministry he was having, he received an astonishing reply. "Success? Who cares about success?" The missionary sucked on his pipe while Gene regained his composure. "Why, then, are you here?" "The pay is better here than in Germany," came the reply. This was undoubtedly true: it was only seven years since the end of the Second World War. This was Gene's first exposure to dead orthodoxy, if even that. He was by now becoming familiar with squabbling and theological confusion on the part of some of his colleagues in the region, but here was a person who had no passion for the ministry that he had chosen, a missionary without any calling at all on the payroll of a state church. Merensky, who had established five mission stations in South Africa and another in German East Africa (Tanzania), would have been greatly disappointed.

At this time, Gene did not see a way to begin to minister in Sekhukhuneland. He drove back to Pietersburg, unaware that seven years later he and his family would see God do great things in the area. On

4. van der Merwe, "Merensky."

another occasion, Gene and Phyllis explored ministry in Chuniespoort. There were very large villages in this beautiful area, which lay to the south east of Pietersburg through a pass in the hills and just beyond the Chunies River. Gene and Phyllis did not go to Chuniespoort very often, however, due to the distance. But when they did, they would hold meetings in a school building. A schoolteacher would ring the school bell to alert the villagers that the missionaries had arrived. The chief in one of the villages would also attend the services, but he proved somewhat of a distraction. He would stumble into the meetings drunk and then sit down where his villagers could see him. During the meetings, he would suddenly stand up and wave at people, and often he would talk out loud in the middle of a sermon. The people found this marvelous entertainment and came out in part to see the antics of their chief and in part to hear the Gospel. When the Grams turned to ministry in other villages, Albert and Louise Louton continued to travel to Chuniespoort.

7

Village Ministry

"'Not by might, nor by strength, but by my Spirit,' says YHWH of hosts" (Zechariah 4.6)

DESPITE FORAYS FURTHER AFIELD from Pietersburg in 1952 and 1953, the Grams came to focus their ministry in three nearer areas in particular. Two were villages in what was referred to as "Molepo's" (or "Ga-molepo"). "Molepo" means "grass rope" or "loop" in Sepedi, but possibly it referred to someone's name. Molepo's consisted of about five villages and is today called "Molepo's Location." It lies east of Pietersburg about thirty miles, just south of Moria. The third village, Motlala, was in the same region. In Sichuana, the language of the Bechuana people, "motlala" means "track." This was an appropriate name, since it could be reached only by dirt roads that eventually gave way to tracks through the grass. Gene had to remember directions by turning onto the various dirt paths after a certain tree or a distinctive bush or rock formation. After the Grams returned to the United States for their first furlough in May of 1954, Albert and Louise Louton continued ministry to these villages as well. In Molepo's, the Loutons helped with the erection of a church building.

In the villages, Gene and Phyllis met traditional Africa. The twentieth-century had barely touched the people's lives. In a letter dated the 18th of April, 1953, Gene described the Bapedi people with whom they had been working in several villages. This tribe occupied an area about two hundred square miles around Pietersburg. They were a brown-skinned people of average height with curly black hair.

The men, Gene continued, were polygamists, if they could afford it. The average price for a bride was a considerable amount of money at the time, about ten head of cattle or $200. The men counted their wealth by the number of wives and cattle that they owned. They had the responsibility to plough the land, but they were often seen gathering in groups drinking beer and talking to one another near the entrance to the village, like the village elders of old sitting "in the gate." While this seems painfully unfair to the women, it did serve the function of passing on the oral history and traditions from one generation to the next in this non-literary culture.

The women of the village worked constantly, and they did so together. Thus they too passed on the oral history and traditions of the culture. They were the life-givers of society, producing children, crops, and daily food. It was their responsibility to hoe the soil, sow the seeds, and harvest the crop, which always included maize, their staple food. The maize meal was mixed into a hard, corn meal porridge called "mielie meal." Versions of this are found throughout Africa under different names. In addition to mielie meal, the Africans enjoyed meat and vegetables. They would eat any sort of meat except pork or rabbits: saying that such food "had the devil in it." Eggs were also off the menu, and when Gene suggested that it was good food, his audience wrinkled their faces in disgust.

The women could also be seen working in the fields with babies on their backs, carrying grass for the roof of a hut, or plastering the hut walls with a mixture of mud and cow dung. Ever working, they were the unsung heroes of village life. Boys were also put to work in the village areas as herders, and the girls would look after the younger children while also playing their way into the roles their mothers held in the villages.

Each family had its own circular enclosure made of stones, thorns, and, possibly, wire. These family enclosures stood within the village itself, and within each enclosure could be found one or more windowless, low, round mud huts with thatched roofs. To enter a home, one had to stoop down to pass through a small, doorless opening. Outside the huts in the enclosure was a yard large enough to keep the cattle and any other animals. The animals would be enclosed during the night to protect them from wild animals and thieves. During the day, young boys would take the cows out to pasture while the girls remained around the village.

Gene and Phyllis were bringing the Gospel to Animists—people who believed in a spiritual world and the continuing presence of ancestral spirits. They believed that spirits inhabited things, such as trees and mountains. The witch doctor was a powerful person in the village, able to see into the future, give advice, and offer healing or protection. If a young man was leaving the area to work in one of the towns or cities, he would ask the witch doctor for a medicine to protect him and help him find a job and a good boss.

The chief would live on the highest ground in the village. Some of the larger villages sprawled out across valleys and hills and contained thousands of people, but one always knew where the chief lived.

Gene and Phyllis visited one of these large villages every week. It had an estimated twenty-five thousand people in it. They would drive out to the village towards the end of day. Gene would often take his trombone along with him and begin to play, pointing his musical instrument toward each point of the compass to call people for a meeting. As the sound of "Onward Christian Soldiers" or some other song in Gene's repertoire echoed through the valleys, people would begin to make their way to the meeting place. With the sun setting, lanterns could be seen swaying in the dark along the paths. It could take up to an hour and a half for most of the people to arrive. Up to three thousand would frequently assemble on these occasions.

The villages that made up Molepo's lay east of Pietersburg off the road that continues on to Tzaneen. To this day, the side road to Molepo's still terminates at the village. In one of the Molepo villages, the headman gave his life to Christ. Headmen ruled areas under the chief. He began to consider what being a disciple of Jesus might mean for him. One day, Gene noticed three new, large rondavels not too far away from the headman's own. The man told Gene that he had had a vision in which the Lord told him to release three of his wives and live only with his first wife. He would provide for the livelihood of the other three and take care of the children he had had with them, but he firmly believed that he should have only one wife.

CAPSULE: POLYGAMY

When Paul advises believers who wish to be overseers and deacons in the church that they should be the husband of one wife (1 Tim 3.2, 12), he almost certainly is speaking about divorce and remarriage. But this passage is always brought up for discussion when people discuss polygamy. The Old Testament, of course, gives evidence of the practice of polygamy in the cultures of the ancient Near East, although by the time of the New Testament it had been abandoned in Israel and was not a practice of the Roman Empire in general. The other option could be that Paul was counseling people not to remarry after a spouse died. While there is evidence of respecting those who remained single after a spouse's death in the culture and in Paul's writings, Paul fully accepts remarriage in such cases (Rom 7.1-6; 1 Cor 7.39; and 1 Tim 5.14). Thus the requirement for overseers and deacons to be married to one wife must refer to not remarrying after a divorce.

All over Africa, however, the question still arises, "What should Christians teach about polygamy?" The answer that is usually given is that a man should marry only one wife, although those who come to Christ are not usually told to separate. Polygamy can, actually, be a form of divorce. A wife may tire of her husband and work to secure him a second wife so that she can have greater distance from him, and a husband may tire of his first wife and seek another to be his closer companion. But polygamy is not always a result of worn out marriages, and in the case of a headman or chief it is essentially required as an indication of his status, authority, and wealth.

A typical practice in Africa is to reserve positions of church office for men with only one wife and to counsel believers not to marry more than one spouse. Polygamists who come to Christ are typically not told to change their situation (cf. 1 Cor 7.17, 20, 24).

This headman was one of the first in the village to become a Christian. During one of the early meetings at Molepo's Village, on a Saturday afternoon, the headman brought the village witchdoctor to Gene. The witchdoctor was himself very sick, and the headman told Gene only that this man was very important to the village. "Will you pray to God for him?" he requested. Gene enthusiastically agreed to pray for the man. But when Gene placed his hands on the witchdoctor, he was immediately shocked, as though he had grabbed hold of a live electrical wire. He struggled to free himself from the witchdoctor but could not. He silently cried out to God to help him and, after awhile, was freed. Gene quickly walked to his car and, trembling and fearful, drove down the dirt road to his home some thirty-five miles away.

Phyllis was at home all this time. She was pregnant with their first child and was not feeling very well. While she sat at the kitchen table writing a letter, the room suddenly grew dark at three o'clock in the afternoon. The darkness increased until it seemed as though it was the middle of the night. Phyllis became fearful and began to pray. She could feel the power of darkness about her and knew that Gene was in some terrible sort of trouble. The darkness was so oppressive that she could not say any prayer, so all she did was repeat the name of Jesus. She did this until the dark presence dissipated.

When Gene pulled the car into the driveway, Phyllis ran out to meet him. Gene was surprised to find out that she had experienced the power of darkness at the same time that he had in the village. In the years to come, this encounter with satanic power early in their ministry would prove beneficial. The young missionary couple knew what they were up against, and they had learned that the power of Satan could not overcome them. Not that they themselves were powerful, but the Lord, to whom all authority in heaven and earth had been given, was omnipotent and was indeed with them (Matt 28.18–20). They had learned the power of prayer, and they often spent time in prayer for the ministries in which they were involved. Indeed, Phyllis had learned that, even if she could not accompany Gene into the villages, she could minister alongside him in prayer.

When Gene returned to the village the next week, the witchdoctor again approached him for prayer. This time, Gene did not lay hands on the man, but he first prayed for boldness and then prayed for the witchdoctor. Phyllis had also come this time and joined in the prayer. The Grams had, of course, been fasting and praying during the previous week, and the result was wonderful. The witchdoctor was set free from the clutches of Satan, to whom he had until then devoted his life. He accepted Christ as his personal Savior, and from that time on served God. He no longer had anything to do with witchcraft and demonic power. And he was miraculously healed from whatever illness he had had.

Over the following weeks, the former witchdoctor was able to tell Gene and Phyllis more about himself. The Grams were surprised to learn that the man was well educated. He had had considerable power, such that people came to him even from surrounding countries. His power and fame had proved to be quite lucrative, and in this ever so traditional African village at the end of a dirt track, he drove a brand new car.

Sometime later, Gene asked the former witchdoctor if people still came to see him. He replied that they did, and he used such occasions to tell them about Jesus. He would then pray to God for their healing, and he used no witchcraft. Moreover, he took no money from the people who came to him for help. (Gene once heard of an unscrupulous minister who charged five Rand per minute for prayer!) He was no longer a wealthy man and lived, like the rest of the villagers, off the land.

Some African theologians have suggested that Jesus be presented to Africans as a great witchdoctor in order to Africanize the Gospel.[1] Moreover, the argument is often heard that witchdoctors are just traditional healers and people with special gifts to help people. But the experience of the Grams with witchdoctors, and seeing their transformation after coming to Christ, did not for a minute lead them to think of the witchdoctor as a positive figure for contextualizing the Gospel. Gene and Phyllis were greatly encouraged by the transformation of both the headman and the witchdoctor of Molepo's villages after they acknowledged Jesus as Lord. God's mission, it was clear, would result in contextual expressions of Christianity, but not by altering Biblical teaching or by giving credence to any power apart from Christ, and it was not advancing apart from the church.

CAPSULE: THE MISSION OF GOD

Andrew Kirk states that

> the theology of mission is a disciplined study which deals with questions that arise when people of faith seek to understand and fulfil God's purposes in the world, as these are demonstrated in the ministry of Jesus Christ. It is a critical reflection on attitudes and actions adopted by Christians in pursuit of the missionary mandate. Its task is to validate, correct and establish on better foundations the entire practice of mission.[2]

Our interpretation of Scripture and our contexts and experiences in mission combine to form various paradigms for mission.[3] Problems result when we have too narrow an understanding of God either from our reading of Scripture or from our experience of mission. Various interpretations of God's identity have led to different mission theologies, such as God as sovereign, God as power, and God as love. Any one of these understandings of God can go a long way to develop a robust theology and practice of mission, but none of them on its own is sufficient. Perhaps these can be brought together and balanced when God

---

1. See the discussion in Schoffeleers, "Folk Christology."

2. Kirk, *What is Mission?*, 21.

3. Bosch, *Transforming Mission*.

and his mission are understood in reference to God's glory and grace in Christ Jesus and where both can be experienced in contexts of the church's ministry.

A "God is Sovereign" theology of mission fails to present satisfactory explanations of the lostness of humanity, the need for evangelism, the requirement of responding to God's work of salvation, discipleship, and prayer. What God designs, whom he calls, and what he decrees become the way to frame our understanding of mission.[4] To be sure, such a theology of mission has its strengths. Mission is God's mission, it proceeds from his will, and we are not to compromise ourselves or presume upon God's sovereignty in efforts to reach the lost, such as through gimmicks and clever rhetoric. The missionary is but an instrument, a catalyst, a backdrop to God's own story.

Nevertheless, such a mission theology struggles to find a reason for action, a heart for the lost, and an urgency in mission. Evangelism becomes little more than calling out those whom God has already chosen. Some versions of such theology believe in double predestination, the teaching that God has chosen some to salvation and others to eternal punishment. Surely such a theology takes the very wind out of the work of missions.

A second understanding of God and his mission is more Pentecostal. It understands mission more from the conviction that "God is all powerful." God is certainly sovereign to do whatever he, in his infinite power, wishes to do. But the missionary goes out in that power to confront the rebellious yet inferior powers of this world. In a demonstration of God's power, people come to accept the salvation that he offers. Salvation is not simply a forgiveness of sins or a change of convictions that ingratiate one to God. It is a real breaking of chains that enslave one to passions of the flesh or the powers of darkness. Such a theology sees the whole missionary enterprise as stemming from God's infinite, sovereign power, but it is a power that woos the sinner and must be sought and received. And it is a power that can be seen in signs and wonders. This understanding of mission begins with prayer for God's power to save. Scripture is preached to demonstrate God's saving power. And mission rests upon the testimonies of those who have experienced God's power.

---

4. Piper (*Let the Nations Be Glad*) suggests that the key theological notion to consider in missions is "Divine Sovereignty."

Problems for such a perspective on God and mission arise when the message of the power of God becomes a message of triumphalism, as though every believer ought to live in triumph over sickness, poverty, and the circumstances of life. The practice of mission can, moreover, devolve into a forcing of the Gospel in ministry that ultimately denies God's power in the weakness of the cross.

A third option is to understand God's mission with the understanding that God is love. Such a theology of mission emphasizes Jesus' incarnation. It involves an emphasis on ministries of compassion, justice for the poor and marginalized, concern for the unity of the church, and a passion for peace and reconciliation. For John, the most profound understanding of God is that he is "love" (1 John 4.7–11). A problem with a theology of God's mission that is wholly based on love, to the exclusion of other notions, is that it struggles to account for God's holiness and judgment. In practice, these are often compromised or even ignored in order to secure a mission of love. There is no central theological theme that unlocks everything. Rather, theological ideas derive from the stories we tell about God's mission.[5]

However, God's sovereignty, power, and love can be brought together rather than held in tension in our understanding of the mission of God. This can be seen in both the Old and New Testaments. In one of the primary Old Testament revelations of God, Moses sees the glory of God in a cloud and hears a voice that reveals God's gracious character:

> And YHWH came down in a cloud and stood with him [Moses] there. And he proclaimed the name, YHWH. And YHWH passed before him. And YHWH proclaimed, "YHWH, a god compassionate and gracious, slow to become angry, abounding in covenant love and faithfulness, guarding covenant love to the thousandth generation, taking away guilt, transgression, and sin. Yet he does not cleanse the guilty. He visits the guilt of the fathers upon the children and upon the children's children until the third and fourth generations." (Exo 34.5–7)

Mission in the world is a proclamation of God's identity, of his glory and grace. In the New Testament, a clear statement of this in Ephesians

---

5. Richard Bauckham takes just such a narrative approach to mission theology in *Bible and Mission*. He believes that key Biblical stories are brought together and clarified in the story of Jesus and that the various stories can be summed up in the theme, "To all by way of the least."

can be found in the repeated phrase "to the praise of his glory and grace" (vv. 6, 12, and 14). The advance over Exodus 34 in Ephesians is the realization that God's intention from the foundation of the earth has been to reveal his glory and grace through Christ Jesus and in a holy and blameless people, the church, in love (Eph 1.4). God's mission is brought to a head in Christ (Eph 1.9–10) and revealed in the church (Eph 3.8–10). Any theology of the mission of God that looks for God's mission outside the church or apart from Christ is not Christian and does not understand how the revelation of God in the Old Testament comes to a head in Christ and the church.[6]

The mission of God that reveals God's glory and grace is a mission that is seen in his sovereign plan, power, and love. The *sovereign* plan of God from the foundations of the earth is to accomplish this work of grace through Jesus Christ in a holy and unblemished people (Eph 1.4; 5.27), who are themselves God's temple built up by the Holy Spirit, a people in whom he dwells (Eph 2.19–22). The *power* of God, manifested in God's raising Jesus from the dead and seating him at his right hand to have authority over every power (Eph 1.20–23), is a power in the church to administer God's grace (Eph 3.10). And the *love* of God (Eph 1.4; 3.17; 5.2) is poured out lavishly on us through Jesus, the Beloved, by whose shed blood we have redemption, the forgiveness of sins, and reconciliation with God and one another (Eph 1.6–8; 2.16). Thus God's sovereignty, power, and love are made known as God reveals his glory and grace in Christ and through the church. To participate in this mission of God is to be a steward of grace. Such is the mission of God.

---

6. Thus Walter Brueggemann's experiment in contemporary missiology (*Hope for the World*) could not be more wrong-headed as he seeks a definition of the mission of God that is neither Christ-focused nor church-focused. He states, "It is clear from any critical reflection that old missional assumptions and practices are no longer credible or productive, but the way ahead is not yet clear. The reality of religious pluralism, moreover, requires that mission be reformulated to recognize that God's mission is much larger than the horizon of the church and that consequently the church's mission cannot be conceived or practiced in absolutist or triumphalist terms. Recognition of the larger scope of God's mission and acceptance of a nontriumphalist posture for the church mission, moreover, may free the church for a generous agency in the world as a hope-bearing, hope-generating servant people" (9). The statement of a position is not an argument for that position. Brueggemann needs to explain what understanding of theology leads him to read against Scripture rather than from it when articulating a theology of mission.

~ ~ ~

God's sovereignty, power, and love came together in an expression of God's grace early in the Grams' ministry in Molepo's. Towards the end of 1952, a group of men approached Gene and Phyllis during one of their visits. They took the missionaries to a death hut, a round hut hastily constructed for a person who was expected to die. According to tradition, evil spirits would come after the death of a person and haunt the hut in which a person died. So it was very important to construct a death hut, which would be burned once the person passed away. Before the death hut was constructed, the witch doctor would be consulted. He would sell to the family various objects of witchcraft that were said to ward off evil spirits who could cause sickness and even death. These items were to be placed in the ground, by the entrance, and in the grass roof of the hut. But when it was decided that there was no longer any hope for the sick person, he or she would be placed in the death hut.

The men said to Gene and Phyllis, "If your God can do something with this young lady at the point of death, then we will believe that what you are telling us about God is true." Gene's sermons in Molepo's had emphasized the power of God to change lives, to heal, and to save. But until that point, there had been very little response to the gospel.

Inside the death hut, there was a young lady who appeared to be in a coma. "She will die today," the men told Gene and Phyllis. They looked at the death hut. It had no windows and only a little door just a few feet high. Gene and Phyllis stooped low and crawled on their hands and knees through the doorway. The men remained outside. After some while, the missionaries' eyes adjusted to the dark just enough to make out the form of the young lady, who was lying on a piece of canvas on the ground. She seemed to be about eighteen years old and not much more than a skeleton. There was a potent and repugnant odor in the hut. She was unconscious, and Gene thought that she probably was dying of tuberculosis, which was circulating in the area at that time. Others claimed that the girl had cancer. Stooping low, Gene moved around to the other side of the girl while Phyllis bent over at her feet. He turned to her and said, "What happens today will determine whether or not the people of this village will turn to Christ." They joined in prayer for the young lady with the burden of the whole village on their hearts. They asked God to show His mighty power, to show this village His power to save and set them free. They asked the God of all compassion and comfort to heal the young woman. They prayed that His will would be done for this girl and for the entire village.

Outside the death hut, they said goodbye to the waiting men and promised to return the following week. During that next week, the young missionary couple continued to pray earnestly for the girl in the village. One week later, when Gene and Phyllis arrived at the village, they found her waiting near where they always parked their car on visits to the village. She said to them, "Do you remember praying for a young lady last week in a death hut?" "Yes," they replied, unaware that it was her. "And what is the news?" "I am that young lady," she replied. Then she related how she saw Jesus take her by the hand and lift her up on the very day that they had prayed for her in the death hut. She also said that she had been aware that they had entered the hut and prayed for her. And she showed them the ashes of the objects of witchcraft that her family had purchased from the witchdoctor: she had burned them to declare that she had turned from any trust in the power of witchcraft to a newfound faith in Jesus Christ. Gene and Phyllis found the village willing to listen to the Gospel now, and many accepted Christ as their Lord and Savior.

8

Old John

"Will the judge of all the earth not do what is right?" (Genesis 18.25)

ON A TRIP BACK to Pietersburg one night from Molepo's village in 1954, Gene, Johannes Mukwevho and Jack Maponya were talking about the remarkable prevalence of demonic power in a particular region of the countryside. The two African ministers told Gene that such power sometimes manifested itself in burning bushes. That is, there would be fire in the bushes, but the bushes would not burn. As they spoke, they suddenly saw the phenomenon. Gene parked the car on the side of the road, and the three of them walked over to the bush. Mukwevho repeated Jesus' name as they approached and, just as they got up to the bush, the fire disappeared. Upon close inspection of the bush, they observed that not a single leaf had even been singed.

One day while visiting Molepo's, a man called "Old John" asked Gene to walk with him a ways. Old John had become a Christian in one of the meetings. He had a stump of a tree for one of his legs, and it was attached to his body with some leather straps that he grasped as he walked. Gene was young and fairly fit, but he struggled along the winding trail alongside the old man, who kept a steady pace. It was a hot day, and the ground was not only dusty but also stony. There were also many thorn bushes along the way that one had to avoid. After half an hour of labor along the trail, Gene asked how much farther they were going to walk. "Not far," was the reply. In cultures of honor and shame, as opposed to guilt, the right answer is the one that the audience wishes to hear. So, Gene kept expecting that "not far" meant they would soon arrive at their destination, but they walked on for another half hour on the dirt track. Finally, they arrived at the cemetery. On top of the graves in the cemetery were belongings of the deceased, from cups to tooth-brushes. It was a large cemetery, and Gene followed Old John to the far end where, by a fence, lay two graves.

"These are the graves of my parents," Old John explained. He began to cry. "Old John, why are you crying?" enquired Gene, as they had been deceased for many years. "Because of what I have found in Christ as my Savior," he replied. "My parents never heard the good news of the gospel. Why did no one ever come and tell them?" "I can't give you an answer," Gene said, "except this, that as far as God is concerned, the Bible says, 'Will not the judge of all the earth not do what is right?'[1] We can only trust that God will do what is right."

Then Gene asked, "Old John, did you not believe in a superior be-ing before you heard the gospel?" He was wondering in his own mind how much faith in God one needed before hearing the gospel itself. "Oh, yes, I did believe in God," the old man replied. "What made you believe in God?" Old John took some grains of corn from his pocket. "Who makes this grow?" he asked. But then he said, "I believed in God, yet I knew nothing of God." The young white missionary and the old black African stood beside each other in front of the graves of two much-loved people who had never heard the gospel. After another five minutes, they returned up the dusty path, taking one and a half hours this time be-cause of the ascent. "Will the judge of all the earth not do what is right?" Old John embraced this trust in God's justice for his parents, while being equally grateful for the mystery of God's grace now revealed to him and all in his village.

Old John's question was once posed to the Grams in a church ser-vice in New Pietersburg. On this occasion, a very old woman came to the services in the township. Before giving her life to Christ, she would disrupt the services by standing up and saying strange things. Whenever they would see her rise to speak, Gene and Phyllis would hold their breath, wondering what bizarre things she would say. But one day, she stood up and testified that she had become a Christian. She spoke of the unspeakable joy that filled her heart since she had given her life to

---

1. Gen 18.25. The context of this passage concerns God's considering judgment on Sodom. Abraham asks God if he will destroy the righteous with the wicked: will God not act justly? God's reply in the next verse assures Abraham that he will not destroy the righteous. While this does not solve the missionary question, "What will God do with those who have never heard the gospel?" it does point to an assurance that, whatever God does, it will be just.

Jesus. Then she ended her testimony by asking, "Why didn't you mis-sionaries bring us this message of salvation sooner so that we all could have been saved?" The question cut to the heart and spurred Gene and Phyllis to redouble their efforts as stewards of God's grace in the towns and villages of the northern Transvaal. They themselves had rushed to the mission field at a very young age. Still, they were troubled with the question posed by this woman and Old John. Why had it taken so long for the gospel to come to this region of the world?

CAPSULE: EDUCATION FOR MINISTRY

Sometimes people wait to enter ministry while they go through a long process of training, as though ministry can be studied and later applied. This is not, however, how most ministry works: it is best "learned" as an apprenticeship, rather like Jesus' disciples. One of the most prominent Biblical scholars from Europe in the twentieth-century believed that our scientific age could no longer be so juvenile as to continue to believe in miracles; one day of real ministry in Africa would have shaken his as-sumptions to the core and made him a far better scholar.

Learning of any sort must never be denigrated: neither academic education nor practical training is ever wasted. The challenge is to grow evenly in both areas of learning. Pentecostals sometimes failed to see the value of formal learning in these early years (although they did estab-lish Bible schools). They were, after all, a reformation movement of the church that was based not on a new academic approach to Scripture but on a new encounter with God and a new experience of spiritual gifts. Their spiritual experience propelled them into worldwide missions. This new zeal was also fueled by the conviction that the Lord's return was imminent. Where in all this was room for years of academic study? And what good had such academic study done in those denominations that prided themselves in advanced academic study for ordination?

Ironically, one of the passages used to encourage people to study for ministry has been misinterpreted. The passage is 2 Tim 2.15. In the King James Version, it is translated as follows: "Study to shew thyself approved unto God, a workman that needeth not to be ashamed, rightly dividing the word of truth."[2] This has been one of the most misused texts

2. References to the King James or Authorized Version of the Bible in this book are to the 1769 Blayney Edition of the 1611 King James Version of the English Bible (Online Bible Foundation and Woodside Fellowship of Ontario, 1988–1997).

of Scripture. "Dividing the word of truth" has been understood by some to mean discovering divisions in Scripture, such as dividing the timeline of redemption history into "dispensations."[3] Understood in this way, the passage has been used to support a "Dispensational" interpretation of Scripture, which teaches that God has dealt with humanity in different ways during different periods of history. However, the passage rather refers to a proper handling or explaining (not finding divisions) of the gospel. The mistaken view is a good example of what happens when one does not study adequately, such as in checking what the Greek says, but relies on a translation the English of which we do not even correctly understand. Secondly, by "word of truth," Paul is referring to the gospel, not the Bible (let alone the New Testament, which had not yet been written). Moreover, the word "study" in the King James translation also creates a misunderstanding for English speakers these five centuries later. The text actually says, ". . . eagerly present yourself to God as one approved (or tested)." The point is that the verse says nothing about studying anything.

The importance of study, however, can be illustrated from the same New Testament epistle. Later, Paul approvingly reminds Timothy of his upbringing, how he had been acquainted with the Scriptures from childhood (2 Tim 3.15). And, in the letter's conclusion (2 Tim 4.13), Paul asks Timothy to bring to him his books and parchments—undoubtedly meaning portions of the Old Testament. Moreover, Paul was himself a scholar: he had been trained under one of the major teachers of his day, Gamaliel. His pragmatic epistles, written to address real churches in their negotiations of the Christian life, are the product of a man who was steeped in and adept at interpreting the Scriptures. And, for all their brilliance, they remain the substance of academic theology two thousand years later.

Untold harm has often been done when missionaries arrive at their field of ministry full of zeal and without adequate preparation. Having a thorough knowledge of Scripture and an ability to interpret it is only the beginning of the training missionaries need. All too often missionaries arrive at their field of service unable to handle cross-cultural communication and living, poorly prepared spiritually or even psychologically, and without good mentors. The eagerness of responding to a missionary call often overrides adequate preparation, and once in their new situa-

3. In particular, see Scofield, "Rightly Dividing the Word of Truth."

tion, the demands of day-to-day ministry often result in little further development over the years to come. Perhaps training on the field might be the ideal solution, but training wherever it is done must not be viewed as optional.

However, the weakness of academic training in early Pentecostalism, compared to the seminaries in which future ministers trained for the mainline denominations, oddly enough sometimes brought a benefit. The benefit came in that *the* book to be learned was the Bible itself, and learn its content they did! Throughout the past fifty years, students training for ministry increasingly, many have felt, know less and less of the Scriptures prior to entering seminary. Then, as seminary focuses on an academic study of Scripture at a master's level, it aims to provide students with the right tools for a lifetime of study. But in this approach to training, would-be ministers can sometimes graduate without a thorough knowledge of the content of Scripture itself. Not many graduating with a master of divinity degree today could hold his or her own against the average Pentecostal student of the mid-twentieth-century when it comes to a knowledge of the content of the Scriptures themselves, even if they were often unprepared to interpret it.

The importance of preparation for mission work, formal or informal, cannot be overstated. Academic study should not be pitted against practical training and simply knowing the content of the Scripture. All such education is useful.

But it is not the only factor in effective ministry. Missionaries sometimes demonstrate another important factor in ministry: simply showing up! The missionary needs more than anything else simply to be present where there is a need, and to rely on God's working through him or her to do His will. This the Grams did throughout their years of ministry in South Africa. They never ministered on the basis of their own strengths, but they were willing to be in the villages, on the mine compounds, and with the people during times of unrest. If there was work to be done, they were prepared to help because they knew that it was God who gave the increase (1 Cor 3.7), it was the Holy Spirit who gave them the right words to speak (Matt 10.19–20), and it was the Lord Jesus Christ who was powerfully present with those who went to all nations with the gospel (Matt 28.19–20).

CAPSULE: URGENCY IN MISSION

If an eagerness for ministry and a sense of end-time urgency propelled Gene and Phyllis into ministry early in their lives, the church has not always felt that urgency. In answer to Old John's question, or to the elderly woman's question in New Pietersburg, as to why missionaries had not brought the good news of Jesus Christ earlier, the only answer to give is that the church did not always respond with Paul's vigor and resolve to the call of Christ to missions. There are exceptions throughout history, of course, and each Christian group has its own wonderful stories of missions to new territories. But it is also true that the church has often misunderstood its missionary purpose.

The Roman Catholic Church mobilized great efforts not to convert Muslims but to overcome them by conquest in the Middle Ages. During the sixteenth and seventeenth centuries, Lutherans, Calvinists, Anglicans, Catholics, and the Orthodox typically saw their goal to be securing the borders in which their respective churches could hold power (and that at a time the Roman Catholic Francis Xavier was engaged in—in many ways—exemplary foreign missions). The lead in foreign missions among Protestants was taken in the 1700s by the Moravians, going to the Americas and Africa to spread the good news.

In fact, the first missionary society in South Africa was the Moravian Mission, with its ministry to the Hottentots of the Cape in the early 1700s. In 1737, Georg Schmidt was sent to the Cape to work among the Khoi-Khoi. The Anabaptists in Europe in the 1500s also refused to understand Christian faith as something into which one was born, as subject to a certain territory, but rather as something that had no borders. For them, the gospel was good news that Christians were to carry to the ends of the earth. They rejected other Protestant interpretations of the Great Commission (Matt 28.18–20), that Jesus' words of mission applied only to the first disciples and not to the church through all time. This mission of the Anabaptists was, however, largely confined to Europe as it took place under extreme persecution from other Christian groups.

It remains one of the saddest stories in the history of Christianity that Africa stood on the doorstep of Europe and remained largely unevangelized until recent times. Islam, of course, cut off land access to Africa from the seventh-century onwards, but when ships began arriving in Africa from Europe, they arrived to collect cargoes of African slaves for the Americas rather than to deliver the gospel for the Africans.

Pentecostalism has been known for its emphasis on the gift of speaking in tongues, but this was really an outward sign of what it believed was its new contribution to the church and its mission: the outpouring of the Holy Spirit to empower believers for a worldwide mission in the last days. Thus Old John's question did not apply directly to Pentecostal missions, which had arrived in his village in remarkable time since the movement's inception in 1906.

≈ ≈ ≈

CAPSULE: EARLY PENTECOSTALISM IN SOUTH AFRICA

In 1904, an associate of John Alexander Dowie by the name of Daniel Bryant went to Johannesburg, South Africa, where he baptized about thirty people. Most of these were blacks, and from this initial ministry numerous indigenous African Zionist movements were spawned throughout the twentieth-century. The largest of these Zionist movements was the Zion Christian Church, an off-shoot of the 1908–1912 ministry of John ("Jack") G. Lake in the country. Like Bryant, Lake was an elder from Dowie's Zion Catholic Apostolic Church in Zion, Illinois. His arrival in South Africa in 1908 seems to mark the arrival of Pentecostalism in the country, with a mission to both whites and blacks.

It was only shortly after receiving the gift of speaking in tongues that John Lake travelled from Indianapolis to South Africa with his family and three other missionaries, Thomas Hezmalhalch, J. C. Lehman, and Louie Schneiderman,[4] and their families. More Pentecostal missionaries were also sent out at this time or very soon afterwards. G. J. Booysen, for example, is another Pentecostal missionary that worked in South Africa for a number of years beginning in 1908.[5] Along with their daughter, Mallie, the Booysens were ministering in Louis Trichardt, a town north

---

4. Louie Schneiderman was Jewish and remained to minister among Jews in London before following the rest of the missionaries sent out from Indianapolis to South Africa. See his articles, "Called to the Jews," 2–3; "News from Natal," 2–3. Also Lillie Schneiderman, "A Letter from South Africa," 2. A sizeable ministry among Jews was part of the early Pentecostal movement in Doornfontein, Transvaal and Vryheid, Natal, South Africa in 1908.

5. A request for prayer by G. J. Booysen in his continuing ministry in South Africa after eight years identifies him with ministry in South Africa in 1908. See Booysen, "An Appeal from South Africa," 13.

of Pietersburg, in 1916.[6] Verna Barnard was an American Pentecostal missionary from this time, working at Doornfontein, Johannesburg,[7] where the Pentecostals began their ministry.[8] Some persons already serving as missionaries in the area "got their baptism," as Lake put it, and became Pentecostal missionaries.[9] Lake's, Hezmalhalch's, Lehman's, and others' efforts entailed a remarkable healing ministry[10] and the spread of the Pentecostal experience. Their work led to the establishment of the Apostolic Faith Mission in 1913.[11] In the same year, the black branch of this ministry was founded by Ignatius Lekganyane. It is known today as the Zion Christian Church.

Lake's fellow missionary, J. C. Lehman, began the Pentecostal Holiness Church in South Africa in 1913. Yet another Pentecostal church, the American Assemblies of God, was recognized by the government in 1917 when it became involved with the work of R. M. Turney in South Africa.[12] Like Thomas Hezmalhalch, Turney was from the Azusa Street

---

6. Dugmore, "From Johannesburg, South Africa." In this article he tells of the healing of "Mother" Booysen and the spread of Pentecost into Rhodesia through an unnamed African minister.

7. Verna Barnard, "A Letter from South Africa," 3. See also Lake, "Asleep in Jesus," 4.

8. For a description of the ministry in its first year (ministry among the poor, healings, speaking in tongues to crowds that understood the languages, conversions, as well as the fraud and opposition), see Kerr, "Has Pentecost Come to Johannesburg?" 27–31. For another description, see Lehman, "Missionary Work Amongst the Natives in the Mines of Johannesburg," 1–2. Lehman's description concurs with Kerr's and also notes that missionaries from America traveled widely in South Africa from an early date.

9. Lake mentions a Chinese missionary from Canton, a Brother Ingram of the "Baker Missionaries," a Dutch missionary by the name of Mr. van Marile, and a missionary serving in Natal by the name of Miss Radford. See Lake, "A Call for Helpers," 7; John G. Lake, "Asleep in Jesus," p. 4.

10. See Lehman, "Apostolic Revival in South Africa," 1–2.

11. The Apostolic Faith Mission in South Africa took its name from the ministry at Azusa Street, also called the Apostolic Faith Mission. See Clark, "Contrasting Models," for a description of AFM and Assemblies of God models for missions in South Africa. Another early Pentecostal group in South Africa, the Church of God and Saints of Christ, owes its origin to a Jamaican missionary, Bishop Albert Christian. Part of his ministry was to the African village of Mapela, near Potgietersrus. While the Grams had heard of this ministry as something that preceded theirs, they had no contact with it. The denomination continues, and it's history is briefly told at http://www.cogsoc.org/our-origin/ (accessed 14 April, 2009) For further details on the AFM, see Anderson, *Introduction*, 106–110.

12. Cf. Synan, "The Origins of the Pentecostal Movement." Also see Anderson, "Signs and Blunders."

revival, went to South Africa in 1910. The Turneys, along with Hanna James, established a mission station in Middelburg, Transvaal, and set up ministry in other places as well, including Doornkop, Marquassi (on the border with Bechuanaland, now Botswana), Natal, and, apparently, Pietersburg.[13] The government recognized the American Assemblies of God denomination in 1917.[14] A loose fellowship of churches made up of the American Assemblies of God and other Pentecostal groups came together under the name "Assemblies of God" some fifteen years later. Missionaries from various countries served together, and churches were established among all the racial groups of South Africa. Each missionary was responsible to his or her own sending agency, but everyone tried to cooperate in joint ministries. Of Turney's work in the country, John S. Richard's wrote the following:[15]

> The work of the Assemblies of God in South Africa was begun by the late R. M. Turney, a former Baptist minister in the United States, who came to South Africa as a pioneer missionary thirty years ago. The first mission station was at Doornkop, where the first outpouring of the Hoy Spirit upon the native people in South Africa took place. From here the work quickly spread, and various assemblies were started. One of the evangelists found his way to Mapela (Potgietersrust),[16] where he came into contact with a brother of the then reigning chief. The chief's brother with nine others had received the Baptism in the Holy Ghost while in a prayer meeting, while as yet none of them knew or had "heard whether there be any Holy Ghost". It was three months after this outpouring that the Doornkop evangelist came in contact with them and taught them the way more fully. Under the leadership of the chief's brother, the work quickly spread. The light was carried to the newer places including Houtboschrivier, where

13. These places are areas of ministry noted in a letter by R. M. Turney to *The Christian Evangel* (November 2, 1918), 10. Ministry in the "Vietersburg" District is also mentioned, but this must be "Pietersburg." Turney also mentions a Bible School in Middelburg. Ministry in Pretoria, the administrative capital of South Africa, is mentioned in a subsequent note in the September 20, 1919 edition, p. 10. See also Carmichael, "Progress" 7–8. This article mentions a number of the Assemblies of God missionaries present in South Africa about the time covered in this book.

14. However, according to Allen Anderson, the Assemblies of God in South Africa was formed in 1925; cf. Anderson, "Pentecostals and Apartheid."

15. The quotation appears without citation in chapter 15 of Stanley Frodsham, *With Signs Following*. Frodsham was editor of the *Pentecostal Evangel* for many years.

16. Potgietersrus is sometimes spelled "Postgietersrust."

another outpouring of the Holy Ghost took place and a number received the Baptism in the Holy Spirit.

On Brother Turney's arrival in Pretoria he found a group of believers who had received the Baptism. He formed the group into the first Pentecostal church in that capital. This he pastored until later he was succeeded by Archibald Cooper. From this assembly many workers were ordained and sent forth, including Brother Stoddart of India.

Several other early Pentecostal missionaries in South Africa included Charles Chawner (associated with the Pentecostal Assembly of Canada),[17] John J. Ingham (who served with the South and Central African Pentecostal Mission),[18] the Andersons, and Kenneth E. M. Spooner.[19] Mrs. Ingram mentions in a 1916 article that the fifth annual convention of the Pentecostal mission was held in Pretoria, with over four hundred in attendance.[20] Some of the early ministry was also conducted in Zululand, Natal.[21]

Along with the European and American missionaries were native South Africans, equally called in mission to the country, people such as Ezra Mnobambi and Johannes Mahlangu.[22] Lehman notes that Africans from the mines took the Pentecostal experience and message back to their home areas.[23] Mr. and Mrs. Joseph K. Blakeney ministered in Durban and recorded a story of an Indian, a Mr. Mullen, from the Wesleyan Church joining the ranks of early South African Pentecostalism.[24] Still,

17. Anderson, *Introduction*, 109.

18. Ingham has an article, "Black Diamonds" about ministry in Benoni, Transvaal in 1918.

19. Spooner tells of a powerful outpouring of the Holy Spirit in 1922 in Naauwpoort, near Witbank, Transvaal, in "Outpouring."

20. Mrs. John W. Ingram, "Glorious Convention," 7, 9.

21. Missionaries involved in Zululand included W. F. Dugmore, Mr. le Roux, Mr. Burton, Mr. Wick, Mr. and Mrs. Saunders, Mr. Hibbert, and Ms. Moodle.

22. Dugmore, "A Visit to Zululand." Dugmore mentions the names of all those noted above between "Dugmore" and "Mahlangu" in 1914.

23. J. O. Lehman, "Missionary Work," 1–2. He also mentions, with deepest regret, the necessity of dividing services for blacks from those of the whites, due in large part to the blacks' intimidation by the whites and to the limited times that the blacks in the mines were given for these meetings.

24. Blakeney, "Durban, Natal, South Africa," 12. The account of Mr. Mullen is given in the February 2, 1918 edition, p. 5, in another note from Blakeney, "An Encouraging Word." Blakeney also told of interracial worship in the city in 1917.

the largest, black Pentecostal movement was Lekganyane's Zion Christian Church, spawned by Lake's ministry.

On one occasion, Gene Grams and his brother-in-law, Edgar Louton, paid a visit to the Zion Christian Church's headquarters at Moria. This group represented the earliest introduction of Pentecostal missions to South Africa through John Lake. Moria was about twenty-five miles east of Pietersburg and only five miles north of Molepo's. They had heard of the meetings held there. Actually, everyone in the area knew about them since the roads would be filled with busloads of people making a pilgrimage there to the Easter services. At these times, people would confess their sins and be re-baptized by fire hose. The early Christian document, the *Didache*, encouraged a practice of baptism that used running water, perhaps to illustrate the "living" water that symbolized the spiritual cleansing that brought new life in Christ. But a fire hose offered a whole new way to consider the symbolism of baptism, as did the practice of being frequently re-baptized. Baptism was not a symbolic participation in Christ's death and resurrection (Rom 6) but seemed to be a cleansing in itself, with the most stubborn sins blasted off by the pressure of a fire hose. Gene and Ed could see people being drenched and knocked off their feet in the short time they were able to visit Moria, but they were fairly quickly ushered off the campground property.

Another practice of the annual pilgrimage at Easter was the collection of an offering. After Easter, banks in Pietersburg closed in order to count the money. There was never an opportunity for the Grams to link up with this essentially indigenous African church, and, in any case, Gene was fairly critical of the display of wealth he witnessed of its leaders as well as of their theology and other practices. Gene's parents had occasionally found their lives affected by the ministry in Zion, Illinois, while they never joined this movement. Strangely enough, thousands of miles away from Zion City in Illinois, Gene once again found himself a neighbor of Zionism, this time in African form. While there was no linking of arms with this movement, a number of the Zionist Christians left it over the years and joined the Assemblies of God or other Pentecostal churches in the country. Even so, the ZCC grew to such great numbers that the post-apartheid government held consultations with it.

While Pentecostals came to South Africa early in the history of the Pentecostal movement, the question posed by Old John and the elderly lady from New Pietersburg remains the great missionary question to the church throughout the nearly two thousand years since Jesus founded his church. Two related missionary questions are, "What will God do to those who have never believed the gospel because they have never heard it?" and "What will God do with those believers who have never helped to take the gospel to those who have never heard?" This last question again and again drove Gene and Phyllis to labor indefatigably in fields that they found to be white for harvesting.

9

Faith

Blessed be the God and father of our Lord Jesus Christ, who, in accordance with his great mercy, has given us new birth into a living hope through the resurrection of Jesus Christ from the dead, into an incorruptible inheritance, both undefiled and unfading, kept in the heavenlies for you, who are being kept by the power of God through faith for a salvation ready to be revealed in the final time. In this you rejoice, although for a little while, if necessary, you have been grieved by various trials, so that the testing of your faith—more precious than gold, which perishes, and is tested by fire—might be proven to be for praise and glory and honor when Jesus Christ is revealed (1 Peter 1.3–7)

EVEN AS THEIR MINISTRY turned from the poor township of New Pietersburg to the even poorer villages of the northern Transvaal, Gene and Phyllis found themselves in their own situation of poverty. They had only been married three months when Gene mentioned in a newsletter to supporters that they had been through "some severe financial tests." For two months, their car stood in the driveway for lack of fuel. Gene borrowed a bicycle to get around town. Every day, Gene went to the mailbox and opened it while uttering a prayer. "Nothing. Nothing for several weeks now." He walked back to the house to face another meal of beets from their garden. Beets for breakfast, beets for lunch, and beets for dinner. He determined never to eat another beet in his life when they finally emerged from this hardship.

He ascended the steps and entered the house. Phyllis looked up hopefully. "Nothing," he said. "Well, come and have something to eat," she suggested. He had planted a garden, but only the beets were left to eat. Gene's boundless energy and knowledge of farm life, his careful preparations and constancy—some called it "stubbornness"—could not alter their predicament. That week, they had searched the house for coins to find enough money to buy some milk, but they were not able to do so.

"I can't understand it," Gene said, "Pa should have sent some money from the churches that support us by now. There has to be something wrong." He looked at Phyllis, pregnant with their first child. How could she and the baby live on beets? All he could do was reach across their little table and take his young wife's hand. They bowed together and gave thanks for their dinner of beets that day.

Gene had noticed over several days that there was some paper lying up against their fence. He had thought that it was rubbish and decided to pick it up at a later time. He also walked daily to the post office to check for mail, about one mile away. After a week, Gene finally picked up the paper along the fence. He discovered that it was an envelope. Looking at the address, he was amazed to find that all it read was "Eugene and Phyllis Grams, South Africa." Some space had been left in the address, as though the sender had intended to fill in the rest of the address before mailing it but had forgotten to do so. There was no return address, but inside was a little note, which read, "We are so happy to be able to send you the enclosed check. We believe that the Lord wants us to do this, and we hope it will be a blessing to you." The note was from Phyllis's home church, Christian Trinity in East Detroit, Michigan. With it was a check for $200! That day, the young couple danced to the faithfulness of God through His people.

CAPSULE: FAITH

There is a qualitative difference between Christians when it comes to the practice of faith. Some have faith without really needing it: they believe that God has acted remarkably in the past to bring spiritual salvation, but they themselves do not live in faith, a daily trusting of God for food, shelter, safety, and empowerment for ministry. Others think of themselves as people who live in faith minute by minute, but they too do not really need it: they are comfortable, not facing adversity, and going through life well fed, well housed, healthy, educated, and in all ways most comfortable. They might give sincere thanks to God for their happy lives, or they might even form the view that material blessings and health are the rightful inheritance of believers—a "prosperity gospel." They say that God blesses them because of their strong faith, and those who are less fortunate in the circumstances of life are less fortunate because they lack the faith that God will grant them the desires of their hearts. Such views of faith, on the face of it very different, are in important ways similar: they are not practical theologies of faith born in the cauldron of need but of comfort.

Alternatively, some views of faith are developed in the context of great suffering, desperate circumstances, and challenging ministries. Here too, however, different views might be maintained. One group may share the prosperity gospel of wealthy Christians, but in this case the theology is held in desperate hope for a better life. It is more of a "rescue theology" than a "prosperity theology," although the rattling of supportive Scripture passages for either theology is the same. Both "prosperity" and "rescue" theologies hold that "faith" is not just a spiritual matter but pertains to the whole of life. Yet they lack any theoretical or practical answers to the suffering of the faithful and righteous.

The practice of faith that Gene and Phyllis were developing in the early years of their marriage and ministry was altogether different. They had to trust God for sustenance; they did not trust him for prosperity. Their faith in God's call had thrust them into a situation of need, and their trust that God would meet their needs was intertwined with their trust that God had called them to service. They were, moreover, finding a greater need than ever to trust God as they stepped into a context of ministry in the villages of northern South Africa that called for divine empowering to bring light to darkness. Thus their faith was not based on any sense of divine entitlement, as though their ability to believe really hard would open the treasure houses of heaven for them, as though their claiming for themselves Scriptural passages that refer to divine blessing could catapult them into such blessings because God's feet could be held to the Scriptural fire. Their faith was, rather, a faith that they had been called to this service, and God would enable them to do it. Their practice of faith, then, meant continuing to live in their calling no matter the challenges that came their way.

In the same June newsletter to supporters in which Gene mentioned their severe financial tests, he also spoke of their new ministry in the villages. Gene referred to one of these villages as the "uttermost part of the earth." This was the village of Motlala. The trip there and back, including the service, could take six hours. Gene and Phyllis would turn off the main road and follow what was little more than a dirt path. The road was narrow, winding, rocky, dusty, and it crawled up and over the hills. When they arrived, they would shake the powdery dust out of their clothes and try to clean off the car's windows a little for the return journey in the dark.

Gene and Phyllis planned their arrival at dusk so that people would be finished working in the fields and could participate in the services. As they approached the village, one of the village school teachers would announce their arrival by ringing a bell. Sometimes the number of people gathering would reach over five hundred, and they would sit attentively under the stars to hear God's Word preached. Gene and Phyllis were also able to pass out literature in Sepedi, and the Bible Society made Bibles available in the people's own language at almost no cost. The Grams delivered hundreds of these Bibles to the villages, and the people were so happy to receive the Word of God in their own language that they cried and hugged and kissed their copies. During this time, many committed their lives to Christ.

When the Grams left these meetings, the car had to crawl slowly from the village as it was thronged by the joyful children. "How lovely on the mountains are the feet of those who bear tidings, who proclaim peace, who bear good tidings, who proclaim salvation, who say to Zion, 'Your God reigns'" (Isa 52.7). These were joyful days, not only for the Grams but also for the people, many of whom had not yet felt the bite of apartheid or the challenges of life in the cities.

Cleaning the car after these trips was part of the ritual. On one occasion, Gene hired a young man to clean the car "inside and out." After a little while, Gene went to check on his progress, only to find that he was throwing buckets of water into the car. The car was so soaked that it had to stand open for several days before it finally dried out.

Gene sold this car—his imported, black '51 Ford sedan—to an Indian storeowner in Potgietersrus. The Indian had fallen in love with the car. Gene wanted to sell it because he had been told in Cape Town that the spotlights that were mounted on each side were illegal; only the police could have spotlights on a car. Without the spotlights, the car had a hole on each side of the car where they were supposed to be mounted. Gene also realized that he could make money by selling the car. He would be able to exchange the pounds that the Indian man paid for the car for dollars from other missionaries. By using dollars, he would be able to purchase a new car at a greatly reduced price from a General Motors factory in Port Elizabeth, a city in the Cape Province. The Indian man somehow managed to get permission to mount the spotlights on the car legally as long as he covered them. He also loaned an old car to Gene and Phyllis for a couple of months until they could purchase their new car.

However, the car that had been loaned to Gene and Phyllis had a bad radiator. It would easily boil over and need to cool along the side of the road, and then water had to be added before the trip could be resumed. On one occasion in July 1952, while the Grams were returning to Pietersburg, the car's radiator boiled over far away from any town. Gene assumed that, at the bottom of a steep slope beside them, there might be some water. So he scrambled down the precipice with the only container they had—a small Coke bottle. He did find a polluted pool at the bottom of the slope, but also a great number of mosquitoes. During the forty or so trips up and down the precipice with his Coke bottle, Gene was bitten numerous times. While they were able to complete their trip back to Pietersburg, Gene fell ill with malaria a short time later.

The malaria gave Gene such a bad headache that he thought his head would split open. He shook from the fever and lay unable to move during the afternoon and evening. Gene and Phyllis were at the Louton's home in Potgietersrus when the illness overtook him. That evening, Albert and Louise Louton, together with Phyllis, prayed for Gene's healing.

CAPSULE: PRAYER AND HEALING

Pentecostal prayer at this time had certain distinctives. As Scriptural passages on prayer and healing came to mind they would be worked into the prayer to bolster faith and appeal to God by analogy—"as you healed so-and-so, we believe that your mighty hand is able to heal Gene this very moment," and so forth. As the King James Bible was the only translation in use among Pentecostals at the time, prayer was typically offered in King James English. The prayers were lengthy; this gave the persons praying time to reflect on God's character, His power and goodness. Meditation on God's character increased faith, and with an increase in faith came a louder and bolder prayer, often in a singsong voice. Yet the prayers were spoken in a pleading voice, perhaps different from the prayers one sometimes hears in certain Pentecostal and Charismatic circles today, where the bold voice of prayer has a certain air about it, as though one can demand healing because some Scripture or other is thought to hold a divine promise to heal in every instance. But the prayers of former times often meant wet faces: they were an emotional seeking and beseeching of our miracle-working and all compassionate God.

One passage of Scripture often cited in prayer, however, was Isaiah 53.4–5 (*King James Version*):

> Surely he hath borne our griefs, and carried our sorrows: yet we did esteem him stricken, smitten of God, and afflicted. But he *was* wounded for our transgressions, *he was* bruised for our iniquities: the chastisement of our peace *was* upon him; and with his stripes we are healed.

This passage became the crux of a Pentecostal doctrine of healing that found healing to be based in Jesus' suffering—"with his stripes we are healed." The passage is interpreted metaphorically in 1 Peter 2.24: "healing" is understood as Jesus' dealing with sin. This is also how most interpreters understand Isaiah 53's poetic language. The suffering servant of the passage takes upon himself the people's sin as though it were a disease. Yet Matthew 8.17 quotes the same passage in reference to physical healing. Matthew, however, applied the verse from Isaiah to Jesus' ministry of healing, not to healing in his death.

But the Pentecostal understanding of Isaiah 53 located healing in the atoning work of Christ on the cross. One always heard in prayers for healing words such as "we plead the blood [that is, from his stripes and death] of Jesus."

For all the difficulty in trying to locate such a theology in any of these passages of Scripture, there is a dimension of this teaching that is Biblical. It is also a way to understand how Matthew could apply Isaiah 53.5 to Jesus' earthly ministry of healing. The key is to understand Jesus' work more broadly than just what we find in a theology of the cross. On the one hand, Jesus' earthly ministry entails more than the cross. He ushered in the rule of God, which begins with his healing ministry, casting out demons, leading people out of captivity in their sins, calling people to obey the ethics of the Kingdom, and including Gentiles in the new covenant. All this comes to a climax when Jesus goes to the cross. On the other hand, what Jesus accomplishes on the cross is more than just an atonement for sins. What Colossians and Ephesians in particular state is that the cross, resurrection, and exaltation establish divine power in the world, particularly Jesus' overcoming sin and the spiritual powers.

The pre-cross work of Jesus in ushering in the Kingdom of God and his post-cross work of being resurrected and exalted above every power are related: Jesus' ministry brings to all creation the powerful rule of God. By understanding Jesus' entire ministry, including his passion, as accomplishing more than just the forgiveness of sins but also as a work of restoration in the broadest sense, Pentecostals touched on a truth that highlighted a wider understanding of the work of Christ. Being in Christ meant, for Paul, a "new creation" (2 Cor 5.17). Redemption would one day mean not only forgiveness of sins but also resurrection, and not only resurrection for those in Christ but also the redemption of all creation groaning in its bondage to decay (Rom 8.21–22). Or, in the language of the Gospels, Christ's entire work was an ushering in of the reign of God, and His work came to its climax in His death, resurrection, and exaltation.

However, if the "healing in the atonement" theology is understood in the same way as salvation from sin, it becomes the basis of a "name it and claim it" theology of healing. If the atonement means that we are saved by faith in the work of Jesus, who took away our sins on the cross, then people only need to believe in Christ to be saved. If the atonement also means that we are healed by faith in the work of Jesus, then healing is waiting for us to claim through our faith. The inevitable result of such reasoning is the conviction that those who are not healed do not have enough faith, and so they need to believe harder. Also, people praying for healing begin to demand the healing from God that has already been paid for by Jesus: our relationship with God becomes consumerist, and we begin to act like consumers waiting for our goods to be delivered.

An alternative would be to understand healing more generally as a defining characteristic of the Kingdom of God that Jesus proclaimed to be already breaking into this world but not yet fully established. This was in practice the view that Gene and Phyllis Grams always held, even before the theological language of an "already/not yet eschatology" was available to articulate it. Thus when the Prosperity Gospel, with its teaching that every believer should have health and wealth, came along in later decades, Gene and Phyllis opposed it. They found it not only unbiblical but also offensive: who were we to demand anything of God, and who were we to insist on prosperity when our Lord had no place to lay His head and stated that the life of discipleship meant the same for us (Matt 8.20)?

What really distinguished the early Pentecostals' view on healing from so many others was that they truly believed in healing. They actually believed that, when they prayed, something might well happen.

Soon after that evening's prayer over Gene, his headache began to subside. The next day, he felt fine. At a later date, he had a blood test that revealed the presence of malarial parasites in his system, but he never again suffered a relapse of the disease, which those who have contracted the disease often do.

Once he had recovered, Gene focused on purchasing his own, reliable car. From the sale of the Ford, Gene was able to buy a beige '51 Chevrolet sedan at the General Motors factory in Port Elizabeth, and there was also enough money left over to purchase living and dining room furniture. Gene had to hitchhike the 1,000 miles to Port Elizabeth to pick up the car. He found rides from about ten different drivers over the course of the journey. On the first part of the journey from Pietersburg to Potgietersrus, he and Phyllis hitchhiked together. Phyllis then stayed with her parents while Gene continued the journey. His next ride was from Portgietersrus to Johannesburg, and he was delighted to find that the driver was Justus DuPlessis, an Apostolic Faith Mission pastor. He was the brother of David DuPlessis, known also as Mr. Pentecost. David DuPlessis was a popular South African conference speaker who maintained that Pentecostals needed to engage the wider church. Years later, when the Grams lived in Johannesburg, they enjoyed fellowship with Justus DuPlessis and his family.

After only six months, Gene realized that he could again make money by selling his Chevrolet. He now purchased a brand new, green '53 Chevrolet pick-up in Port Elizabeth after again hitch-hiking the 1,000 miles.

This time, on the journey to Port Elizabeth, Gene hitchhiked with a free-lance reporter from Holland. They ended up sharing a hotel room together in Grahamstown. During dinner, they discussed what the bowls of water beside their plates might be. Could they be intended for the cats running around the restaurant and even jumping up on tables? A waiter explained to them that they were called "finger bowls" and intended for washing one's fingers after eating with them. Neither had ever seen cats or finger bowls in a restaurant, and the reporter decided to add it into his story about travelling in South Africa.

Gene nearly lost his life in May of 1953 in this pick-up truck. When Laura Waite asked Gene to travel the 90 or so miles to her orphanage near Tzaneen to fix a broken washing machine, Phyllis stayed behind. While on the way to repair the machine, Gene drove too fast for the roads. As he came over a rise, he was horrified to find in his path a sharp, short decline that was immediately followed by a bridge some one hundred and fifty feet long. On each side of the bridge there were stone pillars three feet wide and three feet high, and the two-lane road narrowed to a single lane for the bridge.

Gene would have had difficulty negotiating the bridge at his speed of approximately ninety miles per hour, but he quickly realized that he faced an impossible decision. In the middle of the bridge was an ox wagon pulled by ten oxen with three men riding upon it. Gene had to decide between driving the car off the road and into the dry riverbed that dropped a further fifty feet below the road or aim the car for the oxen while breaking as hard as he could. Figuring that his chances were better if he stayed on the road and just killed some of the oxen—he knew there would be a crash—he chose to stay on the road. He braced himself and instinctively closed his eyes in anticipation of the impact, praying the name of Jesus as he did so. Almost immediately he opened his eyes and was surprised not to see the oxen in front of him. The bridge was gone. He looked back and saw that the bridge was now behind him, and the ox wagon was still in the middle of the bridge. The three men on the wagon were standing up, looking backwards, and waving their arms at him to keep moving. Whatever they had seen left them convinced that they did not want a further encounter with this driver.

On the return journey, an ox damaged Gene's car. Cattle, goats, and sheep were often seen grazing along the sides of the roads—or walking on the roads—so one needed to drive defensively as a rule. After the incident on the way to Laura Waite's, he was driving particularly carefully and uncharacteristically slowly. On this occasion, a large ox on the side of the road suddenly backed down a slope right onto the road just as Gene's brand new '53 Chevrolet pick-up came humming along. Neither could stop in time, and so Gene skidded into the beast. The pick-up's fender was dented and the headlight broken, but the ox just walked away without any sign of injury. Perhaps there was a little justice for the oxen that day.

One day in July of the previous year (1952), Phyllis and Gene were approached by a woman in one of the villages. She could see that God had blessed them with a baby, as Phyllis was now beginning her second trimester. The woman asked them to pray for her, since she was barren. In Africa, one married to produce offspring. In some areas, failure to produce children may mean the end of the marriage or even that it was never truly a marriage at all, whereas once a woman bore a son, she would be known as the mother of this boy. Children would care for their parents in old age and remember them when they died. Generations to come would venerate their ancestors. Barrenness, then, was a curse, and the woman's sense of worth as well as her actual worth depended on producing a child. Among the Bapedi, to be childless in society meant not being able to move up in status from being an initiated woman with a mature status (*kgarebe*) to a woman with children (*mosadi*), the seventh level of status. So, the young missionary couple prayed earnestly for the woman. By September, they learned that she was expecting her first child. The two women rejoiced together as they were now both expecting their firstborn.

However, within a month, the Grams' joy was turned to sorrow. Faith Dawn Grams was born at five and a half months on the 6th of October, 1952. Phyllis's doctor could not be found when the birth began. The nurse at the nursing home in Pietersburg, where many mothers went to have their babies, said that a doctor needed to be present during the birth, and so she tried to keep the baby from being born rather than assisting appropriately. When the baby was born, it was clear that her head had been damaged—most likely because of the nurse's intervention. The nurse then put Faith aside and told Phyllis and Gene that the baby was dead. Gene went to look at his little girl and discovered that she was alive. He could also see that she had been severely injured. He called for a blanket for his daughter, and the nurse obliged. Faith lived about two hours before she died. There was no money for a coffin, and so she was buried privately in a small box in her grandparents' back garden in Potgietersrus.

The birth had damaged Phyllis to the extent that her doctor told her that she would never be able to have children again. As Phyllis and Gene struggled with their sorrow, they also faced a new challenge. The Grams needed twelve pounds and twelve shillings to have Phyllis released from the nursing home, and they did not have the money. So Phyllis remained in the nursing home for a week while Gene asked around for a loan. The manager of their bank refused his request, and eventually Albert Louton agreed to loan him the money. It took the couple six months to pay it off.

The loss of a child, a first child, an only child—who but those who have experienced this pain can understand it? It tears at the heart and leaves an ache that can still be felt half a century later. It leaves a feeling of emptiness that lurks in the shadows of joyful occasions and pounces in times of loneliness or weakness. It is a constant reminder that life is neither safe nor fair. But for the believer, such pain is not without hope, and Gene and Phyllis would from time to time find themselves eager to be reunited with their little Faith Dawn in the resurrection life to come. That is why they named her Faith Dawn Grams, for they had faith in God that they would see their daughter again at the dawning of the new age, when Christ would come, and the trumpet would sound, and the dead in Christ would be raised along with all those who had put their faith in him. They would be caught up together to meet him in the air and so be with the Lord and each other for eternity (1 Thess 4.15–17). Or, if they too died before his coming, they had faith that they would somehow see and be with their little girl in the presence of their Lord (Luke 23.43; Phil 1.23).

To see one's child's life slip away is a suffering that can either leave one ruined, unable to stay the course in life, and without hope, or, despite the pain, it can produce an endurance—a constancy in life that develops character and hope. Gene had already suffered a similar loss eight years and two months earlier when his beloved sister Arlene died. He and Phyllis together now faced this agony with a trust in God that enabled them to continue in ministry. Indeed, the very essence of the Gospel spoke of the Father giving his only and beloved Son to die for the ungodly (Rom 5.6–11). Faith's death, of course, was not redemptive, but Gene and Phyllis knew that their suffering was one that God himself knew full well.

Start of New Pietersburg Church (1952). Johannes Mukwevho
is in a suit and Christopher Damme is wearing a hat.

Call to worship in northern Transvaal village
(1952). Gene Grams plays his trombone.

Burning witchcraft paraphernalia, northern Transvaal (1959).
Phyllis Grams and her three boys are on the left of the picture.

Baptisms at Machachan (1959). Phyllis Grams and the three boys
are in the middle of the picture between the waterhole and
the villagers, with the village in the distance.

Tent evangelism in a South African township.

An altar call in a tent meeting. Gene Grams is on the left.

Baptism for new believers from Meloding, Kutlwanong, and Thabong (1957).

New Goldsfield Church building dedication, 26 October, 1957.

Dedication of Lorraine Memorial Temple, Thabong, Welkom (1961).

Dedication of Loenser Ebenezer Temple, Meloding (1961).
Rev. Philip Molefe is in the center.

Grams family (1962).

Women's ministry (WMC) initiated in Assemblies of God, South Africa
(1961). Phyllis Grams (right) and Martha Pettenger (left) are on the
right of the banner.

10

Tshediso

Leha nka tsamaya kgohlong ya moriti wa lefu, nke ke ka tshoha bobe leha bo le bong, hobane o na le nna; lere la hao le seikokotlelo sa hao ke tsona tse ntshedisang. (Psalm 23.4 in Southern Sesotho)

Le ge nka sepela molapong wa moriti wa lehu, nka se boife bobe, gobane o na le nna; molamo wa gagwe le lepara la gagwe di nkuša pelo. (Psalm 23.4 in Sepedi)[1]

Even when I enter the valley of darkness, I will not fear evil, for you are with me. Your club and staff—they comfort me. (Psalm 23.4)

1952 HAD BEEN A difficult year, particularly with the death of Faith. Someone thought that a dog would help the Grams at this time. So, while Phyllis was still recovering at the nursing home, Gene was given a dachshund. The little dog became so attached to Gene that, when Phyllis returned home, the dog would not allow her near Gene. So the dog had to go, and a few months later the Grams bought another dog for two pounds. Prince was a Doberman Pinscher. He was already their third dog, the first having been a Rhodesian Ridgeback that an African chief had given them as a gift. They named this first dog "King," but shortly before Faith was born, the dog went blind and had to be put down. Prince, however, stayed with the family for a number of years, and the Grams family would from this time on usually have at least one dog around the house.

1. These translations have been posted at http://www.seghea.com/pat/bible/language.html#sesotho, (accessed 5 March, 2010). Note the final word in the Southern Sesotho translation: one can see that it relates to the title of this chapter. While not used in the northern Sotho translation of Psalm 23.4, "tshediso" is also a northern Sotho word meaning "comfort," "consolation," "sympathy," or "pity."

1953 was to be a mixture of opposition in ministry and great joy and consolation. In January, Gene and Phyllis were astounded to find out that they were again expecting a baby. What they had been told would be impossible was now a reality. Cautiously hopeful and faithful in prayer, they thanked God for the miracle that He was working for them.

With a small group of believers in the New Pietersburg church, the congregation set about trying to raise funds for a church building. They believed that a larger place of worship might draw more people to the services. They did all they could to raise funds but, after several months, could only produce $40 of the required $1,500 for a building. It was not until the late 1960s that a building was erected for this church through funds raised by Albert Louton and built with Ed Louton's oversight. Until a hall was rented in 1954, however, the Sunday School class had to be held outside. While the weather often obliged during these outdoor meetings, the drum beating, filth, and stench in the area made lessons outside unbearable.

The missionary couple continued in their study of the Sepedi language and, to some extent, in the villages. In one village, the chief wanted to stop the meetings, but when the people asked him to permit them to continue, he relented. Many times during these trips to the villages, Gene travelled alone. Phyllis's second pregnancy was not going well: she was often sick and overall spent about five of the nine months in bed.

In May of 1953, Gene travelled out to Motlala alone, the village just a little beyond Molepo's that could only be reached by dirt tracks. Many would eventually become Christians in Motlala, although no church building was constructed for years to come. Meetings with around five hundred people would be held in the open, just outside of the chief's kraal. However, on this occasion Gene played his trombone and was surprised to see that not a single person came. So he went to one of the chief's attendants and requested an audience with the chief. Usually, a meeting with the chief had to be scheduled several days in advance, but on this occasion he was given immediate access. The chief spoke directly. "We believe that you have brought a curse to our village," he stated. "We see you coming over many months, but you have no baby. You speak of God and want our people to believe what you believe, but you have no children. You tell us about God's power, but your God did not save your baby. How can we listen to you? Now you have brought a curse to our women, for they also are not having children." Gene had no choice but to leave the village.

Meetings in a hall in New Pietersburg began in June of 1953. Gene was pleased not to travel out to the villages so much without Phyllis, especially given her difficult pregnancy. On the first night of meetings in the hall, he discovered that it had also been double-booked with another Christian group. So, the two groups tried to hold a meeting together. The other group showed a movie about how smoking stunts one's growth. A number of people in the audience, including Gene and Phyllis, could not help laughing at the movie, which produced pictures of very short people smoking cigarettes as evidence. When this was over and many from the other group had departed, Gene preached a sermon to those remaining. On the second night the hall was not double booked, and Gene showed a filmstrip that presented a Bible story. While he was working with the filmstrip projector, he sensed something was happening behind him. He turned around to discover three men, hands extended, about to grab him. The men were so surprised when Gene turned that they ran away. Gene continued to hold meetings in the township, often riding his bicycle the several miles from his house to the hall. One of the original members of the church, Sister Motau, translated for him into Sepedi.

On the evening of the 22nd of August, 1953, however, Gene and Phyllis knew that their baby was about to be born. While Phyllis was struggling through her labor pains, Gene prepared himself by polishing his shoes. "What are you doing?" Phyllis gasped. "I'm polishing my shoes," he replied, matter of factly. "Why?" she asked between contractions. "Well, I have to look my best," he replied. Phyllis suggested that he rather leave directly to find the nurse.

Since there was no telephone in the house, Gene drove his '53 Chev pick-up to the home of their nurse, Mrs. Smit. She stayed for several hours to make sure that everything was going well and then returned home. Gene was to call on her again when Phyllis's labor pains were coming every four minutes. On the 23rd of August, about 4:00 a.m., Gene returned to Mrs. Smit's home, and she telephoned Dr. Nell to meet them at the Grams' home. Everyone waited at the house while the baby took its time to arrive. Gene found himself in an agonizing discussion with the doctor in the early hours of the morning about South African sports, rugby, cricket, and soccer, while Mrs. Smit stayed with Phyllis. Dr. Nell evidently loved sports, and he loved to talk about it. Gene, who had actually enjoyed following and playing American sports while growing up, smiled politely and added occasional comments when he thought he could contribute something to the conversation. At 7:00 a.m., with the sun just on the rise, Darrell Mark Grams was born. He weighed six pounds exactly, and Gene was fearful that he would not live.

Phyllis and the baby were, however, fine. But Gene was suddenly overwhelmed with one of the most severe headaches he had ever had and eventually took to bed himself. Whether it was caused by the all-night vigil, the strain on his nerves as he feared for his wife and child, or the conversation about sports, nobody knew. The Guthrie's, who lived a few blocks away, took news to the Loutons that they were now grand-parents. Albert and Louise Louton were at this time living at the mission station in Saaiplaats, about sixty miles from Pietersburg. They arrived later in the day, and Louise was able to help take care of Phyllis and Darrell for several days. Although Darrell was at first a weak child and suffered from colic, he grew stronger each day. Gene and Phyllis were overjoyed to have their first child after such a difficult time.

After several meetings in the hall in New Pietersburg, Gene decided that tent meetings should be held to increase the size of the congrega-tion. So, Gene went to the superintendant of the location for a permit to hold a tent meeting, but he was turned away. Gene asked if there was any appeal process that he could follow and was told that only the town clerk for Pietersburg could override his refusal. Returning home, Gene said to Phyllis, "I think I don't look old enough to get any respect from the officials." So he took a soft lead pencil and darkened the light moustache that he had recently grown. He then went to the town clerk and asked for a permit to hold tent meetings in New Pietersburg. The clerk refused to grant Gene's request. He gave several reasons, including the fact that the officials knew nothing about Gene. Just what was he teaching the people? Gene explained his Gospel message, but the man still refused.

As he was leaving, Gene turned and said to the clerk, "Why is it that the South African government has permitted me to do mission work, has stated in my passport that I cannot do any other work in this coun-try, and yet you will not permit me to do this? I feel that my hands are tied. What can I do?" The clerk looked at him and replied, "How long would you like to do this work?" Gene answered, "Three weeks." The clerk then granted him permission for the meetings, and, as it turned out, the length of time was repeatedly extended. This tent campaign lasted in all about three months.

Ruth Williamson loaned her tent for these meetings. It was about sixty by forty feet and could accommodate three hundred or so people. Two poles and large ropes held the tent up. Seats were made using cement blocks with planks on loan from a lumber company, and the children just sat on the ground. Albert Louton loaned his generator and lights, as well as a large, wooden pulpit.

In November, 1953, the evangelist, Johannes Mukwevho, came from Venda in the north to help in the tent meetings. He brought his wife and their baby daughter. Hundreds of people came to the meetings—in Africa, it has usually been easy to gather a crowd at almost any venue. Albert Louton assisted in these meetings, bringing his loudspeaker equipment so that the crowds could hear well both inside and outside the hall. The results were very positive, since a number of people gave their lives to serve Christ and several were healed of various illnesses. By May, 1954, about one hundred and eighty people formed the church of New Pietersburg that had begun with five praying women.

Mukwevho had already been an evangelist in the Transvaal. He was a truly anointed servant of God with a fruitful ministry. He was also a very gifted linguist who could speak seven languages, including Tshivenda (his first language), Sepedi, Sesotho, XiTsonga, Zulu, Afrikaans, and English. The movement of tribes in South Africa, due in large part to wars and mining in the previous two hundred years, meant that people often knew several languages, but Mukwevho's command of languages was exceptional. His very black color as a Venda distinguished him from the other African tribal groups in the region of Pietersburg, which were typically browner. The Venda were from the northernmost area of the country of South Africa, and Mukwevho knew the people and region of the northern Transvaal well. Gene Grams and Johannes Mukwevho became good friends and would minister together not only in the Transvaal but also eventually in the Orange Free State.

The meetings were packed from the first night. Phyllis did not usually participate in this tent campaign since Darrell was so young at the time. One night, the tent began to shake violently. The lights swayed back and forth between the tent poles, and Mukwevho went outside to investigate. He returned, shaken, and said, "We are in trouble. There are men out there with big knives. They are shaking the tent and will cut the ropes." Gene replied, "I'm going out." He answered, "No, they will kill you." But Gene thought, "We will die inside in any case. I had better confront this gang." As soon as he was outside the tent, the gang of about fifty men surrounded him. They began to push him, knocking him back and forth. There was a full moon that night, and Gene could see its reflection off the knives that the men were carrying. As he was knocked around, the gang moved him farther and farther away from the tent until he could no longer see it's lights or hear the loud generator.

Gene was convinced that this was his night to die. He thought of Stephen in the book of Acts, the first martyr of the church. Then, surrounded by the gang in an open field, he prayed, "Please, God, take care of my wife and little boy." Suddenly, he heard noise, opened his eyes, and saw the gang members scrambling and running in all directions away from him. They could not get away from Gene fast enough. Every one fled, and Gene found himself alone beside a stream. He had been turned around so many times that he did not even know which direction he should walk. As he thanked God for saving his life, he also prayed for direction to return to the tent.

Back at the tent, Gene looked around for the evangelist. The people in the tent were still there, singing and praying, but Mukwevho could not be seen at all. Gene went back to the platform and found him hiding in the large pulpit. Still thinking the danger was imminent, he said, "Moruti[2] Grams, we are going to heaven tonight." Gene, who already knew what had happened, replied jokingly, "Well, if we're going to go to heaven tonight, you had better get out from under there."

After this incident, large crowds gathered at the tent for services. A number of those who became Christians had belonged to gangs in the township. There was always danger lurking in the townships. Not long after Gene's encounter with the gang, a Pentecostal Holiness minister asked him for a lift back from the tent meeting to the other African location outside Pietersburg. Another man asked to ride along too, and he jumped in the back of the pick-up truck. When Gene let the minister out, the man in the back of the truck climbed into the front seat. The man leaned forward and announced that he intended to travel home with Gene. At these close quarters, Gene realized that he was inebriated. Gene thought quickly and suggested, "It is not permitted by the law." "Who cares about the law," the man said. Gene noticed that the man had

---

2. "Moruti" means "minister," "preacher," or "missionary" in Sesotho.

a knife on him. The man then grabbed some tracts on the front seat and tried to set them alight. Gene was, however, able to throw him out of the truck and escape from this dangerous situation.

A few days later, as people were leaving the tent meeting, a man grabbed Gene by his shirt. Gene saw a knife coming down towards his chest and was able to grab the man's hand in the nick of time. Others quickly came to his rescue, and Gene survived the attack without a scratch. Somehow the man had been angered by something Gene had said in the service that evening. Gene could not think what he might have said that could anger anyone, unless the Gospel itself had been the offense. The incident was quickly over, and the man returned home.

Opposition to the meetings was offset by the stories of transformed lives and the growth of the church. The greater the opposition, the greater was the sense of victory through Jesus. Some struggles that Gene and Phyllis faced had no happy endings, such as Faith's death in 1952 and a co-worker's turning away from Christ in 1953. Yet there had been considerable victory as well.

Six months after Darrell was born, in February, 1954, Gene returned to the village of Motlala and again had an audience with the chief. The chief was delighted to hear the news that the missionaries were now parents, and he set a Saturday for them to visit his village again and to present the baby to the people. On the appointed day, the people gathered in a large group of about 2,000 people. They jumped and shouted for joy, while passing Darrell from person to person. Darrell seemed to enjoy the attention, but after a little while Gene and Phyllis did not know where he was in the crowd. They eventually found him in the arms of a woman who had a necklace of beads that he was happily sucking. The joyful people gave Darrell the name of "*Tshediso*," meaning "Comfort" or "Consolation."[3] It was a good name. Despite the hardship and opposition that the Grams had known over the previous year and a half, they had found consolation and comfort in a thriving church in New Pietersburg, crowds eager to hear the Gospel in the villages, and a healthy baby boy.

3. Edgar Pettenger dedicated Darrell at the November 1953 conference in Witbank.

11

Furlough

> While they were worshiping the Lord and fasting, the Holy Spirit
> said, "Now, set Barnabas and Saul apart for me for the work to
> which I have called them." (Acts 13.2)

JUST BEFORE GENE AND Phyllis celebrated their second anniversary,
and just two months before departing for their first furlough in the
United States, they wrote about the state of their work in South Africa. It
was the 15th of March, 1954. Their work in New Pietersburg had grown
from the faithful five women praying for a church to a large group of
believers of all ages. In January, 1954, the Grams and the Mukwevhos
ministered together in a tent campaign. Children's services were held
in the afternoons, and meetings were held every night with all ages in
attendance. The tent seated about 300 people, and each meeting was
packed to capacity, often with many having to stand outside. There was
a moving of God on the people to the extent that the dry, dusty ground
was wet at the altar from tears of repentance at the end of the meetings.

After the tent campaign, the new church moved into the largest hall
available in New Pietersburg. It could hold about five hundred people.
Here, women's meetings, young people's meetings, Sunday School classes, and nightly services were regularly held—except when the proprietor
of the building decided to rent it out for other purposes, such as boxing
matches. The young church now needed its own meeting space, which
was a wonderful problem to have. While Gene and Phyllis had appealed
to supporting churches for extra funds to pay a minister for the New
Pietersburg church, not enough money was ever raised. However, the
church was now large enough to support its own minister, and they
called Johannes Mukwevho as their pastor.

The Grams also continued their work in the veldt. While they had seen dramatic results, they were concerned about whether the people had, in Paul's words, truly experienced Christ's indwelling through faith in him, had truly comprehended the enormity of Christ's love, and had truly been filled with the fullness of God (Eph 3.16–19). Where were they in their walk of faith? Were they rooted and established in the love of Christ and for one another? Would they stand firm in the Spirit's power, held fast not by the visits of missionaries but because they now belonged to the Father, knew the Son, and were strengthened by the Spirit?

An incident gave Gene and Phyllis a peace that, indeed, the work in the rural areas of the Transvaal was not their own but a work of God. Not long before their return to the US, they were present beside the wife of a village headman in her last hour of life. She turned to her husband, speaking softly and saying that she was ready to die. "But I do not want to leave you and the children at this time. I want you to know Jesus as I have known him." Her husband spoke kindly to her, saying, "Know that I will raise our children as Christians. And I myself will follow him." Assured, she replied, "I know that my sins are washed away." A short while later, she said, "I see the people of heaven coming for me." With that, she closed her eyes and went to sleep in Jesus.

Gene and Phyllis were thankful that they had had the great privilege of serving in God's field and seeing the fruit of their labor after just a couple of years. They were thankful for serving shoulder to shoulder with servants of God like the Mukwehvos. But they needed to return to the United States for a while. They were eager to show Gene's parents their first grandchild, Darrell. They were eager to report back to the sending churches and friends who had faithfully supported them. They wanted to be appointed with the Assemblies of God Foreign Missions Board so that they were not unaffiliated missionaries. And they needed to raise more funds. Financially, their two years in South Africa together had been very difficult, and now they had the added expense of a little boy. But they also hoped that they could raise additional funds for their ministry, whether for a church building in New Pietersburg or a co-worker, and perhaps bring back some donated clothes for the poor.

The young family of three departed for the United States on the *Africa Sun* from Cape Town on the 24th of May, 1954. The trip was most demanding. Almost from the moment that they had left the harbor, the ship was tossed about like a cork in the Cape rollers. With waves rising and crashing in every direction, Gene and Phyllis were overwhelmed with seasickness for two days. They were so sick that they could not take care of Darrell, who rolled back and forth in the cabin in his stroller with each wave. A kind steward by the name of Abie Abrahams appeared at the door, understood the situation, and carried the nine-month-old little boy with him on his chores throughout the ship. Over the next two days, Mr. Abrahams and Darrell became fast friends.

Back on their feet, Gene and Phyllis conducted a service on the freighter for the crew and any other passengers. On such occasions, one seldom knows whether anything said will take root in someone's heart. Some thirty-five years later, Gene and Phyllis visited the Lansdowne Assembly of God church in Cape Town. There, to their amazement, they met Abie Abrahams. He told them that, on his next voyage after he had cared for Darrell, he remembered his previous voyage and the Gospel message that Gene had preached. He bowed his head in prayer and asked to follow Jesus. Abie's grandson, Wayne George, would become a graduate of Cape College of Theology, the theological college that the Grams would establish in the late 1980s. Ministers rarely know the privilege of seeing the fruit of seed sown years earlier. Their hope typically looks to the distant future, when they will stand in the presence of Jesus and learn what work had produced fruit. As Paul said,

> . . . what is our hope or joy or crown for boasting before our lord Jesus in his presence? Is it not indeed you? For you are our glory and joy (1 Thess 2.19–20).

Meeting Abie Abrahams again those many years later was Gene's and Phyllis's foretaste of this moment before their Lord.

Three days before reaching Boston, the *Africa Sun* encountered a heavy fog. The ship's horn blasted constantly to warn other ships in the vicinity until the difficult journey came to an end. The difficult furlough, however, had just begun.

Gene and Phyllis stayed with Gene's parents, William and Martha Grams, at 8341 Coyle Avenue in Detroit, Michigan. When they visited their primary supporting church, Christian Trinity, they discovered that another missionary from South Africa had reported to the church that the Grams had lived extravagantly. For a couple that had spent one week eating nothing but beets, this was as humorous as it was hurtful. Apparently, the story came about because the Grams had some canned food that they would serve visitors if their garden did not yield anything at the time. To the other missionary, having canned food available seemed extravagant. A story such as this was easily sorted out with the people of Christian Trinity, but the Grams had to work through the pain of an unkind and untruthful report from a fellow missionary as their first order of business in the United States.

They also faced financial struggles in the United States. Their little salary had stretched farther in South Africa, and so furlough posed a greater challenge. Gene had to take work inspecting windshields at Motor Products, an automobile parts factory, and Phyllis at Hudson's Department Store in downtown Detroit. Gene's mother took care of Darrell during the day.

At Motor Products, Gene found that he had considerable time on his hands, since he was required to inspect only twelve windshields in eight hours. The task took no more than an hour. This only added to his agony: here he was, inspecting windshields, sitting with nothing to do for seven hours a day, living in the United States, struggling to get appointment with the Assemblies of God, struggling to raise support . . . . The words of Old John rang in his ears, "Why did no one ever come and tell my parents about Jesus?" Whenever they could, the Grams traveled to churches and met with pastors, mainly in Michigan and Wisconsin, to raise support for their return to South Africa.

Getting appointed as Assemblies of God missionaries also proved to be a major challenge. Gene was now 23 years old—the required age for mission appointment—and Phyllis was one year younger. So Gene went to see Charles W. Scott, the Superintendant of the Michigan District of the Assemblies of God. Scott served in this capacity from 1944–1957, and so he had already been in office nine years when this young missionary couple that had so far thwarted the system of missionary appointment walked into his office in Dearborn, Michigan. He supported missions: the whole Michigan District was known for its strong support of missions. So, while Phyllis carried Darrell around the office and fed him Graham Crackers, Gene and Phyllis poured out their hearts about their calling and missionary service in the Transvaal over the past few years. Scott listened patiently and then declared to Gene, "You have to pastor a church in the US before you can be appointed as a missionary. That is our system. You are just a schoolboy out to see the world. If you are not willing to comply with what I am telling you to do, then I am not interested in helping you."

The young couple was shocked. They were devastated. The opinion of one man in an elected capacity, whose days were spent in an office, held power over their future ministry in fields white for harvesting. They had, to this point, worked in missions in a freedom of the Spirit that did not have to negotiate power and position in denominational structures, although they had had their moments with the South African authorities and some other missionaries. Scott had completely misread them, not for their clear and passionate appeal, but because he could not see past the rules and procedures with which he had been entrusted to conduct denominational work in decency and in order. In the not quite fifty years since its inception as an end-time, enthusiastic thrust in missions, parts of the Assemblies of God were showing signs of institutional calcification. Where was the body of believers meeting together in worship and fasting to determine whether it seemed good to them and to the Holy Spirit to set this couple apart for the work to which God had called them (Acts 13.2)? But the Grams did not give up their hope of being appointed with the Assemblies of God. They had begun to see the importance of being connected with others on the field, and they certainly could use an endorsement from the churches of the Michigan District as they tried to raise funds from Assemblies of God churches in the United States.

A few months later, Gene, Phyllis, and Darrell visited churches in Wisconsin, where Gene was also known because of the "Grams" name in Assemblies of God circles there. While in Wisconsin, Gene and his father attended the Assemblies of God camp meetings at Spencer Lake, near Waupaca. One day, a man ran up to Gene while they were waiting in line in the cafeteria: it was the General Superintendant of the Assemblies of God, Ralph Riggs. He had just that year been elected to this post. Riggs threw his arms around Gene and gave him a big hug. Like the Grams, Ralph and Lillian Riggs had at one point been young missionaries to South Africa. They met there and, again like the Grams, were married in South Africa—in 1920.[1] Also like the Grams, the Riggs had worked in the northern Transvaal. Ralph had recently paid a visit to South Africa and met Gene and Phyllis there. As he hugged Gene, he said, "My South African brother, you are eating with me tonight." Riggs's heart was still largely in Africa: they had even named their daughter "Venda" after the

1. Gohr, "Whatever Happened to Lillian Riggs," 7.

tribe where they had served. That was the same tribe from which Gene's good friend and co-evangelist, Johannes Mukwevho, came.

Over dinner, Gene explained their desire to be appointed as missionaries with the Assemblies of God and also told of their disappointing meeting with Scott. Riggs simply replied, "I can certainly understand why you would want to get back to the work in South Africa and not waste time pastoring a church here in the US for several years. Leave this with me."

Shortly thereafter, the Foreign Missions Director, Rev. Noel Perkins,[2] contacted Gene and Phyllis. He stated that he had been made aware of the conversation with General Superintendant Riggs. "Moreover," he continued, "members of the Foreign Missions Board of the Assemblies of God in Springfield, Missouri have met to pray about your request for appointment. While doing so, the Holy Spirit indicated to us while we were kneeling in prayer that we should not require you to take the normal route to the mission field, but that we should proceed with an appointment right away." Whether the directive came from high up in the Assemblies of God or higher up still, the result was the appointment of Gene and Phyllis as missionaries with the Foreign Missions Board of the Assemblies of God. The Grams were delighted that decisions about missionary appointments were still being made by people listening to the Holy Spirit while praying on their knees.

Now the Grams could raise funds on the basis of their appointment with the Assemblies of God. William Grams once again helped to set up meetings in the churches, and the churches not only gave financial contributions through offerings and pledges of support, but also collected items for the Grams to take back to Africa for the nationals. There were clothes and literature, among other things, that people contributed. The missionary movement within the Assemblies of God was now behind this young missionary couple.

And so was the Grams clan. Tom Grams, Gene's uncle, was pastor of the Assemblies of God Church in Rice Lake, Wisconsin, about two hundred miles north of Milwaukee. Gene and Phyllis had driven from Detroit, Michigan to visit supporting churches in Wisconsin, and on the 6th of September in 1955 they joined a Labor Day picnic with Rice Lake Assembly of God Sunday School. A softball game provided the highlight

2. Noel Perkins served as the Assemblies of God Foreign Missions Director from 1927 to 1959.

of the day's fun, and Gene joined in. As always, he gave his all and, after a rather poor hit to center field, he tried to beat out the play by sliding into first base. A bit of rock protruded from the ground just in front of the base so that, when Gene slid over it, he shattered part of his left hipbone.

That night, Gene could not sleep for the piercing pain. No matter whether he stood, sat, walked, or lay down, he was in agony. Phyllis had not yet learned to drive a car, and so Gene attempted to drive on to the next meeting in Superior, Wisconsin on Tuesday night, unaware that he had actually smashed his hipbone in a number of places. He managed short distances, and then he would have to stop to walk about due to the pain from sitting. They just managed the trip and spent the next night with the pastor, Rev. Staudt. As it happened, Staudt was himself recovering from a heart attack. Gene again had a sleepless night, but he could not cry out from the pain for fear of disturbing his host.

Finally, on Wednesday, Gene went to the doctor. X-rays revealed that his hip was indeed shattered, and the doctor said that there were so many bone chips that needed to be moved into place that Gene's only hope was to have surgery at the Mayo Clinic in Rochester, Minnesota. But Gene and Phyllis did not have money to pay for major surgery, and, in any case, Gene could not drive anymore. The decision was made to have Gene's father go by bus from Detroit to get the car and drive it back after Gene returned to Detroit by train on a stretcher under Phyllis's care. The car was left with an elder in the church. Upon their arrival in Detroit, Gene and Phyllis were met by Jack Rettinger, Phyllis's uncle and pastor of Christian Trinity, and Gene's father. The grueling trip was over, but the pain was relentless.

Gene saw another doctor on Monday, one week after the accident. The doctor stated that he did not believe that Gene's leg could be saved. "If there is any hope, you will find it at the Mayo Clinic," he said. But there was simply no money for this. The impossible situation continued week after week. Meetings to raise support had to be cancelled, and Gene found himself looking into a black hole. With a baby boy and wife to care for, little money, a shattered hip that was somehow healing with the bone fragments out of place, a possible amputation, constant pain, and the knowledge that by Christmas that year their visa to South Africa would expire, things looked hopeless.

Every day, Gene's father would drive him half an hour to see a chiropractor in Lincoln Park. The chiropractor could hold the hip in such a way that Gene could have some relief from the pain, but as soon as he released his grip, the pain returned. Over the next five and a half weeks, Gene lost 40 pounds. He would roll back and forth in bed, and Phyllis would feed him there: all this agony was with painkillers.

One Sunday, the painkillers ran out. William went to the drug store and managed somehow to get into the store and convince the pharmacist to give him another prescription. The pharmacist was worried about continuing Gene on the drug and stated that he would not renew the prescription in the future.

That night, Gene was left alone in the house as Phyllis travelled with her in-laws to the evening service at Tabor Tabernacle. Gene found a station on the radio that was broadcasting Revivaltime, an Assemblies of God program hosted by evangelist C. M. Ward. Gene had heard Ward speak when he was a student at Central Bible Institute. The choir that sang for Revivaltime was mostly made up of CBI students. Gene felt a connection with the people in the program. The theme of the radio broadcast that evening was divine healing. A woman testified that she had had a shattered hip. Prior to her accident, she had enjoyed walking in her garden. After the accident, she wondered whether she would ever be able to do so again. She then stated that God healed her, and Ward followed the testimony with a message on the power of God to heal. He then asked his listeners to come "to the long, long altar" where Jesus was waiting with salvation and healing for any who came. Gene had preached many such a message in Africa: now the minister was in need of the message. That night, Gene came in prayer while lying in bed to that long, long altar. He prayed, "Father, as you healed this woman of the same shattered hip that I have, please heal me."

While he prayed and thanked God for healing, Gene fell asleep. He slept for four hours, until 2:00 a.m. The pain in his hip had awoken him, and he saw that Phyllis had returned from the meeting and was asleep beside him. He was surprised that he had slept for so long and had not even awoken upon Phyllis's return from the evening service. But his pain was again unbearable, and he could not sleep for the remainder of the night.

At 8:30 Monday morning, William called outside the room that it was nearing time to leave to drive to the chiropractor. Gene stepped out of bed and hopped on his good leg slowly towards the door. Suddenly, the pain became overwhelming, and Gene screamed at the top of his voice in utter agony. His father, ever mindful of what the neighbors might think, told him to be quiet. But Gene replied, "I'm being healed!" He could feel pieces of bone shifting, as though a tweezers was moving them one by one into place. William replied, "I've been preaching healing most of my life, and I have never seen or heard anyone ever healed this way before! Be quiet, or the police will come and arrest us!" But Gene was healed that moment. Some sciatic pain remained until the 10th of October, but after that Gene never had a further problem with his hip. The 10th of October was the date that had been set by the Foreign Missions Board in Springfield, Missouri for the Grams to receive their official appointment as missionaries.

Now Gene and Phyllis concerned themselves with their need to return to South Africa by the 23rd of December. Since meetings had been cancelled over the past five weeks, they still needed much more support than what they had raised. William called pastors he knew to pledge support, and Christian Trinity increased their support substantially. During their first few years in South Africa, the Grams tried to live on $1 per month. Now their budget, set by the Assemblies of God Foreign Missions Department, was $600 per month. With the help of some thirty churches and about fifteen individuals, they reached this goal. Some supporters gave $1.00 per month. Among their supporting churches in Michigan were Christian Trinity and Tabor Tabernacle in Detroit, and in Wisconsin were Calvary, Bethel, Evangel, and Lakeview in Milwaukee. Much of their support came from the German District of the Assemblies of God, particularly from churches in Benton Harbor and East Detroit in Michigan, Cleveland and Akron in Ohio, and churches in Chicago and Milwaukee.

Gene and Phyllis also had many other supporting churches. One aspect of raising support in a missions-minded denomination was that churches often wanted a large number of missionaries on their support roll. But this could lead to low levels of support to individual missionary families from these churches. While greatly appreciative of the support and interest in missions, including the assurance of greater numbers of believers praying for missionaries, this meant extra effort at raising support and then in reporting back to all the churches. Faith missions have, consequently, long since given up the term "furlough" and replaced it with "home assignment"—often an exhausting and difficult time for missionaries.

On the 22nd of November, just 8 days before their scheduled departure, Gene and Phyllis wrote to these supporters with the good news that their monthly support and passage fare had come together. They were now ready to leave for a second term of ministry in South Africa. The Grams sailed on the 30th of November from New York and arrived in Cape Town on the morning of the 23rd of December, 1955—the very last day that they could renew their visas, which would expire on the 26th of the month.

Unlike their previous trip, the ocean was calm for the entire journey. Albert and Louise Louton, and Phyllis's brother, Ed, and her sister, Joy, were all there to meet them. They had traveled the 1,200 miles from Pietersburg to Cape Town to welcome them home after their long and eventful absence.

The customs official, however, had a problem with the freight: what was "popcorn"? The Wisconsin District of WMs (Women's Ministry) knew about one of Gene's great pleasures in life—popcorn. They contributed fifty tins of popcorn to this noble cause for world missions. Gene justified this luxury when he found that the tins were helpful for intercontinental packing. He was able to place a can of popcorn wherever there was a gap. In all, they packed twelve drums and several crates. The custom's official learned that popcorn was corn seeds, and this raised an even greater problem: no foreign seeds were permitted to enter South Africa. He insisted that every can of popcorn be removed and shown to him.

Gene, Ed, and Albert Louton started the hunt for the fifty cans of popcorn. They had to unpack everything to find them. Finally, just before noon on Christmas Eve, when the offices would shut down for the Christmas holidays, they presented the fifty cans of popcorn to the customs official. He looked them over and then crossed out the word "popcorn" on the import declaration form, writing "spaghetti" in its place. Gene saw this and protested that he could not sign something that was not truthful. The official looked at him and stated in his thick Afrikaans accent, a twinkle in his eye, "What you call popcorn in your country, I call spaghetti! Sign here." Gene signed the form, and the company was finally free to proceed to the northern Transvaal in their two cars.

Mr. Johnson, their Christian shipping agent, had access to the docks, which were about to be closed for the holidays. He graciously offered to work over Christmas and pack up the crates and barrels and then put the freight on a train to Pietersburg.

Gene and Phyllis had also returned with their green '54 Plymouth, a V8, four-door sedan. They drove into the Karoo Desert, hoping to find a place to stop for the night at Laingsburg, Colesburg, or some other town. But there was no accommodation available anywhere, and so they had to travel the entire distance to Pietersburg without stopping. The three men shared the driving between them. The desert was at its hottest that time of year, and the lack of sleep added to their ordeal. At one point, Gene swerved to miss what he thought was a bicycle. Of course, it was not there in the middle of the desert. Not long later, Ed thought he saw animals on the road, which also proved not to be there. To make matters still worse, the group of missionaries could not find a restaurant, but they were able to purchase some food from a small store open over the holidays. They arrived in Pietersburg on Christmas day in the afternoon, having driven for over twenty-four hours.

12

Welkom

Now, may the God of patience and encouragement give to you the same way of thinking among yourselves that accords with Christ Jesus so that, together, with one mouth, you might glorify the God and Father of our Lord Jesus Christ. Therefore, welcome one another, just as Christ also welcomed you, for the glory of God (Romans 15.5–7)

O N NEW YEAR'S EVE, the New Pietersburg church was filled to capacity, and the Grams had a joyful reunion with their African friends. They were also introduced to people who had come to faith during their absence, and on the following Sunday they witnessed seven new converts enter the waters of baptism. This was a good beginning to a second term of service in South Africa.

They were also pleased to be reunited with Phyllis's parents, Ed, and Joy. Yet Gene and Phyllis could tell that Albert and Louise Louton were concerned about how their ministries among the Africans now overlapped. They had picked up ministries that Gene and Phyllis had left when they went on furlough, and they had also occupied the Grams' home in their absence. Would they begin to work together, or would new places of ministry need to be found? At the beginning of January, Gene and Phyllis attended a meeting of the Assemblies of God churches in Johannesburg at Fairview Assembly over the New Year's holiday. This proved to be the beginning of a whole new location for ministry in South Africa.

During the conference, they stayed at the home of Edgar and Mabel Pettenger, fellow Assemblies of God missionaries and the parents of Vernon Pettenger. On one of the days of the conference, Phyllis stayed behind with Darrell, who was sick. Gene heard August Kast, a Swiss missionary based in Basutoland (present day Lesotho), make an appeal for missionaries to begin work in the new gold mining region of the Orange Free State. Just a few years earlier, the area had been little more than veldt and farmland, dotted here and there with some small towns. It was now a booming region of the country. The goldfields of the Orange Free State lay nearly four hundred miles to the south of Pietersburg—well out of the way of missionaries in the northern Transvaal. While driving back to the Pettengers that evening, Gene gave some thought to Kast's appeal. He soon ruled the idea out: the move would be too complicated. But by the time he arrived at the Pettenger's home in Brakpan on the east Rand, he was of the opinion that they should take up the challenge. After discussing this with Phyllis and praying together, she too felt that this was what they should do. So, within a month of their return from the United States, the Grams found themselves trying to set up home in the new mining town of Welkom.

CAPSULE: MISSIONARIES: PLACES, MINISTRIES, AND PEOPLE

It seems as though missionaries seldom land where they intend to go. Adoniram Judson intended to be a missionary to India and ended up being the great pioneer missionary to Burma. Paul's famous "Macedonian call" landed him in Macedonia for only a few weeks (Acts 16.9–10). His "long term" appointment was not to Macedonia but in Corinth, far to the south. Even so, he stayed in Corinth only about one and a half years. Many missionaries do not tend to stay in one place for very long. They are seldom like that typical Presbyterian pastor who gives his life of ministry to one or two congregations. Scripture nowhere mandates that missionaries should move about, of course, but countless missionaries have followed in Paul's footsteps. Of the years of Paul's ministry about which we do know something, from about AD 49–64, the longest he ever stayed anywhere was three years.

The movement of missionaries is quite remarkable, since local church mission committees that support them make so much of the place where their missionaries serve. The Grams were able to tell supporters through the decades of their ministry that they were missionaries to South Africa, but they moved frequently. In the twenty-first century, movement in missions is even intercontinental. Missions in the nineteenth and twentieth-centuries was often more focused on a given area in the world, being somewhat wedded to a Western view of the world through colonial eyes. With the great expansion of Europe into Africa in particular went missionaries from the countries that settled the continent. Thus missionaries went to certain mission "fields" in the colonies, and missionaries were therefore part of the colonial machine that scrambled for territory.

One alternative way to understand missions would be to think first about the gifts a missionary has been given for ministry, such as evangelism, church planting, teaching, and so forth. But even here, missionaries do not usually have only one gift, and circumstances are continuously changing on the field that demand different efforts, retraining, and even new spiritual gifting. This calls for a vigorous program of life-long learning for missionaries—whether formal or informal. The Grams' ministry developed from evangelism and church planting to development of denominational infrastructure and administration to formal theological education to local church seminars over the years from 1951 to the present.

A third way to understand mission support seems best of all: support based on the missionary as a person and his or her calling to be a steward of God's grace. When mission committees determine to tie support to a place of ministry or to a specific type of ministry instead of the person of the missionary, they fail to understand this more fundamental approach to mission support and partnership. Had Paul been restricted by supporters wishing him to focus on a single place or type of ministry, he never would have evangelized, planted churches, nurtured believers, studied and written deeply theological letters, and engaged Jews, Greeks, Romans, and others in a proclamation of the Gospel from Jerusalem to Illyricum to Rome and perhaps even Spain.

So the Grams moved to Welkom in January, 1956. Ten years earlier, in 1946, gold had been discovered in the region of Odendaalsrus, which had until this time been a small village in the middle of farms and veldt. It had been established in 1912 but became a boomtown in the mid-1940s. Welkom, 10 miles to the south, was founded in 1948 by the mining magnet, Sir Ernest Oppenheimer. It is located about one hundred miles north of the city of Bloemfontein, the judicial capital of South Africa, and about one hundred and fifty miles south of Johannesburg, which was the second largest city in Africa after Cairo, Egypt. Welkom soon became the largest of the towns in the Orange Free State goldfields.

About twenty miles southeast of Welkom was the town of Virginia, positioned along the Sand River and the railway between Bloemfontein and Johannesburg. The town of Virginia also grew up quickly after the discovery of gold there in 1955. Virginia received its name from some graffiti on a rock scribbled by two railroad engineers from the state of Virginia in the United States of America in 1890. Another 50 miles south of Virginia was the oldest town in the Orange Free State, Winburg, established in 1842. Odendaalsrus, Welkom, Virginia, and Winburg became the principle areas of ministry for the Grams over the next few years.

In the area between these towns, there were around twenty mining compounds. Each had about three thousand African, male workers living on site, without their families. The African miners came from Eastern, Central, and especially Southern Africa, and the mix of tribes meant that people needed to communicate with one another in a mining language, already developed in the Johannesburg area. This language, made up mostly of Zulu, is known as "Fanagalo." The mines attracted some rather rough characters. In Welkom, empty bottles of liquor were strewn along the main road, Stateway, which had been paved on only one side by the time the Grams arrived in 1956. When it rained, cars and trucks would get stuck in the mud on the unpaved side of the road. Construction of roads, houses, shops and mining compounds meant that the area was bustling with workers and trucks.

To find a place to live in this mining area, the Grams visited Welkom immediately after the conference in Johannesburg. They travelled with their fellow missionary, Vernon Pettenger. Vernon and Martha Pettenger and Gene and Phyllis Grams were to become fast friends, and both couples would give their lives to missions in South Africa. Their long friendship was also helped when the Pettengers lived in Pretoria and the Grams lived in Johannesburg in the 1960s and 1970s. The two cities were only about forty miles apart. Both couples were about the same age and were to have three children close to the same ages. They were both involved in tent evangelism, church planting, erecting church buildings, and nurturing congregations through missionary involvement in a variety of ways. Both Martha and Phyllis trained teachers for the Sunday School program in their regions of ministry, established the Women's Missionary Council (WMC),[1] and helped to set up "Missionettes," a church-based program for girls.

1. The Women's Missionary Council of the Assemblies of God was established in about 1961 in South Africa. This woman's organization held bake sales, made blankets,

While Vernon faced many health struggles throughout his ministry, he had one of the best senses of humor on the mission field—a key quality for anyone involved in ministry. He saw God's miraculous healing in his body several times. On one occasion he was healed from pulmonary thrombosis. He had numerous blood clots throughout his body, and the doctor was stunned to learn that he had survived a trip over six hundred miles in this condition. Later, the Pettengers would learn that God had awoken Emma Jacobson of Trinity Temple, Las Vegas in the night to pray for him at the very time Vernon was making the long trip to the doctor.[2] Also, after taking prednisone for a number of years, his skin became very fragile to the touch, and he bruised and bled easily. The medication also left him with other side effects.[3] However, while in the hospital in 1972, God miraculously healed Vernon so that he was able to discontinue his medications and continue his ministry in South Africa for another twenty years.

Gene had been with Vernon and Martha at Central Bible Institute, but at that time, Gene did not know that he would be a missionary with them in South Africa. Vernon and Martha, however, were both born in South Africa and were planning on returning there as missionaries upon graduation from the college. Like Vernon, Martha had grown up in South Africa, although her parents were South Africans and not American missionaries. When Gene was only six years old, he met Vernon's father, Edgar, who had come to speak at a missions service in Ripon, Wisconsin, where Rev. Williams Grams pastored a church at the time. After the service, Gene excitedly approached Rev. Pettenger, who put his arm around the little boy. Gene said to him, "Some day, I hope that I can be a missionary where you are." Edgar replied, "Maybe the Lord will guide you to be a missionary to South Africa when you grow up."

---

and did whatever they could to raise money for the churches. Money was used to help pay pastors' salaries, to finance tent campaigns, purchase furnishings for the church buildings, and so forth. The women also held weekly times of prayer and invited special speakers to address their meetings. The WMC program was first established in 1925 in Houston, Texas by Etta Calhoun.

2. Pettenger, "Missionary Healed," 14. The healing took place on the 6th January, 1964.

3. One side effect was blindness in his remaining eye in 2000. He had been injured in the other eye while working in the mines as a young man, and he eventually had to have this eye removed.

CAPSULE: SOME EARLY ASSEMBLIES OF GOD
MISSIONARIES FROM AMERICA IN SOUTH AFRICA

The story of the Assemblies of God in South Africa begins with missionaries already in South Africa who sought affiliation with this newly formed (1914) American denomination. Henry and Anna Turney had been Baptist missionaries in the country along with a single woman co-worker, Hannah James. Pentecostals worked together from various countries and with a variety of sending bodies. There appears to have been a unity of work also with the more denominationally organized Apostolic Faith Mission. In 1917, the Assemblies of God in the United States recognized the Turneys and Hannah James as missionaries in South Africa, and in that year they registered the name "Assemblies of God" with the South African government.

The Turneys and Hannah James established a Pentecostal church in Pretoria in 1911. In the same year, they were asked by the son of a chief to establish a Pentecostal mission in Doornkop, near Middelburg. From that time on, they also established outstations around the Transvaal. So they moved to Doornkop, and the church in Pretoria was absorbed under the Pentecostal Mission of George Bowie.[4]

Bowie was the leader of the mission to South Africa from Bethel Pentecostal Assembly in Newark, New Jersey, arriving with his wife Eleanor in 1909. In their Revival Campaigns, the Bowie's ministry emphasized "Bible signs"—healing and gifts of the Spirit—and the alleged fulfillment of prophecies in their day that, they believed, indicated the imminent return of Christ.

The Assemblies of God now had missionaries in the country. Other missionaries with the Assemblies of God from America prior to its organization in the country in 1925 were J. H. Law, Fred and Anna Richards (who went to South Africa in 1912), and Austin and Carrie Chawner. An early picture from the Doornkop Mission included other missionaries: Alex and Iva (Elliott) MacDonald, W. H. and Mrs. Elliott and their three other children, and Edgar Slaybaugh. But the Assemblies of God was not present as a mission there. Instead, they worked closely with the Full Gospel Church in South Africa and remained uncertain about whether they wanted their own work in the country. Then, in 1925, the Assemblies of God missionaries reorganized as the South African

4. Watt, *From Africa's Soil.*

District of the Assemblies of God in America. J. H. Law was the first chairman, and its secretary was J. H. Bennett.

Other Assemblies of God missionaries were arriving about this time. In the 1920s, there were John Harvey, W. A. DuPlooy, and John Scoble (who married the widowed Anna Richards). Mary Johnson worked in Pondoland, South Africa in the 1920s. Upon graduation from the Bethel Bible School, Austin Chawner went to South Africa with the Pentecostal Assemblies of God of Canada at the end of 1925. He ended up working mostly in Maputo, Mozambique among the Shangaan people. Fred Richards had died of malaria in Swaziland in 1915, but his wife Anna remained in the country and their son, John, who had grown up in the country, was appointed as a missionary to South Africa with the Assemblies of God at the age of eighteen in 1924.

Edgar Pettenger and Fred Burke arrived in South Africa on the 4th of June, 1921. Edgar was a graduate of Bethel Bible Training Institute (BBTI) in Newark, New Jersey.[5] The college was established in 1916 by Bethel Pentecostal Assembly, a great missionary and Pentecostal church dating from 1907. Instrumental in establishing the church, the training institute, and the Ossining Gospel Assembly in New York was Minnie Draper, an associate of A. B. Simpson. Simpson was for a time associated with the Assemblies of God, but she is best known as the founder of the Christian and Missionary Alliance denomination. Minnie Draper remained a part of the Christian and Missionary Alliance until 1913. BBTI eventually merged with Central Bible Institute in 1929.[6]

Edgar Pettenger was 22 years old when he travelled to South Africa with Fred Burke, who was one year younger. Burke had prepared for missionary service at Beulah Heights Missionary Training School in North Bergen, New Jersey.[7] Like Bethel Bible Training Institute, this school had been established in 1912 by the efforts of a key female minister in early Pentecostalism, Virginia Moss. She had already established Beulah Heights Assembly.

5. Some of the information about early Pentecostal missionaries in South Africa and about Bethel Bible Training Institute came from a conversation with Vernon Pettenger on 27 June, 2008. Also helpful is McGee, "Three Notable Women," 3–5.

6. Deans of the college included William W. Simpson, Frank M. Boyd, and William I. Evans. Pastors of Bethel Pentecostal Assembly included Allan A. Swift and Ernest S. Williams. But a key figure in this great ministry of early Pentecostals was Minnie Draper, who remained in the Christian and Missionary Alliance until 1913.

7. Rill, "Blessings," 4–5, 25.

The two young men were sent out by the South and Central African Pentecostal Mission, the missionary arm of Bethel Pentecostal Assembly. They initially studied Zulu and worked in Zululand for two years on a mission station established by John and "Mother" Guthrie. Mother Guthrie was from Topeka, Kansas—where American Pentecostalism was born in the USA. These were the parents of the John Guthrie who had married Gene and Phyllis in Potgietersrus.

After his two years in Zululand, Edgar moved to Benoni on the East Rand. He spent most of his ministry in the gold mining region of Johannesburg. Before coming to South Africa, he was engaged to a young woman by the name of Mabel, who arrived two years after Edgar had arrived in the country. Once she did come, she spent six months in Zululand before she and Edgar were married.

Ralph and Lillian Riggs, like the Pettengers and Bowies, were sent to South Africa by the Bethel Pentecostal Assembly. The Riggs ministered in Vendaland in the northernmost part of South Africa. Ralph had trained at the Rochester Bible Training School, started in 1906 by Elizabeth Baker (who also began Elim Faith Home). He was a missionary prior to his marriage in 1920. He had also taught at Bethel Bible Training Institute,[8] along with W. I. Evans, Frank M. Boyd, and Ernest S. Williams, all major names in the early years of the Assemblies of God. The Riggs served six years in South Africa and, in 1953, Ralph Riggs became the General Superintendant of the Assemblies of God in the United States. Thus several key individuals and missionaries to South Africa in the Assemblies of God were connected to the ministry of Bethel Pentecostal Assembly and Bethel Bible Training Institute. Evans, Boyd, and Williams were some of Gene's teachers at CBI.

The interest of the Bethel Mission in South Africa stemmed from an awareness of the ministry of John Lake in that country, beginning in 1908. The Bethel Mission was started in April, 1910, and in South Africa it eventually became the Full Gospel Church of God in Southern Africa.[9] This mission-minded church amalgamated with the Church of God, Cleveland Tennessee, USA, in 1951.

8. Watt, *The Assemblies of God.* According to Watt, it later became Barrington College, which eventually became part of Gordon College in Massachusetts.

9. These historical notes come from "Full Gospel Church in Southern Africa," http://www.fullchurch.co.za/history.htm (accessed 21 December, 2008). The Full Gospel Church was a missionary force from South Africa to other countries in Southern Africa as far as the equator.

Assemblies of God ministry in South Africa in 1928 was reported in Doornkop, where ministry had begun; Witbank, about twenty miles away from Doornkop; Zeerust, where the Bennett's ministered; the villages of Braklaagte, 12 miles north of Zeerust, and Mamasilu, Ramarea, and Pampier Stad; Johannesburg; Robinson; Randfontein; Duivelskloof, in the northern Transvaal, where John Richards and his wife ran a mission station;[10] the villages of Dumere and Mtimkulu; a "splendid work" with about two hundred believers at Potgietersrus, under the charge of the chief's uncle, Petros Langa; and new ministries at Levubye, where the DuPlooy family lived in a rondavel, and Shingwedzi, where the Chawners were working at the time.[11]

In the 1930's, Archibald Cooper and his wife worked in Pretoria. In 1935, James and Mary Mullan moved from the Congo to South Africa to work in the Emmanuel Mission in Nelspruit, Transvaal, with Hubert Phillips. From 1937, this mission worked with Nicholas Bhengu, a prominent African evangelist, under the loosely related network of groups that comprised the Assemblies of God. At this time, Fred Mullan, James's brother, was the Chairman of the Assemblies of God.[12]

Vernon Pettenger grew up in the Transvaal, since his parents ministered primarily in the goldfields of Johannesburg. This was an excellent way to minister, since African laborers came from every tribe and region in southern Africa to mine half of the world's gold. The idea of working with the miners was part of the initial strategy of the American Pentecostals that arrived in 1908. Vernon worked for six years in the mines before going to Bible school in the United States. While other persons serving with the Assemblies of God in the 1920s–1940s might be mentioned, and while other places of ministry might be mentioned, this brief historical record identifies a number of the missionaries and the growth that was taking place through the years.[13]

10. See John Richards' story up to 1932 in "Miraculously," 20–22. This story gives an idea of the work that preceded the Grams in the northern Transvaal. Some of the paternalistic attitudes towards the "natives" are also expressed even as the evangelistic and miraculous work of missions in the area is told.

11. "Report," 11. See other missionary names and places mentioned in Hooper, "God's Blessings," 13–14.

12. Chandomba, *History,* 55.

13. Some other (in addition to names mentioned) Assemblies of God missionaries from the late 1940s and 1950s with whom Gene and Phyllis Grams ministered were: Irene Dietrich, Merlin and Myrtle Lund, John and Erline Garlock, Hilda Olsen, Peggy

~ ~ ~

So it was most fitting that Vernon Pettenger, Edgar's son, should be the one to drive Gene and Phyllis to the new goldfields of the Orange Free State. He had himself already visited Welkom, holding some meetings in the home of a family by the surname of Scott. He had also negotiated with the town planners to sell a plot of land to the young church in the hopes that someday it would be able to build on it. In this way, he helped to establish a small Assemblies of God church among the whites of the newly established town.

When Vernon, Gene, Phyllis, and Darrell arrived in Welkom, they went straight to the estate agents' offices, trying to find any available house. Housing was in short supply because the area was growing so fast, and the estate agents were not at all hopeful that anything would be available in the near future. Once they had visited all the agents, they returned to the first agent that they visited, Barbour and Thorne. A house had just become available to rent in Bedelia, on the southwest side of Welkom. Everything was settled. The Grams would not be ministering in the villages of the northern Transvaal but in the gold mining area of the Orange Free State. They moved to their new home on the 26th of January, 1956. Because prices were inflated in the gold mining towns, the Grams' monthly rent rose from $30 in Pietersburg to $84 in Welkom.

As they wanted to purchase a house rather than rent, they were delighted when, in July, they were told that there was a house for sale. They packed up their belongings into a truck and drove over to the new house on Graham St. in the Dagbreek neighborhood of Welkom, only to discover that someone had already moved into it. The development of a mining town does not always follow normal rules and procedures. So, the Grams drove around the neighborhood to see if any other house was empty. Just two blocks away, at 44 Pretorius Street and on the corner of Pretorius and Fairbane, they discovered a house that was available. So the Grams family moved from Bedelia to Dagbreek.

Gene and Phyllis began ministry in Thabong, an African township on the outskirts of Welkom. A small house fellowship was already meeting there, and they had a pastor by the name of Johannes Lekoetjie.

Anderson, Hazen and Gladys Wolverton, Stephen and Bernice Van der Merwe, Harold and Margaret Jones, James and Beryl Stewart, Ed and Ruth Rill, Ervin (and his wife) Shaffer, and Lewis and Lenore Wilson.

Johannes was not Assemblies of God, but the Grams were introduced to him and he invited them to minister with him, hoping that the church would grow. To go into the African areas, Gene and Phyllis had to explain to the authorities what they were intending to do, and then a permit would be granted for a few weeks at a time.

In Sesotho, "Thabong" means "Place of Joy." The township was very large. The main streets were tarred, but the side streets were gravel. The average house consisted of four small rooms and was about 25 feet long and 12 feet wide. Each house had a small garden. The township had many beer halls, or "*shebeens*," makeshift places where liquor was sold. Africans were not permitted to drink the liquor of the European population, but they were permitted to make their own beer. Within the township, little shops served the basic needs of the population, but purchases were more costly than in the white areas. The shop owners purchased smaller quantities of goods to sell, and so the retail prices were higher in the first place, but they also charged more because they knew that they had little competition. Africans were permitted to purchase items in the white areas, but they had to travel on public transportation for some distance to do so. When they did this, they had to purchase their items at a different check-out. "Cafes," small grocery shops, in the white areas would not permit Africans to enter: they would serve Africans through a service window.

On Easter Sunday in Thabong, seven people were baptized, and others were being instructed in the Christian life in preparation for baptism at a later time. Gene held Bible studies with all the adult believers, and Phyllis held Bible studies with the women. Fulltime pastors were secured for Virginia's African township of Meloding and for Odendaalsrus's African township of Kutlwanong, so there was some hope for fruitful ministry in the region beyond Welkom as persistent ministry was set in place.

The minister for Meloding was Edward Tsotetse, who had been a powerful witchdoctor prior to his conversion in 1956. He immediately turned from his practice of witchcraft and burned his witchcraft paraphernalia, such as herbs, bones, wire, and so forth. Tsotetse told Gene that, as a witchdoctor, he had been able to call fire down from the sky and travel instantly—but still physically—to other regions of South Africa. During their years in Africa, the Grams never heard of such a thing apart from Tsotetse's claim, but they did believe him. After all, there was such a story about Philip's immediate transportation by the Spirit from one area of Israel to another (Acts 8.39–40). And Gene had had that strange experience of instantly crossing a river in his car when an ox wagon was blocking the bridge. However, whatever power was at work in Tsotetse the witch doctor, it was not from God. So, after his conversion, he left those powers behind and determined to follow Christ. He became a full time minister to Virginia's African township of Meloding. Gene worried about Tsotetse's quick move into ministry after his conversion, including his lack of preparation in Bible School. Paul had warned Timothy that anyone put too quickly into a position of oversight could become puffed up with conceit (1 Tim 3.8), and so he recommended a list of qualifica-tions that would establish a person's faithfulness in and readiness for service over time. So, somewhat predictably, Tsotetse's quick transition from witch doctor to minister was not entirely smooth; but he did prove faithful over the years.

After only a few months of the Grams' ministry in Thabong, the church grew to a large enough size that there was a pressing need for a permanent and larger meeting place. The church moved from meeting in the pastor's house to meeting in garages, with the doors open and the people sitting or standing in the garden. The church now joined the Assemblies of God fellowship, and Gene began to look into the possibil-ity of a church building for it. As he visited government officials to see if a church site was available, he only met with opposition. The officials saw the Assemblies of God as a "sect" to which they did not wish to grant a site for anything. In addition, the white Assemblies of God church in Welkom, the New Goldfields Assembly of God, was a problem from the official's perspective. It had a piece of property in a choice location of the town, but their building was an unsightly prefabricated structure. The officials had initially granted permission for this structure for only 6 months, but the church had been able to extend this permission over several years. So, when Gene requested property for a church building in Thabong, the officials pointed out what a disgrace the white church building was in Welkom.

13

From Every Tribe and Tongue and People and Nation

> . . . you have stripped off the old person with its practices and
> put on the new person, which is being renewed in knowledge
> according to the image of the one who created it, where there
> is no Greek or Jew, circumcised or uncircumcised, barbarian,
> Scythian, slave, or free person, but Christ is all things and in all
> things. (Colossians 3.9–11)

IN ABOUT JUNE OF 1956, three members of the white Assemblies of
God church, New Goldfields Assembly, came to visit Gene and Phyllis.
They were Mr. Scott, Mr. Lugtenburg, and Mr. Postumus. This was the
church that Vernon Pettenger had earlier helped to establish. The three
members explained to the Grams that their pastor had recently left due
to a lack of finances. He had a large family of seven children, and the
church of thirty-six people could not support them adequately, so he left
ministry and began work in one of the mines. The three men from the
church asked Gene to become their pastor. Because this church seemed
to be the major hindrance to future work in Thabong, Gene and Phyllis
agreed to assist the white church in Welkom.

Gene's new role as the pastor of New Goldfields Assembly did not
diminish his work among the Africans in Thabong and surrounding
regions. Tsotetsi moved to nearby Melodeng, the African township for
Virginia, to undertake ministry there. His wife, however, was not granted permission to join him by the authorities. Pass laws in South Africa
not only separated whites, Coloureds, Indians, and Africans from one
another but also different tribes from each other. Even though as blacks
from different tribes the Tsotetsis were permitted to marry each other in
apartheid South Africa, this did not automatically mean that they would
be permitted to live together. So this became a matter for prayer when

the authorities initially refused. Gene made several trips to the officials to plead the couple's case before permission was finally granted.

Gene had also begun work among men in the various gold mines of the region. During much of 1956, Phyllis was pregnant with her third child. When she did not feel well, she would stay at home while Gene went out to minister here or there. She always saw these times not as a matter of her being left out of the ministry but as an opportunity to be present with Gene in ministry through prayer. Sometimes, as she moved about the house, she would worship and pray out loud, or she would kneel beside her bed and be lost in prayer for an hour or so before "the Throne of Grace." Almost every night, Gene would travel out to the mines for a meeting. Darrell turned three years old that August, and Gene often took him along to the mine ministry. The miners were delighted to see a small boy in the harsh and family-less environment of the goldmines, and he enjoyed the attention and the mines very much. At the mines, Gene usually preached to large crowds. Sometimes he would have as many as seven interpreters to translate his message so that the workers from the various tribes of Southern Africa and beyond could listen in their own languages. Miners came from the Congo, Kenya, Tanganyika (now Tanzania), Rhodesia (now Zimbabwe) and other surrounding countries, as well as from all over South Africa. Many of these had never heard the Gospel of Jesus Christ. A five-minute message could take well over half an hour to deliver in the various languages.

Ministry in the mine compounds was successful, but Gene requested prayer from his supporters in the US for the vexing problem of tribalism among the new converts in August, 1956. He noticed that the men had begun to separate into tribal groups and not intermingle as they had when they first came to Christ. The prayer that Gene prayed was taken from Jesus' "High Priestly" prayer in John 17, a prayer that the disciples would have the very love and unity of the Father and Son. It might have been a prayer for the church in South Africa in general, as it was only in Christ that the unity the country so badly needed, with its unjust racial and economic divisions, could be found. But what good was the church for South Africa as long as it not only tolerated but perpetrated apartheid? The test of the health of a church is not growth but "saltiness": does it stand out in its witness to the righteousness of God in the unrighteous world?

African miners from Southern African countries would also come to services in the African locations. They brought with them their traditional, animistic beliefs that held them in superstition and spiritual bondage. On one occasion, a man showed up at the Grams' house to ask for a chicken. He explained that he needed its blood to offer a sacrifice to his ancestors. Gene and Phyllis were able to tell the man the good news that Jesus Christ had shed his own blood once for all to make atonement for our sins. The man joyfully accepted the eternal sacrifice of Christ that not only saves us from sin but also disarms spiritual rulers and authorities by triumphing over them by the cross.[1]

While Gene continued to secure a site for a building in Thabong, the church continued to meet in schools, garages, and the open air. A large shed was used for the Thabong church itself, although one windy day it was blown down. Driving this proliferation of meetings everywhere was a desire to saturate the area with the Gospel. With miners from so many parts of the continent present, converts would inevitably spread the Gospel in the towns and villages of many regions in Africa as they returned home. One prime example of this was Henrique Mugabe from Mozambique. He heard the Gospel in meetings at the mine that some other minister held and became a Christian. A number of years later, Gene became acquainted with him and learned that he had become a minister of the Gospel in his home country once he left the mine. He later became the General Superintendant of the Assemblies of God churches and the President of the Bible school in Maputo, Mozambique.

Almost immediately after beginning ministry with New Goldfields Assembly of God, Gene realized that there were major problems with the membership. The Sunday School director had very recently been dismissed from his job as he had been caught smoking underground in one of the mines—a very dangerous and serious infraction of mine rules. During a church dinner, a number of the women got into a fight and began swearing at one another. So Gene spoke to the church after a Sunday morning service. He said that there was a need for standards of membership, and therefore he was dissolving the membership of the

1. Cf. Colossians 2.13–15: "And because you were dead in trespasses and the uncircumcision of your flesh, he [God] made you alive with him [Christ], thus forgiving all our trespasses, wiping out the record of debts against us with its public decrees that stood against us. And this he took away from our midst by nailing it to the cross, with the result being that he disarmed and made a bold, public show of the rulers and authorities, triumphing over them on it."

church from that moment. He passed out application forms for new membership. Only one third of the original thirty-six members reapplied, and all were accepted. So the church began anew with only twelve members in 1956.

These newly constituted members of the church began to grow in their understanding of Christian discipleship. One vivid lesson they were learning from their new minister was that God loved all people. They could see how Gene and Phyllis spent their Sundays and lived through the week in ministry devoted mostly to the Africans. During a Wednesday night Bible Study class, one of the women gave a testimony of how God had changed her heart towards Africans. With tears running down her face, she told how disturbing it had been to see the Grams work with blacks. But then, she said, God had shown her that Africans too have souls. Everyone faces some hard choices as they choose to follow Jesus in discipleship, and in apartheid South Africa, one of the common challenges was to realize that in God's Kingdom there was no separation of the races.

With the membership sorted out, Gene focused on the need for a building in 1956 and 1957. He approached numerous banks to secure a loan. Eventually, the United Building Society agreed to put up the loan. The bank manager, a member of the Church of England, wanted to know how a church of twelve members that did not support its pastor could expect to make payments on a building. Gene explained that the reorganized church would practice tithing and take up offerings. The manager jokingly asked if Gene would be willing to come to his church to teach on this concept of tithing. He was impressed enough to grant the loan of about 30 thousand pounds.

The largest builder in the city, Mr. Bell, volunteered to build the church's building. He had children in Phyllis's Sunday School, and his mother-in-law was a faithful member of the church. So Bell secured lumber and a beautiful face brick, and the building was completed at little cost for materials or labor. The lovely church building was also in a good location, just off Stateway, on the southeast side of Welkom, just one mile from the city center.[2] The location of New Goldfields Assembly of God was remarkable for one further reason: a neighbor had a chained lion. Children from the church would hope to hear the lion roar during

2. A picture of the New Goldfields Assembly of God can be found in Pettenger, "1500," 16. One taken on the day of its dedication is also found in this book.

one of the services. The building was dedicated on the 26th of October, 1957, and the congregation insisted that Gene's name be placed on the cornerstone.[3]

When Phyllis took over the Sunday School ministry in 1956, she organized five classes for children of different ages, and these were held outside on the church grounds. The program grew to a size of about six hundred children between 1956 and 1958. Apparently, Sunday School classes were not being held in other churches in Welkom, and so people were thrilled to have something available for their children. Flannel graphs were used to tell Bible stories, and there was much singing. With a lion visible from the church grounds, stories about Daniel in the lion's den made a great impression. An adult Sunday School class is unusual in South Africa, and so Gene's Bible class was also a novelty. This single adult class grew to about one hundred people. In addition, the church started a men's ministry, a women's ministry, and a youth ministry. The youth met during the Sunday School hour on Sunday mornings.

Gene's Sunday schedule was as follows:

8:00 am	Meeting in Thabong for pastors from twelve or more churches who would then teach the message he gave in their churches to others.
10:00 am	Bible class at New Goldfields Assembly of God.
11:00 am	Sunday morning service at New Goldfields Assembly of God.
3:00 pm	Service in Thabong, sometimes elsewhere.
7:30 pm	Sunday evening service at new Goldfields Assembly of God.

On Wednesday nights, Gene led a Bible study at New Goldfields. One of his first studies was on fear. He mentioned that some people are

---

3. When the International Assemblies of God split away from the Assemblies of God in 1964, Gene's name was actually chipped off the cornerstone of this church's building, a church he loved so very much. Shrubs were placed in front of the cornerstone to cover the blemish. In 1981, however, he was asked to return for the dedication of a new education wing. Years later, he and Phyllis would visit again, but the church had little or no memory of them. Ministry is, after all, with certain people at a certain point in their lives, not with buildings, institutions, or generations to come. And churches are not buildings but people gathering in Jesus' name.

so fearful that they carry guns to protect themselves. At this, five women in the congregation sitting near the front pulled out revolvers from their purses to show that they were indeed afraid and prepared. Gene had hit on a pertinent topic.

On Saturday afternoons, Phyllis would travel to Whites, a small white town about twenty-five miles from Welkom. The town and an African township had grown up around a single industry, a cement factory. A family by the name of Pearce lived there, and Mrs. Pearce was a member of New Goldfields Assembly of God. She asked Phyllis to have regular children's meetings for the African families in the area. Phyllis was eager to do so: this is why she had come to Africa. Hundreds of children came to these meetings, which were held in a large pavilion.

On Thursday nights, the Grams would hold a service in the Pearce's home.[4] Frequently, Gene also held Bible studies on other evenings at other places, such as at Odendaalsrus and Virginia. During the days, Gene would often go to the mines to pass out literature and hold a meeting, and with other matters of ministry to attend to during the week, Gene was busy day and night, and Phyllis, with her women's and children's ministries and two little children at home, was also very busy.

On the evening of the 29th of October, 1956, the church held a *braai* (cookout), and Gene was responsible for picking up several of the members for the occasion. Unfortunately, Phyllis went into labor at the same time, and so she travelled with Gene in the car while he made the pick-ups. Once everyone had gathered, Pastor Grams opened in prayer and then quickly drove Phyllis home to have her baby. So, that evening, at 10:10 p.m., Dr. Tommy Tucker presented Dennis Dwight to the world. Like Darrell, Dennis was born at home as Phyllis would not go to a hospital after her traumatic experience with her first child. Phyllis's mother, Louise, and her little sister, Joy, were there for the occasion as they had come from Pietersburg to be with the family.

There was also an exciting birth "from above" about this time. Joseph Mojakotsane became a Christian. Sometime around 1951, he and an accomplice had murdered a man whose car they had stolen. The accomplice had been convicted of the actual shooting and was put to death, but Mojakotsane had been sentenced to life in prison. While

4. Some years later, the Pearce's son, Charles, and his wife, Rhoda, became American citizens and then returned as missionaries with the Assemblies of God to South Africa.

there, some unknown Christians regularly visited the prisoners. The Thabong church itself developed a strong ministry to the prison, with several teams going out before the Sunday morning service. Mojakotsane hated the Christians who visited the prison. He even tried to grab them through the bars of his cell. On one occasion, he was handed a copy of the Gospels. He took it and tore pages from it in front of the ministry team, throwing the pages around his cell. But, while sitting on his bed a little later, he picked up one of the pages of the Gospel and actually read it. As he read, he was convicted of his sin and need for God. Since he had heard the prison ministry team speak of repentance, he prayed on his own that God would forgive him his sins. From that time on, he became a disciple of Christ.

Prison officials noticed a change in Mojakotsane's life. He was eventually released from prison shortly before December, 1956 after an appeal for a stay of his sentence had been granted. He became a great witness in the community and would bring new people to the church services. He also helped in the Sunday School program, using his van to collect children from around the location. Often the children that came were simply picked up off the streets. A number of these children became Christians and a vital part of the church. Some years later, Mojakotsane moved to Lesotho as a minister of the Gospel.

As the ministry spread to Virginia and Odendaalsrus in 1956, about ten *tsotsis* (gangsters) became Christians. They testified of the change in their lives, how previously they had lived lives of stabbing people, smoking *dagga* (marijuana), gambling, and so forth. The church also had testimony of healings. In his December 17th newsletter that year, Gene reported that "several who have been bed-ridden with crippling diseases for so long have been instantly delivered . . . . Yes, the blind are seeing, the cripples are walking, and all manner of diseases are disappearing. Praise the wonderful name of our Lord forever!"

By this time, the church in the African township of Odendaalsrus, that is, Kutlwanong, had been granted a building site. This township was only about ten miles north of Welkom. Efforts to evangelize and plant a church in the Odendaalsrus area were clearly divinely assisted. People told of dreams they had had in which they were instructed to attend the church to learn of the way that leads to heaven. Others told of seeing the church's name or the pastor's face in their dreams. Because the church now numbered about sixty members at the end of 1956, authorities were willing to grant a building permit.

The minister in Odendaalsrus lived in a tin shack with his family on the site of the future building. During the day, he would make cement blocks for his house and the church building. After the nightly meetings, the church members would make cement blocks for their future church building until midnight. Funds to move ahead faster were urgently needed, and these would have to come from supporters in the United States. For several years, only a foundation for the church building had been laid, and it would not be until 1961 that the rest of the facility was completed.

14

Lesotho

Remind them to be subject to rulers and authorities, to be obe-
dient, to be prepared for every good work, not to revile, not to
be quarrelsome but gentle, showing every kindness to all people.
For we were ourselves once foolish, disobedient, misled, serving
every sort of passion and pleasure, living in malice and envy,
rancorous, hating one another. But when the kindness and love
for humanity of our Savior God appeared, he saved us, not from
works in righteousness that we ourselves did, but in accord with
his mercy through the washing of regeneration and renewal by
the Holy Spirit, whom he lavishly poured out on us through Jesus
Christ our Savior, so that we, having been made righteous by that
grace, might become heirs according to the hope of eternal life
(Titus 3.1–7)

By July, 1957, several positive developments had taken place. First,
the three Assemblies of God churches of Thabong, Kutlwanong,
and Meloding held a joint baptismal service. The congregations walked
about two miles to a pond of water, singing as they went. As it was the
dry season, the pond was not very deep, and the baptismal candidates
had to kneel in the water for their baptisms.

Second, officials in Meloding (Virginia) had finally given permission to conduct religious services. Their opposition had been an impen-
etrable barrier to expanding the ministry. And the young church was
growing. On one occasion, while the minister there was teaching on the
Holy Spirit, the power of the Spirit fell upon them, and six of the believers were filled with the Spirit. People walking by the building heard the
noise and came in to see what was happening. The Gospel was explained
to them, and some became Christians right then and there.

Meanwhile, the Grams did not like their house in Dagbreek: it was hot in the summer and cold in the winter. So Gene had a new house built in a new subdivision, Naudeville, and, in June of 1957, the Grams moved a third time in Welkom to 36 Lena St. This was only the third house in the new area of Naudeville to be occupied, but houses were being built everywhere as the gold mining town continued to grow. Gene put in the garden, including a mulberry bush in the back garden. Little did the family know as they settled into their new home that the next two and a half-years would have them going around the mulberry bush, as the saying goes. But these would not be wasted years in ministry.

The Grams' new neighbors were the Smith's, but as they were Afrikaners, they pronounced their name "Smit." Mr. Smith detested Gene, calling him a "*kaffir boetie*." "*Kaffir*" is an Arabic loan-word meaning "heathen," but in South Africa it was used derogatorily of the blacks. "*Boetie*" means "little brother," and so "*kaffir boetie*" was a hateful expression for one who befriended black people.

While the *stoep* (porch) to the Grams' house was being constructed, the black builders that Gene had employed made a mistake with the pillars. Gene took a level and held it up to a pillar. "I would like to recommend you as builders to others who need work done on their homes," he said, "but I cannot do so with workmanship like this." The workers could see that the pillars were crooked and agreed that the work would have to be redone. "But I know that this will be difficult for you," Gene continued. They were day laborers: to redo work would mean no pay for a few days, and no pay would mean no food. Mr. Smith was watching from next door. "I'll tell you what," Gene said, "I'll pay you for redoing the pillars, and we can give you food while you are here." The workers were amazed, but Mr. Smith was disgusted.

"*Kaffir boetie*," he called over from next door, "come over here, I want to talk with you." Gene went next door, and Mr. Smith led him into his kitchen. There he instructed Gene in the ways of South Africa—a lesson Gene had heard before. He remembered his first lesson on the subject from that senior missionary on his wedding day. "Let me tell you what I would do with these stupid *kaffir* workers of yours," he said. "I'd kick them, make them redo the work, and definitely not give them any extra pay, let alone serve them food. Man, I know you are an American, but how can you be so stupid?"

"Well," Gene replied, "all I can say is that what I do has nothing to do with being an American. I think about what Jesus would do, and I believe that he would see these poor African workers as no different from us. Every one of us needs his forgiveness, and I have forgiven these workers for a much simpler error than the ones I have committed in my life. I thank God that he has forgiven me."

To Gene's amazement, his irate neighbor began to cry. Gene asked if Mr. Smith would like to pray with him. He nodded. Gene told him to pray after him. "Our Father God, thank you for forgiving us for our sins. Thank you, Jesus, for dying on the cross in our place. Thank you for your sacrifice that takes away my sins. Please forgive me . . . . Thank you for forgiving me . . . . Thank you for saving me." Mr. Smith repeated every word, and from that day on he never again called Gene "*kaffir boetie*," although it was true: Gene was a little friend to the heathen, even the likes of Mr. Smith.

The police too had been watching Gene and Phyllis Grams. From time to time, they would conduct raids on the house to see if any blacks were sleeping over: it seemed just the sort of thing that these missionaries might do with their black friends. Any African caught outside in the white areas after curfew would be arrested, and anyone housing them was complicit in the crime. In these days, Gene and Phyllis could see no end to apartheid South Africa. They lived out a most peculiar role of great privilege as whites while being ridiculed for their close fellowship with blacks.

Thirty one years later, on the 6th of October, 1988, Gene and Phyllis Grams would be invited to a state dinner of the South African government held in their honor and hear the Deputy Chairman of the prestigious President's Council, Mr. Kotze, stand up to say to them before numerous dignitaries in the soon-to-be dismantled white government, "You showed us a way out of apartheid. I am not a prophet or the son of a prophet, but I predict that, within three years, apartheid will be history."

When he said this, the Prohibition Against Mixed Marriages Act had already been abolished in 1985, the Pass Laws in 1986, and various restrictions against races using the same facilities were coming to an end. Mr. Kotze was referring particularly to the 1959 Extension of University Education Act No. 45 that had very recently been repealed in July, 1988. This act had given the Minister of Bantu Education the authority to designate colleges for Africans to attend. Black students had not been permitted to attend the University of Cape Town or the University of Witwatersrand without a permit. Quotas were used to determine how many of any race, if any, would be permitted to attend a college that had been designated as one that could have other races attend. But, with Mr. Kotze's help in Parliament, the Grams had established an interracial Bible college, the Cape College of Theology, already in February, 1987. It had been allowed to operate as a residential college without any quotas at all for the different races. Finally, in June, 1991, the Parliamentary House of Assembly in South Africa repealed the quota system for colleges and universities altogether. It was almost three years after Mr. Kotze's prediction.

In 1957, though, the apartheid laws were still being passed, and it seemed to the officials that the Grams were probably flouting the laws in their work in the African townships and breaking them in their home. If Africans had been found in the Grams' home after curfew, they would quite likely have been deported. But the South African authorities did not prove to be the major obstacle to ministry; rather, the mission authority was.

In 1957, Everett Phillips, the Foreign Missions Director for Africa, and his wife Dorothy traveled by car throughout Africa, visiting the Assemblies of God missionaries along the way. When they visited the Grams in the Orange Free State, Gene showed him their several points of ministry, including the European (white) church building of New Goldfields. Its construction was nearly finished. Gene was very pleased with how the building looked, and he felt that this was quite a remarkable part of his story in ministry: he had helped to turn around a failing ministry, and by ministering to both whites and blacks he was bringing some reconciliation through Christ between the polarized races of South Africa. Gene told the story of this church to Phillips, whom he liked personally. He told how the church had grown from twelve members to one hundred and eighty in attendance in about eighteen months. He told of Phyllis's great ministry to hundreds of children.

Phillips, looking up at the impressive ceiling, said simply, "Gene, you did not come to Africa for white people. So, get out of this as fast as you can. You should go and study Sesotho in order to work more with the black Africans." Gene was devastated. He had even arranged for some African speakers to come to address this white church, thereby bringing together the races in worship and ministry. But the Foreign Missions Director for Africa saw otherwise, and they had no choice but to comply.

The Assemblies of God in the United States had been structured initially more as a fellowship of churches that were quite independent, but it also had set up presbyteries along the lines of Presbyterian churches, and some of its leaders functioned with the authority that bishops in the Episcopal form of church governance wielded. The Field Secretary for Africa would be voted on by the missionaries of the continent he directed, but there would never be an announcement of the results of the vote, since he was appointed by the Foreign Missions Board. The Grams had great respect for Phillips and liked him very much, but in a matter such as this, Gene had no process available to him to appeal Phillips's decision.

So, towards the end of 1957, Gene and Phyllis arranged to study Sesotho at Mount Tabor Mission Station with an older missionary couple. The mission station was located near Mafeteng in the nearby country of Lesotho, a country surrounded by South Africa. Phyllis was expecting their fourth child at the time, and Darrell and Dennis were four years and one year old, respectively. The original plan was to stay in Lesotho for six months and make significant progress in the language, but events did not unfold according to plan.

In January, 1958, the family of four packed their 1955 Plymouth for the three hundred mile trip to Basutoland (now Lesotho). The Grams had been informed that there would be no beds or chest of drawers for the children at Mount Tabor Mission Station. The car's boot (trunk) was left open so that more could be packed, and a crib and wardrobe were also placed on top of the car. Ropes were passed through the windows to tie these items securely.

Five miles out of Welkom, the whole load on top of the car shifted and fell onto the boot. A truckload of miners happened to be passing by, and they gladly helped lift the load back onto the car, singing as they did so. One of the wonderful things about Africa is the music, and one could often hear a work team in the distance keeping rhythm together through their songs as they lifted some heavy object, dug trenches, or constructed roads. The miners also helped tie the load down more securely. A car built today probably could not have withstood such a load: the roof would have caved in. The miners tied the load to the car so well that it became part of the car: nothing could move it.

Nearly three hundred miles later, at about midnight, the Grams family reached the Lesotho border. They turned off the main road onto the road to the mission station. This road was gravel and mostly a single lane. The car came to a river. There was a causeway for cars to cross over, but it was far underwater due to recent, heavy rains. As he could see one pole sticking up above the water along the edge of the submerged causeway, Gene decided to try to drive the car across the flooded river. A little ways into the water, the headlights became submerged, and suddenly this harrowing experience was in almost total darkness. Just then, Darrell shouted from the back seat, "Daddy, Daddy, there is water coming into the car!" The car was flooding quickly, but continued forward for a little ways. Then the engine stalled. Had the car not been weighted down with so great a load and so securely, it most certainly would have been washed away in the fast flowing current, as they later learned had actually happened to someone else at this same crossing point. Six times Gene was able to restart the car and progress a few feet before the engine would fail. The last time that this happened, the battery was very nearly drained of power. But, as the car edged up the embankment on the other side and emerged out of the water, the engine did not fail.

During this whole procedure, a donkey had been watching from the other side of the river. As the car arose from the river in the middle of the night, its headlights bearing down on the poor beast, the donkey turned tail and ran down the road. Braying excitedly as it went, it ran nearly the entire way to the mission station. The Grams family had arrived in Lesotho, announced by a donkey.

The missionary couple that ran the mission station saw the arrival, but did not come outside in the middle of the night or help to unload the car. This would be one of those painful missionary stories. Fellowship with fellow laborers in mission can be as sweet as it can be sour. Gene and Phyllis never did understand why they were so mistreated by these older missionaries whom they had revered so highly over the past several years. The Grams' whole time in Lesotho would accomplish nothing at all.

The family lived in a one-room rondavel, which rested on the side of a rocky hill. Gene would count the flies he killed —usually around one hundred—while Phyllis made breakfast. There were so many flies because the mission station kept cattle nearby, but Africa nonetheless was abundant in flies. While a chief might use a fly chaser made of a stick of wood with a cow's tail attached, a more common sight would be to see flies crawling all over children. Flies would even drink from the corners of their eyes, and the children, accustomed to this, would not so much as flinch. The kitchen was in another rondavel some fifty feet away. Phyllis, now pregnant with her fourth child, had to be especially careful as she moved between huts on the rocky path on the hillside. The "kitchen rondavel" had no refrigerator, but Phyllis was permitted to use the missionaries' refrigerator on condition that they opened it only once a day. This proved a real challenge, as Dennis was not yet two years old and on baby formula.

The arrangement with the missionary couple was that the husband would teach Gene and Phyllis each day. But there were many interruptions, especially those to do with the condition of the road to the station. So Gene, together with others on the mission station, found himself recruited to work on the road on average two and a half days each week. The Grams did their best to study the language, but the primitive conditions, the need to care for two little children, Gene's frequent migraine headaches, and the constant road repairs made language study very difficult. The greatest blow to their plans came in the first week at the mission station. The missionary simply decided not to teach Sesotho to the Grams after only two lessons. He also insisted that Gene and Phyllis remain at the mission station and forbade them to mingle with Africans in the surrounding villages. This would, of course, have been the best way to acquire Sesotho, but the missionary was apparently worried that a competing ministry might develop. Instead, a schoolteacher was appointed to continue the lessons, but he proved to be incapable at instructing English speakers in his language. Gene and Phyllis did struggle along with the language as best they could. Dennis, however, seemed to be picking up Sesotho rather easily as he sat around the campfire at night with some of the Africans at the station. In his early years, he could speak Sesotho just as well as English.

Perhaps it might be said that language learning was not Gene's and Phyllis's forte, or perhaps it was simply not their own priority. Phyllis's managing house under these conditions was demanding. Gene's thoughts were on ministry that he had given up for these few months. After only a couple of weeks in Lesotho, on a trip into town to purchase the week's groceries, Gene and Phyllis noticed the headlines in a local paper: "Another Ritual Murder Find." The practice of obtaining human flesh for witchcraft reminded Gene that people were dying without hearing the Gospel. At the same time, the Grams received word that one of their supporting churches had contributed $100 for a tent for evangelism. To the Grams, Africa was the dark continent—heathen, superstitious, and dangerous. But they had the light of Christ, and sitting on the side of a hill in Lesotho did not seem to be the best way to meet the continent's needs. Evangelistic ministry as they had known it in the northern Transvaal was beckoning.

Before four months were past in Lesotho, the Grams wisely packed up and returned to Welkom. That they had lasted this long was testimony only to their initial resolve. Language acquisition is more than learning a language: it is also about learning a culture, learning to think as others think. It is also a way to demonstrate to people that they are valued for who they are—their way of life, culture, and language—and this is especially important if one is also asking them to change something about themselves, as Christian mission work does. Such arguments for language study were a little weaker in the mining townships of the Orange Free State, though, since so many African languages and cultures were represented. Still, Gene and Phyllis forever regretted their failure to gain fluency in Sesotho.

15

Return to Welkom

But we have this treasure in clay jars so that the surpassing power might be God's and not from us, who are in everything being pressed but not crushed, perplexed but not despairing, persecuted but not abandoned, struck down but not destroyed, always carrying about in the body Jesus' death, so that the life of Jesus might be revealed in our body (Second Corinthians 4.7–10)

THE REST OF 1958 proved to be an exciting year but ended in disappointment. When the Grams family returned to Welkom from Lesotho, they picked up their work with the African townships. In their absence, nineteen persons had been filled with the Holy Spirit and several had given their lives to Christ in the area. At the same time, a number of the church members were transferred to other mine compounds. This meant that church membership changed quickly.

The Grams returned to their house on Lena Street, which they had rented to the South African pastor replacing Gene at the New Goldfields church. As it happened, this arrangement too had been disastrous: the new family failed to clean the house at all in the four months that they occupied it. So the Grams had much work to do on the house upon their return from Lesotho. The pastor continued in the church, but within six months the congregation dwindled from 180 members to about 50. He had also initiated the city government's taking over the church's manse on its adjacent property as a way to deal with the financial challenges that the church was facing.

As New Goldfields Assembly headed quickly in a disturbing direction, the remaining members decided to ask Gene to return as pastor. Without seeking mission approval, he agreed to do so in order to get the church on a solid footing until another minister could be called. So Gene pastored the church for another six months. In that time, he was able to renegotiate the manse property, which to this day is still owned by New Goldfields Assembly of God. The membership did not grow much, though, and many of the earlier members who had gone to other congregations, especially the Full Gospel Church in Welkom, did not return.

One day, the church held a *braai*. As people were leaving, Gene left Phyllis in the car briefly while he went to do something. When he returned, he found Mr. Pierie Stoltz from the congregation standing by the car. Gene sensed something was wrong, and he then noticed that Phyllis was crying. Stolz then turned on Gene. "My wife is in the hospital and you are the pastor. Why have you not been visiting her more often?" He was furious, but also confused. Phyllis had gone to the hospital daily to visit her. "That is not enough," the distraught man replied. Gene suggested that the two of them leave Phyllis and go into the church building to discuss things. As they entered the building, Stolz said, "I'm going to teach you something, little preacher." He was well over six feet tall and perhaps six inches taller than Gene. He rolled up his sleeves. Gene took off his coat and said, "Have you ever heard the expression, 'The bigger they are, the harder they fall?'" At this, Stoltz began to cry. He had become overly anxious and realized that he was acting inappropriately. He apologized, hugged Gene, and from that day the two men became good friends. His wife was actually fine and was released from the hospital in a few days.

Gene also found himself in the situation once again of trying to restore the church's reputation in the town. When he tried to purchase a bed at OK Bazaar, one of the local stores, he was told that no Assemblies of God minister would ever be able to purchase anything on credit. The sales manager tore the credit application form up in front of Gene. With the church in debt, Gene had to return office equipment and supplies that had not been paid for to the stores from which the goods had been purchased.

One purchase the Grams did make at this time was a 1958 Plymouth. Gene and Darrell travelled to Bloemfontein to trade in the 1955 Plymouth that they had brought with them from the United States. The Grams had purchased the 1955 car with the money they themselves had raised for missions, since at the time they had not yet been appointed by the Assemblies of God. When Gene and Phyllis received a letter in 1958 that they were eligible for funds to purchase a car through the mission, they decided to do so. They hoped that this Plymouth would be better than their 1955 Plymouth had been. It would also be a little safer because it was a right hand drive (cars drive on the left side of the road in British colonial countries like South Africa). Gene also purchased a 50 cc motorcycle about this time to get about town. After an accident that knocked him out and threw Darrell through the air, the family was back to having a single mode of transportation.

Money for future cars came from "Christ's Ambassadors," the youth ministry of the Assemblies of God churches. Their "Speed-the-Light" program raises funds for mission vehicles and equipment (such as printing presses, radios, and public address systems) through their own offerings and fund raising events. While many youth programs in other churches today raise funds for their own short term mission trips, this program offers support for long-term missionaries. In this way, it ties the youth into the denomination's mission efforts. According to an article published on the 13th October, 1957, Speed-the-Light had raised $2,268,675.11 since its inception in January, 1945.[1]

Phyllis expected to deliver her baby in late July. Albert and Louise Louton came down from Pietersburg to be on hand, and there was, of course, much prayer for Phyllis and her baby. Louise believed that she had been given a word of knowledge from God that the baby would be a girl. On the 25th of July, 1958, Phyllis gave birth to her fourth child and third son, Rollin Gene Grams. Louise was, to say the least, shocked. After a few days, the Loutons had to return to their home, but it was just at that time that everyone except Rollin fell terribly ill with the flu. They were too sick to leave their beds.

Ed Louton and his new bride, Barbara (Hughes), had just arrived in the country from the United States, and they proceeded directly to assist the Grams family rather than go to Pietersburg to set up house. Upon their arrival in Welkom, Ed asked what might be the first thing he could do. Gene suggested that he take the family dog, which had been unattended for several days, out of the garage for a walk. Ed hurried to the garage. A few minutes later, Gene caught sight of Ed through the

---

1. Short, "77-A-Minute," 14–15, 31. In an article ten years later, on the 30th of April, 1967, it was reported that Speed-the-Light had raised $103,518, 677.63 since its beginning (which it claims was in 1944). In just twelve months in 1966–1967, the CAs had purchased "81 cars, 20 station wagons, 12 trucks, 16 motorcycles, 48 bicycles, 6 buses, 2 boats, 2 trailers, and 1 jeep." See "Operation Demonstration," p. 18.

window: he was flying through the air and bounding down the street as the exuberant animal pulled him along at top speed from the other end of the leash.

With Rollin's birth, the Grams would have no further children. Ed and Barbara, on the other hand, soon began to have children: David, Linda, Valerie, and Barbara. The children had something few missionary families have: grandparents, uncles, aunts, and cousins with whom to enjoy Christmases and holidays.

Towards the end of the six months back in Welkom, Gene contacted Jim Mullan, who had originally come from Ireland to minister in South Africa with his brother, Fred, to see if he knew of a qualified pastor for the New Goldfields church. Both Mullans served in the Assemblies of God fellowship, including on its executive board. Jim Mullan suggested Paul Lange, and he agreed to go. Soon after arriving, Lange unbolted the church pews from the floor so that on Saturday nights they could be placed in a circle for communion services. This service was called an "open ministry," and anyone could speak at the service. This was a growing practice at the time in the Assemblies of God in South Africa.

The American Assemblies of God Foreign Missions Department would eventually break away from the South African Assemblies of God, in July, 1964. There were a number of reasons for the division.[2] The happy times of fruitful ministry in Welkom came to an end when the American Assemblies of God formed the International Assemblies of God in South Africa. The churches that the Grams had worked with remained part of the South African Assemblies of God. But at this time, only the pews were unbolted from the floor in the New Goldsfields Assembly. Differences had not reached a boiling point in the larger fellowship, and the Grams celebrated a second restoration of the Welkom church, which remains a thriving congregation to this day. Only in the 1980s and afterwards would the

---

2. The disputes were over doctrine, church governance, and worship practices. The American Assemblies of God Foreign Missions Department had already decided to close South Africa as a field. The Grams family was going to be posted to Tanzania. But during the discussions, the missionaries appealed to remain. So, they withdrew from the South African Assemblies of God and formed the International Assemblies of God. Morris Williams and Gene Grams rewrote the constitution of the new denomination and registered it with the government. The denomination was divided, however, because of apartheid, and so Gene had to type the constitution four times under four names for each race: the Assemblies of God International for the whites, the International Assemblies of God for the Africans, the International Assemblies of God (Coloured), and the International Assemblies of God (Asian).

Grams find themselves working with ministers in both the International Assemblies of God and the Assemblies of God in South Africa once again. Their insistence that the Cape College of Theology that they had established be for various groups, not just the International Assemblies of God, would be a blessing to many in South Africa.

In September, 1958, the Grams reported several exciting incidents. First, they thanked supporters who had been praying for Dennis over the previous year. Dennis had severe allergies, but he was now completely well. Second, people in the Virginia township of Meloding were turning to Christ, leaving behind lives of crime, drugs, drunkenness, and so forth. A witch doctor was also saved at the time, and he burned his medicines and the other items he had used for his cures and witchcraft. Several children in the Sunday School had been filled with the Holy Spirit. In Odendaalsrus, among several who had given their lives to Christ was a harlot. In Thabong, new converts included several criminals and communists, who were opposed to the government.

Plans were also in place for a new thrust in ministry in these areas. Evangelist Philip Molefe from Sharpeville, near Vereeniging in the Transvaal, would begin meetings with the Grams on the 10th of October, 1958. Four months of meetings were planned, although funds for the evangelistic campaign were still needed. Three hundred dollars were needed for 10,000 gospel tracts, and further funds were needed for advertising, gasoline for the lighting plant, and so forth. Funds had not yet come in to purchase a tent, but Rev. Molefe had his own.

Gene was excited to have Rev. Molefe join him in this tent ministry, and he wrote during the evangelistic campaign in his December, 1958 newsletter:

> Brother Molefe is a very humble minister whom God has raised up to proclaim the message of Christ's salvation among his people. Within the last six years he has been used of God to establish twelve strong churches. Hundreds of criminals and heathen are being converted. The government officials are thrilled about the reports of what God is accomplishing through him and they are thrilled about his coming here. They believe that crime will be drastically reduced in this area as the people are converted to Christ.

The tent campaign lasted two months. Finances proved to be a major problem for running the campaign any longer. But enough ministry developed out of the two months to move to the next phase of working directly with the young converts and the growing churches. In the meet-ings, drunkards, drug addicts, gangsters, thieves, policemen, nurses, teachers, office clerks and others accepted Christ as their Savior. There were signs and wonders from God too: the deaf, crippled, blind, mute, and others were healed. Some three hundred people were added to the church in Thabong.

While the campaign was under way, Rev. Molefe told Gene that he planned to bring ministers he knew to help with the growing ministry. As the conversation progressed, Gene began to feel marginalized: what need was there for him in this ministry other than to try to raise funds from the United States? The partnership fell apart, and Gene and Phyllis decided that they needed to step aside rather than stand in the way. One definition of being a missionary is to be someone who tries to work him or herself out of a job. If they were not essential to the ministry, the Grams would move. And so they did.

16

Into the Bundu: Sekhukhuneland

For this reason, I too, because I heard of your faith in the Lord Jesus and of your love for all the saints, do not cease to give thanks, bringing you to mind in my prayers, so that the God of our Lord Jesus Christ, the Father of glory, might give a Spirit of wisdom and revelation to you by knowing him, having the eyes of your hearts enlightened in order that you might know what is the hope of his calling, what is the glorious wealth of his inheritance among the saints, and what is the abundant greatness of His power for us who believe according to the working of the power of His might, which He worked in Christ by raising him from the dead and by seating him at his right hand in the heavenlies, high above every ruler and authority and power and dominion and every name that is named, not only in this age but also in that to come. And he subjected all things under his feet, and he appointed him head over all things for the church, which is his body, the fullness of the one who fills all things in all ways. (Ephesians 1.15–23)

THE GRAMS FAMILY OF five moved to Pietersburg in December, 1958. They found a house at 105 Magazyn St., on the same street where they as a family of three had lived before, at 40 Magazyn St. They thought at the time that this was a permanent move, but, of course, it was not. This became a base for ministry for only one year. Before the end of 1959 they were right back in their old house in Welkom. The decision to return to Welkom from Pietersburg was quickly made when Rev. Molefe asked Gene and Phyllis to return and help in the ministry there. He would continue as a tent evangelist, and Gene and Phyllis would be involved in discipling the new believers.

The year away from the Orange Free State could be viewed as a mistake. Why could things not have been clarified before a family moved several hundred miles away, especially since Philip Molefe and Gene Grams liked each other and had had a successful ministry together? Whatever one makes of the confusion, the result was that God used this move to advance his work in the northern Transvaal and still allowed the Grams to participate in His amazing work about to unfold in the goldfield regions of the Free State.

A return to the northern Transvaal could have meant an overlap of ministry with others, such as the Loutons. But the region was large, and the Grams either sought out places where others were not engaged in ministry or helped out as they were invited by others to do so. They particularly wanted to minister to the "less privileged" Africans outside the urban areas, in what South Africans call "the bundu," or bush. And they never went to an area just for meetings; they always intended to establish a church. Bible school students would be recruited to serve newly established churches, and the missionaries and African evangelists could move on to new points of ministry. This would mean spending significant time in the bush. So, during 1959, the family often lived in a tent or caravan in the African veldt to minister to the African villages in tent campaigns. They were able to borrow a tent from another missionary for tent crusades while raising the final funds to purchase it.

Fred Burke, their fellow Assemblies of God missionary in Witbank, suggested that the Grams work in Sekhukhuneland. This region in the northern Transvaal was where Dr. Mason had taken Gene to explore ministry several years earlier. Burke was the principle of the Assemblies of God's African Bible Training Institute in Witbank, and one of the students was from this area. So Burke knew that there was a need for ministry there from the student. A possible reason for this area's need for ministry was that just two years earlier, in 1957, the governing authorities of the region had appointed Frank Maserumule to be the chief of a new village, Mohlalaotwane, in the Nebo district of Sekhukhuneland for the Bakone people.[1] In 1958, there was a violent uprising in Sekhukhuneland because the government had interfered by breaking the power of the traditional chiefs and promoting others to be chiefs if

1. This information comes from p. 8 of an untitled study with no author done at the University of Johannesburg, available at http://ujdigispace.uj.ac.za:8080/dspace/bitstream/10210/726/3/Text.pdf (accessed 1 May, 2009).

they complied with their plans. Gene did not, however, know the details of the politics at the time; in his mind, he was going to visit the person who could grant permission to hold tent meetings in an area where there was no church.[2]

Neither did Gene know that, in 1917, H. M. Turney, the first Assemblies of God missionary in South Africa, had wanted to establish a work here. Turney wrote,

> The paramount chief of Sekhukhunaland [*sic*] has [sent] to me [twice] to come and establish a station on his territory, and another chief from that district called on me personally to ask that a school and church might be opened in his village. These are the trials which press so [sorely] on the [missionary] in the field. These are the things which cause him to weep tears of anguish as he pleads the cause of the dumb (Prov. 31:8) before the throne of God. If lack of funds only meant privation for [himself] and his family and workers, it would matter very little, but when he has to look into the wistful eyes of men pleading for the Bread of Life and tell them that because the money is withheld he cannot help them, it is [heart-breaking]. We read continually of [Christians] at home meeting to feast on the Word. But alas! they do not [deem] to remember "to send portions to those for whom nothing is prepared."[3]

Remembering his earlier failure to find an open door for ministry in the region, Gene was more determined now than ever to succeed. He wanted to minister where there was no church, and Sekhukhuneland was a good prospect for that. He headed southeast from Pietersburg on the road to Lydenberg, driving a hundred miles or so to the area that Fred Burke had mentioned. The area was very rural and some seventy miles from Middelburg. The people in this area were a mixture of Bapedi and Ndebele tribesmen. The chief was the only one who could grant permission for the tent campaign, but it took three days to gain an audience with him.

---

2. Apparently, there were Christians among the Bapedi of Sekhukhuneland. But this was a vast area, and Gene's purpose was to go to an area where no church existed.

3. Turney, "Tests," 12. The Scripture reference is to Neh 8.10, which literary refers to sending food to those who have none rather than being a reference to hearing the Gospel. It's metaphorical use illustrates a typical approach to how Scripture has been used in this tradition (and many others), particularly those in which the Scriptures are so well known that Biblical phrases are easily co-opted for use in a preacher's rhetoric.

Gene would arrive in the morning and sit in the car in the hot sun each day, waiting to see the chief. On the first two days the chief's headman did not summon the missionary. Apparently, the chief was too inebriated to see anyone. On the third day, at about 4:00 p.m., the chief was willing and able to hear Gene's request. Gene was summoned and was ushered into the large rondavel. Inside, it was very dark. Chief Maserumule could speak English, and so the two were able to converse without an interpreter. The Chief spoke first, "I know you have come to see me for a reason, but before you tell me why, I want you to pray for my eleven wives." He was half-drunk at the time, or rather sober enough to reflect on his eleven-fold marital problems. As he unfolded the problems he faced with his marriages, one could well appreciate his additional problem with alcohol.

Standing by one wife, Maserumule described in graphic detail the history of her faults and then waited for Gene to utter a prayer. This was not a time to explore possible mutual responsibility in marriage: marital counseling was not on the agenda. The inebriated chief and the missionary moved to stand beside the next wife for a repetition of the same process. As the kraal grew darker in the waning daylight, Gene could not help but feel an admiration for the chief's ability, in his state of mind, to articulate others' faults with such intricate detail. The process was taking considerable time, and some of the chief's complaints about his wives were of a most delicate nature, such that the missionary was glad that the darkness hid his flushed face. He had certainly never prayed like this before.

Afterwards, Gene was permitted to ask his question to the chief: would Chief Maserumule of the Bakone in this Nebo region of Sekhukhuneland permit him to hold a tent meeting in the area? This was a completely different affair from seeking permission for tent campaigns in the Orange Free State from government officials. Here, something had been given by the missionary of potentially immense worth—prayer for the chief's eleven wives—and now the chief had reason to give something in return. Moreover, this chief, who had already been complicit with white government authorities and depended on them for his elevation as a regional chief, may have thought that he was politically wise to grant this white person's request. In any case, a tent meeting, Gene was instructed, could be held for two weeks. Ultimately, this period would be extended two weeks at a time so that the tent meetings actually lasted for what was becoming the usual three months.

As the day to begin approached, the Grams family moved to Sekhukhuneland. They used a nine by twelve foot tent and had army cots for beds. Rollin was only about six months old, so he slept in his baby buggy. The family had purchased a kerosene refrigerator: they felt fairly comfortable in the bush. Chief Maserumule instructed them where they could pitch their tent, as well as where the larger tent for meeting could be erected. As there was no electricity in the area, they had their own generator for lights. Over the course of the next three months, the Grams would travel back to Pietersburg every week or so for a day to pick up supplies and then return to Sekhukhuneland. Once they ran out of water, and so Gene went to the river to dig in the almost dry riverbed just as the women of the village did regularly. When the women saw him on his knees, digging in the mud, they were astounded and broke into uproarious laughter: they had never seen a man do such women's work before in their lives.

In general, they were welcomed warmly. How peculiar this all was, to have a white family living in a tent in this rural region among the Africans. But two witchdoctors were not at all bemused. From some of their newfound friends, the Grams learned that the witchdoctors had tried to put spells on them of one sort or another, but nothing at all happened.

One day, heavy rains fell on the area and began to get into the tent. Gene ran out in the rain and dug a trench around it. Afterwards, he felt tired and lay down on his cot, listening to the rainfall outside. It fell steadily for a long time, and as darkness came, Gene said to Phyllis, "Nobody will come to the meeting tonight. I guess we have a night off." But Phyllis did not play her part as a sympathetic wife. "Dear, what if somebody happens to come?" This little exchange was repeated enough times to make Gene angry, and this left him even less inclined to walk through the now pelting rain to the tent, let alone preach.

Of course, he went in the end. He found that the wind had blown the tin covering off the power plant and rain was falling right onto it. "Ah, there is no way this will start now," he said to himself, feeling his spirits rise a little. The generator always took several tries to start, so Gene prepared himself to go through the routine. He would do what was necessary to prove Phyllis wrong about having a meeting that night. To his surprise, the generator started on the very first try, and light flooded the tent. Gene was still convinced that nobody would show up, but he thought that it would be a good idea to walk around inside the tent and pray for the next evening's meeting before he returned to his own crowded little tent. After all, if he returned too soon, he might have another awkward discussion to face with Phyllis. As Gene paced the tent, praying, someone entered. The man was able to speak a little English, and Gene had by now conquered a little Sepedi. After going over the words carefully in his mind, Gene said, "We will not be having a meeting tonight since nobody else is going to come."

The man began to cry. "What is with everybody?" Gene thought. "This meeting is not going to happen." Just then, the interpreter showed up. He was a Bible school student from the Africa Bible Training Institute in Witbank who had relatives in the area. The interpreter was able to explain a little more of the man's story. The man was Abram Moloko,[4] and he had travelled a very long way in the rain to come to this meeting. That was it, there were no more excuses. So, Gene preached, the interpreter interpreted, and the audience of one listened intently. And Abram Moloko was saved that night. In subsequent meetings, Moloko's three brothers also gave their lives to Jesus. And some time later, about 1970, Moloko became a much-loved superintendant of the northern Transvaal district of what would later be called the International Assemblies of God. He lived into his 80s, dying in 2006.

There was also further opposition to the missionary work. Once, a witchdoctor sent greens to Gene and Phyllis to eat that were poisoned. People were always stopping by to talk to the Grams at their tent during the day, and sometimes they brought vegetables from their gardens. Vegetables had to be cleaned carefully with chlorine to kill the bacteria. Still, this time Gene and Phyllis felt checked by the Holy Spirit not to eat the greens at all. Later, a woman told them that they were surprised nothing happened to them. "Those vegetables," she said, "were poisoned."

Chief Maserumule sent his son, Reuben Maserumule, to see what was happening at the meetings. As the first son of his first wife, Reuben was destined to become the chief after his father. Hearing the Gospel proclaimed night after night, Reuben humbled himself before the cross along with many other villagers. Afterwards, he told Gene and Phyllis

---

4. "Moloko" means "relation," "family," or "relative" in Sepedi.

that by becoming a Christian he knew that he would no longer be considered in line to become chief.

After the tent meetings, various Bible school students from ABTI journeyed out to the area to hold meetings, and eventually a pastor was sent to shepherd the church that had been established. No building was erected, though.

Reuben eventually attended ABTI himself. The school was moved from Witbank to Rustenburg in 1960. Several years later, in about 1965, he married a young woman who had been converted in the first tent meeting that the Grams would hold in Mapetla, Soweto. After she became a Christian, the family cut off ties with her and threw her out of the house. She would wait at the tent meeting until everyone else had left, and then she would return home to sleep in the coal box outside, unseen by her family. She was too ashamed to tell anyone at the tent meetings, and so this went on for some time. Eventually, some of the Christians found out, and they were then able to help her. After a few years, the Maserumules moved to Rustenburg, where Reuben became a teacher at ABTI. He gave up his inherited role as paramount chief to serve his Lord in ministry. Today he is a pastor in the northern Transvaal.

17

Testimonies of Transformation: Middelburg

For by grace you have been saved through faith—and this is not from your doing—the gift is from God, not from works, lest anyone boast. For we are His workmanship, created in Christ Jesus for good works, which God prepared beforehand so that we might walk in them. (Ephesians 2.8–10)

THE MIDDELBURG CAMPAIGN WAS held in March and April of 1959. The Grams had primary responsibility in this ministry, although Fred Burke from nearby Witbank also played an active role. One of the great benefits of a missions approach to ministry in any area of the world is that other partners in ministry could be drawn upon as need be. Paul's letters already provide evidence of teamwork in missions, and he and his co-workers also benefitted from partnerships with other Christian missionaries.

In addition to the Burkes at the Bible School in Witbank were James and Beryl Stewart and Louis and Lenore Wilson, who were also close friends of Gene and Phyllis. The Stewarts in particular would later be closely involved in ministry with the Grams. Several Africans were involved in the ministry as well through preaching and translating. Among them were Daniel Seale and Brother Mahlong. Phyllis held women's and children's meetings during the afternoons, teaching, preaching, and leading in worship. One of her co-workers at Middelburg was Joyce Lebelo, the wife of the African pastor in Witbank, John Lebelo. John also taught at the Bible school. Men were firmly in control in African society—more so than in the European culture of the day. Becoming a Christian opened up a new freedom to the women, many of whom were married to unbelievers. They could participate in ministry, discuss the meaning of Scripture and how it applied to their lives, and support each other in the difficulties that they faced. Students from the Africa Bible Training Institute also participated in the campaign, from handing out flyers about the meetings to participating in the ministry. Choirs from the Bible college also contributed greatly.

When Gene and Phyllis established Cape College of Theology in 1985, they remembered how important it had been for the students to learn not only in the classroom but also in active ministry as part of their studies. They initiated various ministries of CCT itself rather than try to find ministry opportunities in churches for the students. In this way, students were trained to work in teams and initiate ministry themselves. One of the great ministries of those later years would be to the street children of Cape Town. The result was not only a great benefit to others but also that graduates of CCT were well prepared for the practice of ministry by the time they graduated.

One of the Assemblies of God ministers who participated briefly in this campaign was a household name for many in South Africa. He was Nicholas Bhengu, a well-known evangelist who also had a following within the denomination. The Assemblies of God in South Africa was a coalition of various freestanding ministries. Its loose organization was as much a blessing on some occasions as a problem on others. Philip Molefe had a group of followers in Sharpeville, Middelburg, Witbank and other areas; Mbata had his following in the Bloemfontein area of the Orange Free State, and Nicholas Bhengu had his own large following in various parts of the country.

Bhengu was a phenomenal speaker. He was a Zulu and the son of a Lutheran pastor. Bhengu's persistent message—one revealed to him in a dream—was "Africa back to God." His first crusade was in Port Elizabeth in 1940, then in East London, and then throughout South Africa,[1] and for another forty years he held crusades around South Africa. In his meetings, he "declared war" on crime and sin, and he could tell stories of countless thieves, gangsters, and murderers who repented of their sins and accepted God.[2] At times, the Spirit of God would fall on the crowds and people—even on children—and they would speak in tongues and prophesy or lay prostrate in the meetings, unable to walk for the power of God.

1. See the brief historical description on the Assemblies of God webpage, http://www.aogm.org.za/ (accessed 31 March, 2010).

2. "The Black Billy Graham."

There was already a church in Middelburg. This was the area where some of the first Pentecostal missionaries had lived and where they were buried. So, after the campaign, the church was able to follow up with the new converts and opportunities that the campaign provided.

As Bhengu approached death in 1985, he was in the Groote Schuur Hospital in Cape Town. Gene went to see him, and the two reminisced about the various work they had been able to do together over the years, including the Middelburg campaign. He said, "I am happy you will be starting a Bible college here in Cape Town and that we will be able to work closely together again." By the mid-1980s, there was discussion of reuniting the various Assemblies of God groups that had divided twenty years earlier. Before the Assemblies of God split in 1964, Bhengu told his followers to boycott the Africa Bible Training Institute in Witbank (which was later the Africa Bible College and then the South Africa School of Theology in Rustenburg), and he instead sent his followers to Union Bible School near Pietermaritzburg. The conciliatory words from Bhengu to Gene these many years later brought Gene great encouragement as he and Phyllis dedicated themselves to starting the Cape College of Theology that would serve various groups and denominations, not just the American related International Assemblies of God.

The Middelburg Campaign produced some encouraging testimonies, which Gene wrote down in the tent meetings and then reported to supporters in the United States. For a few of the testimonies, he would follow up with the individuals after the meeting to make sure that he had heard correctly. The following are some of those testimonies, as the people themselves told them:

Young Man: "I was a great sinner before Jesus found me. I used to think that it was great sport to torture animals to death. One day I gathered together as many cats as I could find and put them into an oven where they soon died. I did many things like this, but I thank God that he has forgiven me and saved my soul."

Teenager: "I was really working for the Devil; dancing, jiving, drinking, smoking and doing many other things when Jesus saved me. My heart is greatly grieved when I remember my sinful life, but I thank God that now I am his child."

Woman: "God has done a wonderful thing for me and my house. When I heard the Word of God preached here I couldn't sleep for two nights until I surrendered my life to Christ. My husband has found the Lord in this tent, and now our home is altogether changed. I thank Jesus!"

Young Man: "I was a great drinker and a servant of Satan. I carried a knife everywhere I went and was always ready to stab anyone on the slightest impulse. Now, I thank Jesus that here in this tent I was set free, and now I carry a Bible in place of the knife."

Former Drunkard: "I was a drunkard and have often been in jail because of my wicked deeds. I took great pleasure in stealing from the helpless, blind, and crippled beggars who sat in the streets pleading for alms. I thank God that this tent came here for it was here that Christ Jesus forgave me and saved me."

Woman (crying as she spoke): "How thankful I am that this tent was erected here. People of this town know that I have lived a very wicked life, but now my burden of sin has been rolled away, and I am so very happy in Jesus."

Former Thief: "I stole a car and many other things and have had to suffer the consequences at the hands of the law. I always carried a knife with me. I was also a great drunkard and once, when being in this state, I even threatened my own mother with my knife. How I thank God that he has now forgiven me and saved me from my many sins."

Young Boy: "I am only a young boy, but already Satan has had his hand on me. I was smoking and starting to drink when Jesus found me in this tent and forgave my sin."

Girl: "I thank God that the tent came here and we were taught about Jesus. He saved me and healed me. Oh, I am so thankful for all that he has done for me already. People may laugh at us, but we don't care because we have Jesus."

Teacher: "I attended church regularly and was active in religious activities. I prayed and thought that I feared God, but I was unhappy. I was so confused in my mind that I was willing to try almost anything in my pursuit of peace. I even went to the Moslems for help. They gave me a copy of their Koran, but that did not succeed in explaining to me God's great plan of salvation. How thankful I am that one night I decided to come to this tent. I was truly lost, but now I am found by Christ. I was in darkness, but now I have come into His wonderful light. I have found Christ in this tent and he filled my every longing. I thank him with all my heart."

Old Man: "I drank much and my whole body was full of pain, but now I am healed and saved. Thank you, Jesus!"

Mother: "I thank God that he saved me and healed my body from my suffering. I had two daughters that were very sinful and I was greatly grieved over the way that they were living. However, I am thankful to God tonight that during these tent meetings both of my daughters were wonderfully saved also. I am very happy."

Another School Teacher (who became a leader in the church and a high school principal): "I used to think that the people who were associated in any way with this tent were just crazy. I saw another tent in Johannesburg in 1955 and again in 1958. Although the presence of this tent greatly troubled me, I would not venture anywhere near it. I did not want to be classified with these fanatics. When I was transferred to a teaching post here in Middelburg, I was sure that there would not be any tents here to bother me. You can imagine my surprise and anger when I saw this tent being erected here in Middelburg. I made up my mind that I would not attend any meetings, but one day my curiosity got the best of me, and I decided to have just a little peek inside. I didn't think it would hurt me that much; so one night I peeked into this tent, and I am so happy to tell you that because of that little peek, I am now saved and following Jesus. How I praise the Lord that he had mercy on me and saved my soul."

Man: "I did not know how to believe in God, but tonight I want to thank God that here in this tent I learned how to have faith in God and to believe him to set me free from my sin. And that is what he has done for me—I am free."

Boy: "I used to attend Sunday School, but afterwards I used to go out and steal anything I could find. I even have a car battery at home and I will now take it back since Jesus has saved my soul."

Dagga (marijuana) Smoker: "I was absolutely no good. I hated my parents and many other people. I smoked dagga cigarettes and did much to displease my Lord. I am so happy that I saw Jesus on the cross in this tent. It was at the cross that I was set free. I rejoice greatly that this light came to the Africans also. I am now completely changed and will soon be baptized."

Young Woman: "I used to drink alcohol which was intended for medicinal purposes and I was a prostitute, but now Christ has forgiven me and He has changed my whole life."

Elderly Man: "God has done so many miracles here in Middelburg. Before the tent came here the young men and boys were all over this township playing dice and gambling. How happy we are today that many of these young men and boys have accepted Jesus and are here with us in this tent tonight. We don't see the dice playing in the streets anymore. Yes, God is really a great God."

Teenager: "I was an awful sinner. Perhaps the greatest sin in my life was that of lying. It seemed as though I just could never tell the truth. I was stealing whatever I could also. How happy I am that one night I came to this tent, for it was here that I saw myself as an awful sinner and needed to be saved. I thank the Lord Jesus for having mercy on me and saving my sinful soul."

Young Woman: "Although my mother taught me to pray and I attended Sunday School when I was a child, I still grew up to be a wicked woman. I began drinking at an early age and have been living the life of a prostitute. Oh, how I thank God that Christ has forgiven me and changed my life completely."

Teenager: "I was a very great sinner. I am ashamed to say that I put many a girl to shame already and I was also a gambler, but now I am free since Jesus washed all my sins away with his precious blood."

Young Man: "At first, when I attended these meetings, I thought that these people here in the tent were just trying to deceive people. However, one day, when I went home from the meeting, I opened the Bible and my eyes fell on a verse that told me that I needed to repent of my sins. I thank God that I can stand here tonight before all of you and say that I am now a child of God."

At the end of this report of testimonies from the Middelburg Campaign, Gene added, "God gave us a most outstanding campaign in Middelburg. These are only a few of the many testimonies that were given and we were able to record. Some of the worst people in Middelburg were converted and are now living respectable Christian lives. To God be all of the Glory!!!" The most significant signs of successful ministry were repentance, transformed lives, and the planting (or, in this case, the strengthening) of a church.

18

Name Above Every Name: Machachan

"But if by the Spirit of God I am casting out demons, then the kingdom of God has come upon you." (Matthew 12.28)

LATER THAT YEAR, THE Grams family camped in an area between Pietersburg and Potgietersrus, by a village called "Machachan." It was a lovely area that lay beside a river. This time, the Grams had a small caravan that they had borrowed from Fred Burke in Witbank. They brought water with them from Pietersburg, but if they ran out, Phyllis would strain water from the riverbed and then bring it to a boil five times to avoid hepatitis, bilharzias, and parasites. The family used powdered milk and had an ice chest. They were able to buy food from the local shop, and villagers would bring them chickens to cook. There were no toilet and bathroom facilities in the caravan or nearby, so the nearby fields had to suffice.

Darrell was supposed to have started school by this time, and he had actually been enrolled in 1st grade briefly. But one day he returned from school and declared, "I don't want to go to school anymore." Gene and Phyllis had wondered whether he was too young to be in school anyway, and they missed him terribly. So they simply said, "Alright, you don't have to go to school this year!" The future lawyer put down his little school case, took off his school uniform, and returned to that wonderful phase of life of imaginative play.

The village of Machachan has long since disappeared, however. Not long after the Grams went there to minister in 1959, the region was designated a "white" area by the government, and so the entire population was moved about ten miles away. The village itself was bulldozed, and the area became farmland. Machachan was an area well known to the

Grams, not only for being close to Pietersburg but also because they had heard their co-worker in the region, Ruth Monroe, tell of her efforts at bringing the Gospel there. Ruth had ministered at Machachan from time to time over six years, but she knew of only two converts for all her efforts. The community was not without a witness to the Gospel: a Roman Catholic church was there at the time. But the village was known for its animist beliefs, and it abounded in witchcraft. Albert Louton had also been working in Machachan more recently, and he was meeting with more success. So the decision was made to put out more effort and see what God would do in this harvest field.

Gene, his father-in-law, and Johannes Mukwevho held daily meetings with the few converts, and Phyllis held afternoon meetings for the children. Mukwevho stayed with one of the African families in the village. Every so often, the Grams would leave the area to spend a few days back in Pietersburg and then return. There was some opposition to the meetings. One night, for example, Mukwevho was leading the meeting on his own when a group of youths entered the tent, brandishing knives. They forced those who had gathered to disperse. Thankfully, nobody was injured.

On the very first Sunday of the tent crusade, Gene and Johannes Mukwevho encountered a female witchdoctor who was possessed by over fifty demons. After the service, the woman walked up onto the platform while Gene and his co-evangelist were ministering to people on the ground. Gene turned around in surprise when he heard the woman speak to him in an American accent. She was glaring at him from the high point of the platform. "You go back to America," she said. "This is no place for you to be. I do not want to see you." Knowing that a demon was speaking from the woman's mouth, Gene and Johannes began to pray. The woman continued, "We are going to the mountains to get reinforcements. We will kill you." The evangelists replied forcefully, "You are going to leave this woman and no longer live in her. Come out in Jesus' name!"

The demons threw the woman violently to the ground. They spoke in English and Venda, Mukwevho's first language. They made fun of the blood that Jesus had shed on the cross. The woman began to cry. This was nothing like the imagined demon possession Gene had witnessed when in Bible school nine years earlier, when an American pastor thought he was contending with a demon of stubbornness in a woman. This was the real thing, straight off the pages of the Gospels and Acts. But Gene and Johannes knew the outcome of those stories, and they knew that Jesus was more powerful than any number of demons.

After some time in prayer, it was clear that some of the demons had left the woman. The next day, Mukwevho and some others continued to pray for the woman until all the demons had left. During this time of prayer, various demons identified themselves. They did not all leave together, but eventually she was completely free. When all the demons had left, the woman spoke to Mukwevho and Gene in Sepedi, since she knew neither Venda nor English.

The woman's son, who was also a witchdoctor, saw how different his mother was. He also knew that his mother had been healed of some sickness, and so he too came for prayer. Then Gene and Johannes talked to them about what it meant to follow Jesus, including the point that one could not follow Satan and Jesus at the same time. "Jesus," they said, "is more powerful than Satan." Both decided to follow only Jesus in their lives, and they brought their witchcraft paraphernalia and placed the items outside the tent. They also broke down the altar at their home where they had worshipped their ancestors. Just before they were baptized, the witchcraft items were burned in a huge pile on which Gene had poured five gallons of gas. Before the items went up in smoke, Gene picked up a few dolls with the thought of keeping one or two as a memory of this event. But the son said, "If you do, I will not be free." So the items went up in smoke, just as the Ephesian converts had burned their books of magic in Acts 19. About thirty people were baptized that day. Only those who had attended classes and whose faith was truly evident were baptized.

The Grams ministered in Machachan about two months. Later that year, Albert and Gene put up a crude place of worship—a roof on poles, with no walls. The roof was made of corrugated iron. Gene always left his hammer with a claw for pulling out nails at the building site, but one day he threw it in the back of his car. As he was driving back to Pietersburg, he saw in the waning daylight some object in the middle of the road, and so he slammed on his breaks. In front of him was a mound of dirt on the road and, on top of it, a pick-up truck on its side. Gene got out of the car to see if he could help. The man in the pick-up was an undertaker, and he had a body in the back of the truck. He was also a very large man and could not climb upwards to get out of the door of his truck. He was screaming for help when Gene appeared. Gene remembered his hammer and, using the claw, pried open the stuck door. But he was unable to help the man out of the vehicle, and so he drove on to Pietersburg for help from the man's son. The two of them returned and were able to rescue the undertaker without anyone crashing into him. The whole task had taken one and a half hours.

Over time, Albert was able to raise funds for a more permanent building for the new church in Machachan. But after all their efforts at providing the congregation a place to worship, a few years later the government destroyed everything when it moved the people away.

Gene and Phyllis wrote about this time in Machachan in a newsletter dated 17th August, 1959 from Pietersburg. Noting how people ceased to do certain things after turning to Christ, they wrote,

> We will never forget the joy of hearing the demons cry for mercy as they were commanded to the depths of hell in the mighty name of Jesus. They had no option, and had to go at the command of the all-powerful name of Jesus. A number of young people have been saved because they had witnessed the mighty power in the name of Jesus. They began to discard certain things that they felt that the Lord was not pleased with in their lives. It is truly wonderful when the Holy Spirit convicts of sin. It isn't necessary then to make rules and laws forbidding things when the conviction of the Holy Spirit is present. Although the progress is slower than we would like to see, we are gradually moving forward in this place in the name of Jesus! Oh, how we praise Him!

The letter went on to mention that several African co-workers were supported by persons in North America, and then Gene and Phyllis asked others to consider if they would like to contribute as well. "Brother and Sister Philip Frey of Windsor, Ontario" were paying the salary of co-evangelist and interpreter Abram Ramalebana.[1] "Sister Marion Arnold of Richmond, Virginia" was supporting various African preachers, including Christopher Pheme's family.

CAPSULE: SUPPORT OF THE NATIONAL CHURCH AND ITS MINISTERS

Support of African ministers was never ongoing; it was always arranged for a period of time until the ministers could get their ministry established. Then the Old Testament principle of tithing was meant to supply the needs of those ministering to the congregations. Missionaries at the time were well aware of the dangers of developing a church that depend-

---

1. Abram Ramalebana tells the story of his conversion and working with Gene Grams in his testimony at http://www.tcg.org.za/Phaahla.htm (accessed 1 May, 2009).

ed on support from the West. The problems of dependency overlapped with problems of colonialism, inequitable relationships that retarded the move towards maturity of the newly established churches. A number of denominations in the early 1970s saw dependency in their mission programs in various countries as such a problem that they called a moratorium on missions, turning over ministries to nationals. The move was only necessary because missions had been established on the wrong footing in the first place, and the moratorium on missions resulted in a large-scale disinvestment in missions altogether. Many Evangelical mission societies and denominations, however, continued their work in missions rather than call a moratorium on missions. They preferred to approach mission work as partnerships with national ministries. While this proved to be a healthy understanding of missions in many ways, it left many a mission agency with too little an understanding of its own mission, turning not a few into match-making agencies that supplied individual missionaries for job openings abroad. Perhaps the future for missions, as many "mission fields" now send their own missionaries abroad, is that mission agencies will regain a sense of their own unique mission and no longer just be sending agencies unable to initiate their own ministry in a region.

Amidst the triumphs of ministry also came personal trials. Gene continued in his letter to mention that Phyllis had broken her foot after slipping on the back step of their house in Pietersburg while doing the washing outdoors. The cast had caused her so much pain that it was removed, but the leg was still swollen and blue. Dennis and Rollin, moreover, were ill during this time from an allergy in the dusty region of the northern Transvaal. The Christian life is not a road of constant triumphs, of healing, and salvation. It is, after all, a life lived out in a world that still awaits the final victory of Jesus Christ over sin, suffering, sickness, evil, and death. Jesus' cross and resurrection have signaled the end of all this suffering, such that we can say, "Where, oh death, is your sting?" (1 Cor 15.55). Yet, prior to Christ's future coming in final triumph over all His enemies, life slouches inexorably towards death. A broken leg and two little boys' allergies in the midst of dramatic healings and deliverances from demons remind us of this.

19

God's Gold

But thanks be to God, who always leads us in triumph in Christ
and spreads the fragrant knowledge of him everywhere through
us. (Second Corinthians 2.14)

IN EARLY 1960, GENE and Phyllis discussed their plans for ministry
yet again. They had moved many times in the previous years. After
returning from the United States in 1955, they lived in Pietersburg for all
of a month. Then they lived in a house in Bedelia in Welkom for about
four months. Then they lived in their house in Dagbreek, Welkom where
Dennis was born, for just over one year. Then they moved to their third
home in Welkom on June 15th, 1957, the house in Naudeville, where Rollin
was born thirteen months later. But only seven months after the move to
Naudeville, the Grams spent four months studying Sesotho in Lesotho.
Eight months later, they moved to the Transvaal for a year, spending much
of the time camping in the remote areas where they ministered. They then
returned to the house in Naudeville in December, 1959.

But they almost immediately decided that this was a mistake.
Despondent and embarrassed, they faced the facts that stood squarely before them. They simply could not find places to hold meetings, and even if
they did, the local governments were so non-cooperative with their ministry that they could not secure sites on which to build any church buildings.
They had to move again, they thought. So they made plans to return to the
northern Transvaal. This time, they would study Sepedi at Laura Waite's
mission station, Bethesda, about one hundred miles from Pietersburg and
continue ministry in the surrounding villages as before.

Yet this never happened. They would never live in the northern
Transvaal again. Their plans to move had gone very far indeed, however.
They had arranged to rent the house to a minister and his family who

were moving from just outside Welkom. The Grams' household goods were already packed into the garage, Phyllis and the children were outside, and Gene was taking some curtains down. These were the last items to be removed from the house. In five minutes, they would be on their way to the Transvaal. But as Gene took down the curtains, he felt checked in his spirit. God spoke to him in his thoughts. "Who told you to go? You are completely out of order. If you would be patient, you would see great things."

Gene ran outside. As he passed the family, Phyllis asked where he was headed. "No time to explain," he called back to his bewildered wife. He jumped into the car and drove to the Babour and Thorne estate agents. We are not going to leave Welkom," he stated. "We are staying in our house. Do you have any other houses for rent like ours?" The family that was to move into their house was already en-route. The agent looked through his listings and found no possibilities. Just then, a secretary brought a note to the agent that said a new home had come available to rent. "I'll take this one," Gene said, and ran out of the office. The agent called after him, "But you haven't even seen it." "We have no choice," Gene called back. He then drove on the road out of town and, not long later, discovered the moving van. After flagging the vehicle down, he learned that the new renter was in the truck. Gene explained that they could either rent the house on Lena St. or the new house that Gene had found at the estate agent. The family decided to move into the new house—they even thought that it was better—and so the Grams moved their belongings back into their house that same day. Phyllis and the children were happy to move back into their own home.

"Now, what will God do?" Gene and Phyllis asked. A little over a year later, they would write the following to supporters in the United States in September, 1961:

> "Now thanks be unto God who causes us to triumph . . ." (2 Cor 2.14).
>
> On Sunday, September 10th, we witnessed the fulfilment of our prayers, desires and dreams over the past six years. The mountain that seemed insurmountable was conquered. The river which seemed uncrossable was crossed. At long last, we dedicated our beautiful new church in Welkom [i.e., Thabong]. It's all a great miracle which began to unfold in October, 1960.

Gene's friend, the Sharpeville, Transvaal-based evangelist, Rev. Philip F. Molefe, had said to him, "Let me do the evangelizing and you do the teaching." Gene agreed, and the two men, almost the same age, began plans for what would be known as the Meloding Revival. Gene's close friend and former colleague in ministry in the northern Transvaal, Johannes Mukwevho, also joined them in the Free State at this time.

When Gene wrote in October, 1960 in the *Pentecostal Evangel* about the wonderful ministry of God in Meloding earlier that year, he spoke of it as a "revival."[1] The revival lasted most of the year.

CAPSULE: REVIVAL

"Revival" is a loose term. It could be used to refer to bringing a lethargic church back to life, or even an active church closer to God. We might think of the letters to the seven churches in the book of Revelation for such a notion of revival. The term can also refer to a series of evangelistic meetings, where the emphasis lies on bringing people to Christ for the first time. We might think of a Biblical passage like Acts 2 for this view of revival, when Peter addresses a large crowd in the context of miraculous signs and many become Christians. John 3.3, 7 uses the Greek language's double meaning of "born again" and "born from above" to refer to salvation. In 2 Cor 5.17 Paul refers to life in Christ as "new creation." Finally, Ephesians 2.1–7 also captures the idea of revival:

> And you, being dead in your trespasses and sins in which you once walked in accordance with this world order, in accordance with the ruler of the authority of the air, the spirit who is now working in the children of disobedience; in which also we ourselves once walked in the desires of our flesh when we acted out the desires of our flesh and thoughts; indeed, we were by nature wrathful children, just like everyone else. But God, being rich in mercy, on account of His great love with which He loved us, even when we were dead in transgressions, made us alive with Christ—you have been saved by grace—raised us up, and seated us in the heavenlies with Christ Jesus, in order that He might reveal in ages to come the superabundant wealth of His grace in His kindness to us in Christ Jesus.

It is this second sense in which the term might apply to the Meloding Revival, although the actual terms used at the outset seem to have been "tent campaign" or "crusade." Today, the word "crusade" is no longer help-

---

1. Grams, "Revival," 14–15.

ful, being too militaristic a metaphor with associations of church-backed "holy war" against Islam—hardly an image one wishes to conjure up for Christian ministry. Even "campaign" has militaristic connotations, and perhaps "revival" is the best term, capturing the idea of God's resurrection power bringing new life to those who are dead in their sins. As Paul put it, "If anyone is in Christ—new creation!" (2 Cor 5.17).

The revival in Meloding was, moreover, in the Pauline sense, a ministry in word and deed, by the power of signs and wonders in the power of the Holy Spirit (Rom 15.18–19). The change that revival entails is not a mere metaphor: it is seen in the transforming power of the Holy Spirit. Such transformation is a clear demonstration not only of God's new creation but also of his love. All this—new creation, transforming power, love—can be summed up in a single word: "grace." It is a grace found in the death of Jesus on the cross for our sins and his resurrection from the dead. "Grace" and Jesus' cross and resurrection also move us beyond doctrinal concepts of revival. As church historian Richard Lovelace says, "Spiritual life is produced by the presence and empowering of the Holy Spirit, not simply by the comprehension of doctrinal propositions or strategies of renewal."[2]

There were already a handful of believers in the Assemblies of God church in Meloding before the revival was planned. They formed a house fellowship with the pastor, Rev. Tsotetse. The tent campaign was, however, an effort by others on behalf of this little church that did not even have a building. Rev. Philip Molefe came from Sharpeville for the initial meetings in March and April of 1960, and then again in August of the same year. Johannes Mukwevho also came down from Louis Trichardt in the northern Transvaal when he heard that a translator was needed for these meetings. He and Philip Molefe had worked together before in

---

2. Lovelace, Dynamics," 79. This quotation puts us in touch with what some theologians are calling "primary" or "first" theology. In describing this, Kevin Vanhoozer asks, " . . . is God more like seeing or tasting? In other words, should theology begin with abstract propositional knowledge or with concrete, personal knowledge?" (First Theology, 19). He adds, "The postmodern condition has awakened theologians from their dogmatic slumbers—to be precise, from the dream that doctrine or system is the be-all and end-all of theology" (39). He offers instead what he terms "first theology," which he defines as "performance knowledge, a matter of doing the Word, of living, as well as looking, along the text" (39).

Sharpeville, just as he and Gene had also worked so well together. The Assemblies of God work in Sharpeville began about five years earlier than that in Meloding. The initial converts in the revival campaign led by Molefe totalled 325. They were baptized in the river, and then they all marched through the township singing, "I will follow Jesus."[3]

The plan was that Molefe would be the primary evangelist, and Gene would be the primary teacher during the revival. Gene would also raise funds, engage the various government officials in securing sites for church buildings, and interact with the police. Rev. Bethuel Mofokeng, also from Sharpeville, came to speak in the meetings, as did several others. One of these was Rev. John Tlotlalemajoe, who organized counselors, that is, people who could talk with those wishing to give their lives to Christ after a service and pray with them. He eventually became the pastor of the church in Thabong, Welkom.[4] Choirs from established churches came on various nights by bus to sing. Christian films and testimonies also conveyed the Gospel, and Gene later held six weeks of Bible doctrine classes for the new believers. There were speakers who addressed women and children as well. Phyllis Grams had oversight for this work, although, again, a number of persons were involved.

Announcements of the intended meetings began with the help of someone from Mission Aviation. This missionary suggested that pamphlets be drawn up and dropped over Meloding from the air. Gene was not too certain about this approach, but as the man wanted to play a part, he found himself dropping leaflets announcing the meetings from several hundred feet above the township as the other missionary piloted the plane. Later on, Gene was somewhat discouraged when he discovered that the leaflets were being used for toilet paper, but, one way or another, news of the tent meetings did get around.

The handful of believers in the Meloding church used to meet in an unfinished, rented house, and a larger place was needed for the campaign. The local government gave its permission to erect a tent in Meloding from the 5th of March to the 5th of April, 1960. But the revival required extending this period several times so that the tent campaign lasted, as they had in other regions, about three months. The tent itself had to be extended to accommodate the large crowds, which, at times, could even

3. Pettenger, "Sharpeville Massacre," 15.

4. Rev. Tlotlalemajoe has remained the pastor in Thabong all these years. At the time of writing, he is in his mid-eighties.

reach 2,000 people. As the numbers swelled, many in attendance had to stand or sit outside, but they were still able to hear everything over the public address system. The combined attendance over the first weeks of meetings was over 40,000, if one adds up the attendance for each of the nights. Many people returned night after night, but people not only came from Meloding. Others came from all over the Orange Free State, parts of Basutoland, and even the southern Transvaal. By the time that the campaign ended, the tent was in ruins, in part because of the high winds that blew across the area.

On the first night of the tent campaign, Mr. Phera, a member of the Location Advisory Board for Meloding, became a Christian. That day, he had had a quarrel with his wife and had beaten her severely. By evening, he was intoxicated and stumbled to a seat in the tent. During the service, he sobered up and responded to the Holy Spirit's speaking to his heart. His life was forever changed that night. His wife saw the difference in her husband over the next few days and also became a Christian. To have such a testimony from a man of such standing in the local government "stirred all of Virginia," wrote Eugene Grams in a newsletter. Many who came to the tent meetings from the area came because they had heard what had happened to Mr. Phera. Some said, "If God can change a wicked drunkard like Mr. Phera, He can also change me."

Early in the campaign, three or four gang members became Christians. They would sit, night after night, in the front row seats. Alongside the nightly message explaining salvation in Jesus Christ, the campaign had a theme: *God can do anything. There is nothing too difficult for God.*[5] He can make the vilest sinner clean, can transform lives, deliver people from demon possession, heal the sick, and restore broken relationships: God can do anything. Mr. Phera had discovered this the first night of the campaign, and these former gang members could testify to the change in their lives as well.

But one night, about two weeks into the campaign, Gene noticed that the former gang members were not present. He feared the worst: were they, like the seed that fell among the rocks in Jesus' parable of the sower, going to wither and die after a short, encouraging growth spurt? Gene could hardly preach as he turned this thought over and over in his mind.

All of a sudden everyone in the tent heard the worst noise imaginable. All eyes turned to the back of the tent and saw the tent flaps being

5. Luke 1.37; cf. John 15.16.

pulled back. The former gang members walked in, dragging a man who was entirely naked and shrieking. The men delivered him to the front of the meeting, tied up with ropes and belts. He struggled to free himself but was securely bound. Gene looked at the former gang members for some sort of explanation. One young man said, "Moruti Grams, you have been telling us that God can do anything. What about this?" Gene looked back at the man, a wild man completely out of his mind, as close to an animal as a human can become. And yet he was even worse off than that, for Gene could see that the man was possessed by demons. His eyes were clouded, as though in a trance, and he did not seem in control of his own person or able to interact with others at all. He had descended into an internal world of torment. A woman came up and covered his nakedness with her Basotho blanket.

The man was well known in the area. He lived mostly in the cemetery but was also known to wander aimlessly far and wide, through fields and along the roadsides. Once he wandered as far away as Vereeniging, nearly 150 miles away, and back.

As when the paralytic man was lowered through the roof by his friends in the middle of Jesus' teaching in a packed house, this meeting came to a standstill. It is one thing to speak of God's Kingdom, that God was powerfully present, but it is quite another to have to stand up to a challenge to this message. The entire campaign could be discredited: if the God who can do anything could not help this madman, the speakers would be false witnesses, people's hopes would be dashed, and the church in Meloding would be demoralized and perhaps even disband.

Gene and Phyllis, together with some other believers in the meeting, began to pray for the man. They prayed for about two hours while people watched: could God help the wild man of Meloding? Then, suddenly, the man's eyes became clear and he looked around as though to say, "Where am I?" The trance-like state that he had been in for years broke. He identified himself as Thomas Khajwane.

Thomas Khajwane was reborn that evening. He was transferred from demonic possession to the freedom of a child of God. In the following days, Gene and other ministers visited his home and met his parents. Gene's Sesotho was still not strong enough to engage the conversation that he needed to have with Khajwane, and Khajwane did not know any English. So an interpreter was also present. His parents were present too. They showed Gene the paraphernalia purchased at great expense from witchdoctors to ward off evil spirits. Some pieces of red, electrical wire, bought from the witchdoctor at an exorbitant price of 60 pounds were placed at the entrance to the home and in the ceiling—a graphic symbol of power, pointed defiantly towards any invading spirit. But they were powerless to keep away the evil spirits.

The transformation of Thomas Khajwane, needless to say, brought others to the tent campaign. His parents became Christians, as did many others, including a young woman who would become Thomas's wife. The two would not long hence have a baby girl, whom they named Eugenia.

Soon after his conversion, Thomas explained through an interpreter, "Moruti Grams, I have never been to school a day in my life. How can I ever grow in the Lord unless I am able to read His Word?" God proved His power once again in this life. Only six weeks later Thomas Khajwane demonstrated to Gene Grams that he could read both Sesotho and English perfectly. He soon became a member of the church choir and later on was made an esteemed member of the town council.

20

Restitution

Once he was standing, Zacchaeus said to the Lord,"'Look, Lord, I am giving half of my possessions to the poor, and if I defrauded anyone of anything, I will restore four times the amount." So Jesus said to him, "Today salvation has come to this house, because even this man is a son of Abraham." (Luke 19.8–9)

ANOTHER CONVERT IN THE Meloding revival was David Khalu. The man had become a petty thief in the downward spiral of his life, and his conversion, like that of another thief in Scripture, Zacchaeus the tax collector, involved making restitution. He had been a school principal some time earlier, but he had lost his job due to heavy drinking. This problem also cost him his next job as a bus driver. Virtually every night, David Khalu would show up at the meetings with some stolen goods to leave at the front of the tent. Sometimes he would arrive with a wheelbarrow filled with stolen goods, as he did the night that he showed up with the front door of his house. He had stolen it from a building site. "Revival" in these meetings was not merely a matter of asking for forgiveness and being forgiven for past sins. It was also a matter of making restitution. After his conversion, Khalu went on to become a successful salesman, selling rather than stealing things.

On one of the evenings of the tent meetings, Gene asked David Khalu to give the testimony of his recent conversion. He came forward, ascended the platform, and then turned to ask Gene what he should call him. "Shall I call you sir or boss or reverend?" he asked. Gene replied, "How about brother?" He walked over to David Khalu and threw his arms around him. Khalu was taken aback. Here, in the heart of Afrikanerdom, where apartheid was both political policy and doctrine, was a white man asking to be called his brother. "I never in all my life," said David, "thought that I would ever be permitted to call a white man my brother, let alone have him give me a hug." The transforming power of God's revival was also at work in those meetings to resolve the anger and hatred manifested in the deep-seated racism and violent reaction to it that was festering in South Africa at that very time in riots.

In the middle of the initial phase of the revival, the name of Sharpeville became known around the world. The African National Congress and the Pan-African Congress, both opposing the Nationalist Party that ruled the country and composed mostly of non-Europeans, began to organize protests against the pass laws. On the 21st of March, 1960, the day after the eighth anniversary of Gene and Phyllis, 5,000 to 7,000 black Africans converged on the police station in Sharpeville in a peaceful protest that turned ugly. Sixty-nine people were killed and one hundred and eighty were injured when the police opened fire on the crowd. Protests, riots, and strikes sprung up around the country in the following week, and the government called a state of emergency. Sharpeville was known both for the tragedy of the massacre and for marking the transition in South Africa from peaceful protests to violent, armed struggle against the white, Nationalist regime. The success of the revival back in Meloding, however, had the support of the local police, and so the meetings were not disbanded during the emergency. The town council gave special permission for the meetings to continue.

In Sharpeville, the opposition to the government prepared a statement that they insisted was to be read in every church. When ministers in the Sharpeville Assembly of God church examined the statement, they determined not to read it. It called for a violent struggle against the government. The day after the statement was to be read, leaders of the opposition came to the church to inform them that the penalty for not reading their statement would be meted out that night: the church building would be burnt down to the ground. At the time, Philip Molefe was away in Meloding, and John Tlotlalemajoe was left to address the situation. He called the church together into the building, and the people began to pray. While they were praying, people outside brought wood and placed it all around the walls of the church building. They then drenched the wood with fuel. But, try as they might, they could not light the fuel. God miraculously delivered them from the attack. When the people inside realized what was happening, their prayers for protection turned to praise. The building was spared, and the people were left alone.

States of emergency were declared periodically for fear of revolution. During one of these (possibly in 1961), Gene travelled with fellow missionary Ervin E. Shaffer to Douglas in the Cape Province. Shaffer believed that God wanted them to hold a meeting there. When they arrived in Douglas, they reported to the police headquarters to make their request to hold a public meeting. Gene said, "We have a public address system, poles, and lanterns and would like to preach to the Africans this evening in the open air." The dumbfounded police stated the obvious: "There is a state of emergency on and no public meetings are allowed. You cannot do this." Gene replied, "But we believe God wants us to do this. Would it not be possible to hold this meeting if you accompanied us?" The police discussed this for a while and decided to permit the meeting. So the two missionaries were accompanied by twenty-five policemen into the African location. A crowd of hundreds gathered at the sight of the lanterns and the police. Many responded to the message of salvation, including about half of the policemen.

The emergency situation in South Africa at the time of Sharpeville brought about an earnestness among believers to seek God's presence. Fifty-four days after the Meloding Revival began, on the 29th April, 1960, Gene wrote about his Bible classes to Rev. Raymond Brock, editor of the American Assemblies of God church magazine, the *Pentecostal Evangel*. Meetings were also permitted to continue in Thabong, and Gene was able to hold his Bible classes there as well. In his letter, he mentioned that believers came an hour early to the Bible classes in order "to pray and seek God for a great outpouring of His Spirit in South Africa." He also noted that, with virtually all other meetings banned, people who otherwise might not have been interested in Christian meetings were attending: "Many people who want to go somewhere, but find no place to go, come to the meetings. It has resulted in some finding the Lord. The government authorities are" now urging us to "speed up our evangelization program as they are beginning to realize that Africa's only hope is Jesus."

Gene again wrote Rev. Brock on the 30th June and included information about the "continuous revival" in Meloding. He was eager to have Rev. Brock publish an article on the revival to encourage others in the Assemblies of God "to press on to revival." In this he seems to have been keenly aware of the importance of testimonies about God's empowering presence and transforming work for others to have their faith strengthened.

CAPSULE: DYNAMICS OF REVIVAL

Faith that God does work His will, that He lovingly pursues us, and that His power is present to transform us seem to be key elements for revival. This faith, moreover, is expressed in an earnest seeking of God, a seeking God in prayer, a tarrying expectantly in God's presence. Not only had believers in the Orange Free State been meeting more for prayer during the revival, but in this letter Gene says that his information about the revival "may be of special interest especially since all of you [those at the Assemblies of God headquarters in Springfield, Missouri] have been praying in Springfield for a greater blessing on God's work." Prayer is not only an expression of faith, it is also "effective." As James says, "The prayer of a righteous person is ever so effective in its working" (James 5.16).

There is, then, a relationship between repentance, God's transformation of lives, public testimonies, faith, an earnest seeking of God, and prayer. Testimonies about God's work of renewal in people's lives increase faith, an increase of faith is expressed in an earnest seeking of God, of His Kingdom and righteousness, which also involves a boldness in prayer to which God responds. Prayer is both a result of increased faith and a cause for God's gracious, powerful presence among his people. Church historians point out the importance of prayer for revival, and this was equally true of the Meloding Revival. Knowing this, many a church seeks to promote prayer, but all too often without testimony. In the case of the Meloding Revival, testimonies of persons from the earlier Sharpeville Revival, of work God had done in the Grams' ministry earlier in the 1950s in the northern Transvaal, and of those being dramatically changed in the present revival led to a fervency of prayer. And the state of emergency in the country contributed to the people's earnestness in prayer. Thus it would not be incorrect to say that prayer cannot be separated out from true testimonies of God's powerful, loving, transforming presence, from the increase of faith among the faithful, or from a fervent seeking after God's righteousness and presence. If the Meloding Revival can teach us what revival is, it can also teach us something about the precursors to revival: prayer and testimonies that increase our faith in and expectancy before God.

The dynamics of revival involve a changed relationship to God as well as a changed relationship to others. This is why teaching was a major part of the revivals. In South Africa in particular, one of the fruits of salvation was unity among believers despite apartheid. Another dynamic was restitution. Entering into intentional fellowship in Christ that entailed care for one another was a further feature of revival. If God offered healing to the needy, believers were taught in this grace to meet each others' needs. Even if evangelism was the primary emphasis, a holistic theology developed from the dynamics of revival.[1]

The Meloding Revival continued to deliver stories of transformed lives. David Khalu's desire to make things right with God gives us an example of what it might mean to seek God's righteousness earnestly. One late night during the tent meetings, he remembered yet another item that he had stolen. He returned home to find his wife fast asleep in bed. He could not help waking her up as he removed their duvet from the bed. His wife was beside herself. It was about 40 degrees Fahrenheit[2] outside at night this time of year, and her husband had already removed the front door to the house. Now he was taking their bed cover. David tried to explain. He said, "Jesus could return tonight, and we do not want to be found with any stolen goods in our house when he does." This sort of behavior finally proved too much for his wife. She tried to have David committed to a mental institution. Some six months later, however, the powerful transformation in his life convinced her to give her life to Christ as well. She later became the leader of the women's work in the church—a ministry that sometimes involved raising money by making blankets.

There were several physical healings during this revival that also testified to the greatness of God. The parents of a deaf and dumb girl brought their daughter to the meetings from as far away as Klerksdorp, about two hundred miles to the north. As the ministry team prayed for her, she was instantly healed. The next day she began to speak, and she improved in her speaking daily. Another deaf girl from Maseru, about two hundred miles to the south, was completely healed after prayer.

Without any coaxing on the ministers' part, people kept returning stolen goods to the tent meetings. Boxes of wrist watches, jewelry, illegal weapons, coshes, amulets, witch doctor's horns, a primus stove, materi-

---

1. See my article, "Transformation Mission Theology," 193-212. *Transformation,* the journal of the Oxford Centre for Mission Studies in the United Kingdom, is available online through the OCMS webpage: www.ocms.ac.uk. Not only is my article published in this journal, but the journal explores holistic mission theology and practice internationally.

2. That is, 4.4 degrees Celsius.

als from building sites, tables, chairs, beds, dagga (marijuana), daggers—whatever seemed to be of value—were daily collected and placed in the church's nearby rented house. The house actually did not yet have the roof on it, and so a tarpaulin was placed over it to provide temporary shelter. A number of those who became Christians were well-known persons and businessmen in the area, but there were also a number of criminals and *tsotsies* (gang members) who became Christians. Rev. Mofokeng himself had been a *tsotsi* before being saved and becoming a minister in the Assemblies of God. As people came to the front of the tent to repent, a number of them could be seen reaching into their coats to produce some piece of stolen property as discreetly as possible, particularly when they were illegal weapons.

It soon became obvious that a church building of some sort would be needed for the growing church of Meloding. Gene first went to the town authorities regarding a building site for the church. But the white man in charge of such matters treated him with contempt. When he would see Gene coming, he would lock the door and call him derogatory names, cursing him from his window. To him, Gene was someone who was propagating a new religion that loved blacks. Land was at a premium in these booming towns of the Orange Free State goldfields, and the authorities were hardly going to squander it on Gene Grams and his African "brothers." The official called him *"Kaffir bootie,"* the derogatory term in Afrikaans that Gene's neighbor had once used of him.

Gene bore such abuse without much concern. He knew his African brothers and sisters labored under far more misery. For example, Gene one day drove somewhere with an African pastor named Rev. Pemmi. They stopped for food at a drive-in restaurant. When served, the waiter asked if the passenger was a *"kaffir."* Gene replied that his passenger was a pastor. The man responded that *"kaffirs"* were not allowed to eat at the restaurant. So Gene drove off while the restaurant owner shouted after and cursed him. He and the pastor bought some food at a nearby shop and fixed their own sandwiches.

As Gene was getting nowhere with the official about a building site for the church in Meloding, and as the need for a church site was dire, God removed the man for three months. For whatever reason, the official was given an unusual blessing, a three-month holiday. The man who replaced the official deferred to his superior, a Mr. Smit, in this matter of a church site.

Gene's first encounter with Mr. Smit was equally negative. The high winds that whipped across the Orange Free State had displaced some roof tiles on the Grams' house. Gene was on the roof repairing the damage when a telephone call from Mr. Smit came. Gene climbed down from the roof and entered the house. Picking up the telephone, he heard Mr. Smit briefly introduce himself and insist that he come to his office immediately. Gene explained that he was in the middle of fixing his roof, but the man was short and unwavering, "Do not even clean yourself up. I must see you immediately."

When Gene entered Mr. Smit's office, he saw revolvers and pistols on the desk. Mr. Smit then showed him other illegal weapons. Gene quipped, "Well, are you going to shoot me now?" "This is a very serious matter," the man replied. "One of our plain clothed detectives tells us that your people are planning to riot against the pass laws. They have burned their pass books." He said that the weapons in his office had recently been confiscated in the township, and that the police were very concerned about a possible riot along the lines of Sharpeville. Gene had not been at the tent meeting the previous night, but he said, "If this is true, it has nothing to do with those who have given their lives to Christ in these meetings, for a Christian would not do such a thing." Christians do, of course, do such things: some even see it as their duty to oppose unjust laws, and some, sadly, have done so by using violence, as in the American Revolution. But these believers sought to pray for everyone, including government officials, and to live a quiet life in an unjust world (1 Tim 2.1–2), choosing rather to be wronged (1 Cor 6.7) than to defame the name of their Savior. Gene was right: these believers would never do such a thing. When he left the meeting, the matter hung heavily over him.

He enquired of those who had been at the meeting the previous night and found out that there were no plans among the people whatsoever to burn pass books or even to demonstrate. Not long later, Mr. Smit called Gene to his office again. He was deeply embarrassed and began to apologize for his previous accusations when they first met. As it turned out, the detective in question had fabricated the story. He was a member of the Jehovah's Witnesses, and he thought that his false testimony would discredit the revival.

Meetings with Philip Molefe resumed later that year, in August of 1960. Again, people surrendered stolen goods. At one point in the campaign, Gene announced that they would take all stolen goods to the police on the people's behalf. A newspaper reporter from the *Goldfield's Friend* wrote up the story in an article published under the title "Surrendered Loot the Proof of Conversion" on the 28th of October, 1960. A picture of some of the stolen goods showed mostly items taken from building sites. But the night that Gene announced that stolen items would be returned to the police on the people's behalf, a man in a sharp, expensive black suit came forward to receive Christ as his Savior. As he was kneeling at the front of the tent, he pulled out eight large uncut diamonds—illegal, stolen property from the diamond mines of South Africa. The man said stealing diamonds had been his livelihood, and he had made considerable money in the illegal diamond trade. But he knew that following Christ meant giving all this up, and he urged Gene to take the diamonds on his behalf to the police. Gene joked with him, "So you want me to go to jail instead of you?" Mere possession of uncut diamonds would land one with a stiff jail sentence. The man simply said, "I think they'll listen to you." Gene took the diamonds and placed them in his coat pocket.

The next day, Gene went to the Virginia police station with his three ton, Bedford truck—the truck used to haul the tent—piled high with stolen goods. The truck had been purchased from John Richards with funds raised for the tent meetings. About this time, the Grams also purchased a second car for the family, a Messerschmitt. This little car had three wheels, and the entire roof lifted up on the side, exactly like the cockpit of the airplane version of this German invention. Only one person could sit in the front seat but all three children could fit into the back seat, and they loved to take rides. Instead of a steering wheel, the car had handlebars. It could reach speeds up to fifty miles per hour, and it handled like a motorized sidecar to a motorcycle. The Bedford, Plymouth, and Messerschmitt were a strange site in the Grams' driveway (as were the Grams' new pets, Rover the Doberman and Jolly the cat, who often slept peacefully together outside).

At the Virginia police station, Gene found a long queue of black Africans and took his place at the back. The officer at the desk called him forward because he was white, but Gene insisted on waiting his turn in the queue. He was, after all, a "*kaffir bootie.*" He waited about an hour, and when he got to the desk he felt the Holy Spirit check him: this was not the place. So he said, "I think I'm in the wrong place." The surprised officer asked what he needed, but Gene simply replied, "No, I'm very sorry, but I am in the wrong place." Then he left and climbed into the cab of the truck. He prayed for wisdom. Then the idea suddenly came into his head: go to the Criminal Investigations Department (CID)—eighteen miles back up the road in Welkom.

Upon walking into the offices of the CID, Gene was met by a desk sergeant whose primary role in life seemed to be to protect the man behind the closed door, the head of the security force for the northern Orange Free State. "If you write a letter explaining the purpose of your visit, we will inform you within two weeks whether it will be possible to see Gen. Hendrick Van den Bergh," the sergeant explained in the logic of bureaucracy the world over. Gene managed to direct the sergeant over to the window. They were on the second floor of the building, and they could see the truckload of stolen goods below. "That truck is full of stolen goods," he pleaded, "I need to see Gen. Van den Bergh right away." But the sergeant was unimpressed, as though he saw such things every week. Then Gene slapped his arms to his sides in frustration. He had completely forgotten about the uncut diamonds in his pocket from the night before, and thankfully he had worn the same suit the next day. He pulled out the diamonds and showed them to the dumb-founded sergeant. "Now will you let me see the General?" he asked. In less than a minute he was in the general's office.

Van den Bergh rose from behind his desk to greet Gene. To Gene, who was 5 feet 6 inches in height, the General, who was about one foot taller, seemed to keep rising for some time. They shook hands, and Van den Bergh said in his heavy Afrikaans accent, "I've been waiting to meet you for some time now." Skirting over the innuendo that he had been under the observation of the secret police, Gene replied, "Well, it almost did not happen." He produced the diamonds. "Man, this is worth a lot of money," the general said. "Sit down, please. You don't know much about me, but I certainly know a lot about you. Your file is building almost every day." He told Gene that the CID kept sending plain clothed detectives to spy on the meetings to see what was happening. "And when they report back to us, they tell us that they have become one of you!" Gene remembered praying with several policemen at the altar.

Then Van den Bergh buzzed his sergeant and explained that he was not to be disturbed under any circumstances. The sergeant was, no doubt, quite capable of fulfilling this request. For four hours, the two men talked together about Gene's ministry in the area and the current tent campaign in Meloding, the stolen goods, and then more personal matters. Not long before this, Van den Bergh's daughter, Lorraine, had died from cancer. He himself was a member of a church, and he was eager to open his heart to another Christian. But he especially wanted to find out how he could know if, when he died, he would go to heaven. His daughter had become a Christian shortly before her death. He had heard some of the dramatic testimonies of transformed lives from the Meloding Revival. But his own minister had answered this same question about the assurance of salvation by saying that, in fact, we do not know if God will accept us before we stand in his presence on the day of judgment. "I'd be the happiest man in the world if I could know whether I am going to go to heaven," said Van den Bergh. "You can know today, Sir," said Gene. He explained that salvation was not by works but through faith in Jesus Christ, who shed his blood for our transgressions. This was God's doing, not ours, and so we could know that, if we give our lives to Him, He would be faithful to us. And, as we trust in Him, we begin to know His transforming power in our lives here and now. The giant general put his hands and head down on his desk and wept like a child. The two men prayed together.

For the duration of his time in the Orange Free State, Gen. Van den Bergh helped the African believers in various ways. He was eventually promoted to oversee security for the entire country and moved to Pretoria. His questionable role in the apartheid government of South Africa is a matter for the history books, but his role in helping to build two black African church buildings out of his own personal finances will not likely be found there. It is an incredible story: that the future chief of security for the apartheid government would do anything for black South Africans would probably not be believed by the majority of persons in South Africa if it were widely known. But if one were to drive to Thabong, one would find a strangely named church building, the Lorraine Memorial Assembly of God Church, a testimony to the truth of this story.

Van den Bergh had wanted to do something to help the ministry that Gene and Phyllis Grams were undertaking in the area. "Well, if you want to help," Gene replied one day, "we are having trouble finding building sites." "Do you have any money for a building?" the general asked. "Yes, about $100." "Man, you are not going to build much of a building with that!" He himself negotiated the land for the church site in Thabong, telling the officials that, if there was no land, they should donate the police station since the Assemblies of God was doing more to fight crime than the police. While there were no available sites on record, the town council investigated further and discovered that property already committed to a Swiss Mission was no longer needed. This was then given to the Assemblies of God. In the end, not only did Van den Bergh help to build the church building in Thabong, but he also supplied the finances for fifty workers over six weeks to construct the church building in Meloding. After all the difficulty to secure church sites and to finance the buildings, between the 2nd of April, 1961 and the 1st of April, 1962, four church buildings were constructed. In addition to Thabong and Meloding, buildings for Odendaalsrus and Winburg were also built.

21

Fields White for the Harvest

Then he said to his disciples, "The harvest is plentiful, but the laborers are few; so ask the Lord of the harvest to send laborers into his harvest." (Matthew 9.37–38)

WHILE MINISTRY IN THE Orange Free State continued, another evangelistic campaign was planned for Sharpeville in December, 1960. Philip Molefe returned to his home church for these meetings, leaving Meloding after a number of successful months of ministry. In 1964, a report in the *Pentecostal Evangel* stated that Sharpeville was the "evangelistic centre" for the Assemblies of God and that meetings "have been conducted every night in the week and three times on Sunday for more than eight years, and the revival continues."[1]

In a newsletter after the December 1960 convention in Sharpeville, Gene and Phyllis wrote:

> We are still rejoicing in the blessings of the great Convention in Sharpeville from December 24th through New Year's Day. The large tent was too small to accommodate the more than 1200 believers that usually attended the services. We were thrilled to see that about three hundred of that number were from the Orange Free State. They hired trucks and cars to go to Sharpeville to share the blessings of the Convention. Early each morning hungry seekers assembled in the tent to ask God for the infilling of the Holy Spirit. Many dozens met with God's conditions and received the Pentecostal experience. This seemed to have a great effect on all the other services. The spiritual tide was high and often waves of blessing would sweep over the people. We thank God for the many African ministers and evangelists whom

1. "Progress of Pentecost in South Africa," 8.

He has raised up to take the message of "Light" to those who still are sitting in darkness. Together with Brother Philip Molefe, our gifted African evangelist, whose ministry was greatly blessed during 1960, were many others who contributed much to the great success and blessing of the Convention. Our missionaries and visiting ministers who ministered during the Convention included Vernon Pettenger, Edgar Pettenger, Lewis Wilson, Eugene Grams, Fred Burke, Ed Rill, John Garlock, Robert Bolton, missionary to Formosa en-route to the USA, and Don Northrupp, Director of World Missions, Inc. in Africa.

The climax and highlight of the Convention was the great baptismal service in which 197 followed the Lord through the water. Of those 108 were from the Orange Free State. Following the service at the river there was a victory march through the streets of Sharpeville. As the large crowd of more than one thousand marched past the police station we were reminded of the more than seventy dead and nearly two hundred wounded which lay on the same street during the riots last March. What a contrast to see the hundreds of waving Bibles and songs of victory as the saints marched to the tent for the afternoon service. The Lord has certainly given great blessing and revival in the midst of such great trouble.

They continued in the same letter to report that, by the end of 1960, there were over 1,000 in the Sunday School programs for Odendaalsrus (Kutlwanong), Welkom (Thabong), and Virginia (Meloding). In Welkom, there were nearly 600 in Sunday School. Phyllis gave oversight to the Orange Free State Sunday School ministry, from planning curriculum and making it available to training teachers. Her counterpart was Joy Adams in the northern Transvaal, who also worked in child evangelism. Mabel Pettenger had pioneered the Sunday School ministry throughout South Africa for the Assemblies of God by offering courses to train teachers and Christian workers, who would then start new Sunday Schools.

As Gene and Phyllis gave their exciting report of ministry at the close of 1960 to supporting churches, they also divulged plans for ministry in 1961. Early in the year, there would be an Easter Rally with the Orange Free State churches. The church choirs were preparing to sing various songs and then unite their voices in the Hallelujah Chorus. While they reported the need for funds for church buildings, more funds were also needed for the evangelistic services. A tent had already been purchased. It measured 100 by 60 feet. But another $3,000 was needed for seating and a platform, and $1,000 was needed for adequate lighting.

Gene and Phyllis were involved in several places of ministry other than Odendaalsrus, Welkom, Virginia, and Winburg in 1961–1962. A church was started in Heilbron, and a house was used for the place of meeting. Interior walls were torn down, and a brief evangelistic campaign was held to boost membership. Another evangelistic campaign was held in a school in Klerksdorp in the same year to expand the church where Rev. Khumalo was the pastor. Rev. Daniel Seale, with whom Gene would work in years to come, started to have house meetings in Senekal and was able to establish a church. Seale had become a Christian during meetings in Sharpeville that were held by Philip Molefe. The Grams were somewhat involved with these ministries.

But much of 1961 and part of 1962 would be spent in overseeing the building of the four churches in Odendaalsrus, Thabong, Meloding, and Winburg. The church building in Odendaalsrus took four years to build due to a lack of funds. For a long time, this church had nothing more than a foundation. The parishioners tried hard to raise funds for the building project, but they had such meager incomes that hardly any progress could be made. There were no loans available for Africans, as there were for the wealthier whites, and so the church just had to make do with what they had. What they had was a little corrugated iron shack in which to meet, alongside the pastor's house.

Gene's and Phyllis's excitement over the upcoming dedication of a church building in Odendaalsrus could not be measured: they had been frustrated so many times in trying to secure church buildings in the Orange Free State. They wrote the Assemblies of God Field Secretary for missions in Africa and asked him to be the dedicatory speaker. When the building was dedicated, the growing congregation and those visiting brought what they had collected over a long period of time to offer towards the cost. Lewis Wilson, one of the missionaries, wrote about the sacrificial giving that day:

> Although most of the visiting friends had no building in their own town in which to worship, they had come prepared to give in the dedication offering. From their own incomes, most of them had brought a pound ($2.80). In turn, each visiting church delegation marched forward with its gift. When the gifts were counted, it was announced that the cheerful but sacrificial offerings amounted to $930—one third of the total building cost![2]

2. Wilson, "Odendaalsrus," 24–25. Two pictures of the church and its new building may be found in this article.

The building had been completed on credit from the builders, and this offering went a long way towards liquidating it. This was the first African church building to be built for the Assemblies of God in the goldfields area of the Orange Free State.

In his newsletter of June, 1961, Eugene Grams announced the news that in the previous week a church site had been allotted in Thabong to the Assemblies of God by the local government. Just a few months prior, a great wind had destroyed the building that was being used for services. The church then moved to the facilities of a local school, but these were inadequate for the size of the church.

Van den Bergh's role in building the Thabong and Meloding church buildings was known to a few, including some of the Africans, but he asked that during his service in the government his name not be used. Gene visited him a number of times over the years, including at his new office in Pretoria when he was the head of the Borough of State Security for South Africa. After being escorted down four corridors by various security officials, Gene sat down in the office of the chief of national security for South Africa. On such occasions, he was always served hot tea. This symbol of hospitality and culture was wasted on him: Gene hated tea. Of course, he drank it politely and then, as his cup was re-filled, avoided the slightest sign of the agony that this brought him. As the General and the missionary chatted over tea on one occasion, the General said, "These offices are full of all kinds of microphone wires, so let's talk it up for Jesus. Who knows? Someone might listen to the tapes some day and become a Christian." On another visit, Van den Bergh asked his secretary to bring in the file on Gene Grams that the govern-ment was keeping on him. It was massive, containing notes on what he said in meetings around the country, his movements, telephone conver-sations, and so forth. Gene was not permitted to look into the file, but it was a friendly warning that for the Grams family there was no privacy in the apartheid police state.

On the day before the dedication of the church building in Thabong, Van den Bergh asked Gene Grams for a shilling.[3] When Gene gave it to him he explained, "Now, if anyone ever asks you if you paid for this church building yourself, you can tell him, 'Yes'; you just don't have to

3. Van den Bergh's picture at the dedication of the Lorraine Memorial Assembly of God Church can be seen in a brief article about the occasion: see Grams, "Welcome Gift for Welkom," 11.

tell him how much." The funding of this building was the General's memorial to his daughter, his personal thanks to the Assemblies of God's efforts in helping reduce crime through transforming lives through evangelism, and perhaps a "thank offering" to whatever work God had done in his own life. In actual fact, Gene had insisted that Van den Bergh not pay for everything in the construction so that there was a sense of partnership and ownership on the congregation's side. Members of the congregation purchased Coca Cola and meat in large quantities, then placed the items in baskets on their bicycles and sold them door-to-door. In this way, they managed to raise funds for the fence, cement walks, furniture, and paint. The church building was valued at $15,000 and was completed in six weeks. It measured 80 by 35 feet. In addition to the auditorium, it had a choir loft, an impressive entrance, and three offices. The auditorium could seat 400 people and had church pews made of Philippine mahogany.

On the day of the dedication of the Thabong church building, more than 700 people attended, including Gen. Van den Berg. Vernon Pettenger spoke briefly at the dedication of the building and then cut the ribbon and officially opened the doors. Those who could not get in for lack of space gathered around the open windows.

Inside the building, the General Secretary of the South African Assemblies of God, L. B. Potgieter, preached a sermon, visiting church choirs sang, and Paul Masondo of Brakpan, Transvaal, offered the dedicatory prayer. Then P. F. Molefe presented the keys and charged the church board members to be faithful in caring for this building. The pastor appointed to the church was Rev. John Thotlhalemajoe, who had relocated from Sharpeville.

The third church building to be built in one year was in Meloding. While Van den Bergh provided labor for the church building in Meloding, most of the rest of the building costs were funded by a supporter in the United States who said that God told him to give sacrificially for this need. Thus the church building was named after Rev. Karl Loenser, the Superintendent of the German Branch of the Assemblies of God in America. It was given the awkward name of "Loenser Ebenezer Temple." "Ebenezer" refers to the stone of remembrance raised by the prophet Samuel (1 Sam. 7.12). It carried the meaning "Thus far the LORD has helped us," a help that came not only through faithful supporters such as Karl Loenser and through the various ministers that had helped to establish the church, but also through the signs and wonders of God Himself in the great Meloding Revival.

The building site for this church building in Meloding, Virginia was offered to the church by Mr. Smit, the official who was so apologetic for accusing those associated with the revival of plans for political unrest. He offered the choicest site in the entire township to the church in Meloding, right at the very center of town. The cornerstone was laid on the 20th of August, 1961. As the building neared completion, he said to Gene, "There is no electricity in the township as yet. Would you like to be the first to receive electricity?" He brought in electrical lines from several miles away and was honored to flip the switch at the church building on the momentous evening that Meloding received electricity. The crowd cheered as the first light in the entire area flooded the building. Mr. Smit then apologized to the Africans gathered there for mistreating them in the past and asked for forgiveness. It was a joyful repentance, graciously received. Three weeks later, at the young age of thirty-nine years old, Mr. Smit dropped dead of a heart attack.

The tent campaign in Meloding had begun on the 5th of March, 1960. Periodically, groups of converts would be bussed north to Sharpeville to join others for baptism. The reason for this was that the revival that started there in about 1956 was seen as a continuous revival in the southern Transvaal and the Orange Free State. Rev. Molefe pastored the Assemblies of God church in Sharpeville and was the evangelist in Meloding. Rev. Tlotlalemajoe came from Sharpeville to participate in the tent campaign and pastor the church in Thabong. Choirs and others from Sharpeville came to participate in the ministry efforts in the goldfield region of the Orange Free State. So the churches here were related to the Sharpeville church through such partnerships, and the baptismal services were, therefore, initially held in Sharpeville. On the 27th of December, 1960, 258 new converts from the Orange Free State were baptized in a river there.

CAPSULE: BAPTISM AND TRANSFORMATION

A theology of adult baptism worked well in Africa. It lacked the cuteness of a Western, infant baptism, with the child in a baptismal gown, the family gathered around, and the child being named for life in a community of Christians. Baptism was not an occasion for a settled Christian community to affirm its Christian identity as new generations were born. Many in Africa were turning from Animism, witchcraft, and sinful ways, and adult immersion upon confessing Christ for the first time demonstrated the transformation taking place. Baptism was a symbol of radical transformation, a repentance for the forgiveness of sin (Mark 1.4), a participation in Christ's death and resurrection (Rom 6.3–7), a pledge to God for a good conscience that comes as a result of Christ's resurrection (1 Pet 3.21), and an event of being joined to the unity of community in Christ where there were no divisions (Gal 3.27–28).

So these events were large and celebratory. People bussed in from the surrounding regions. Choirs sang. Crowds gathered on the banks of a river. People held each other's hands as they entered the waters so as not to be swept away in the current, but this also symbolized the new unity of those from every tribe in South Africa baptized into Christ. The new converts were fully immersed: this was no less transformative than birth or marriage, even if the stated theology of baptism was that it was not a sacrament but an ordinance in the church. Everything about this shouted: "you are being baptized by the Spirit into a new community in Christ." There was no expectation of a gradual growth into Christ as a child grew up, attended Sunday School, was confirmed at about twelve years of age, and came to "own" a faith already "sealed" by the parents. This was rather a radical change.

Of course, these were Pentecostal churches, closely related to other churches in the holiness movement associated with Wesleyanism. For them, conversion and baptism were not the only transformative events in believers' lives. Sanctification was closely tied to conversion, as the repentance from sin and restitution in the revivals demonstrated. Salvation was never thought of as a human work, as though God would offer salvation to those who had done enough good in their lives. Salvation was by God's grace. But conversion could not be thought of distinctly from living a life of holiness—being separated to God, as though one could be saved and still live a sinful life. No Pentecostal could ever agree with Martin Luther that to be saved by grace alone through faith could mean that the believer could sin boldly, confident in the knowledge of God's sovereign will and grace![4] No repentance was acceptable without restitution and change. No regeneration in a person's life was complete with justification apart from sanctification. Christ's work in salvation meant

4. See Martin Luther's letter no. 99 to Melanchthon on 1 August, 1521 in *Saemmtliche Schriften*, ed. Walch.

not only a change of status but also a moral transformation. While Pentecostals did not affirm complete sanctification as a state the believer could reach in this life, whether by effort or grace, it was a clearly evident process in the life of one who had given his or her life to Christ.

But there was more. The message of Pentecost was that there was indeed more. There was also the present power of God. Christ's powerful work was also restorative: people were healed and demonic forces were submitting as God's Kingdom advanced. The power of God was present here and now, even if the battle still raged and sin, suffering, and death were yet to be finally and completely vanquished at Christ's second coming. The church of Jesus Christ was being built in fresh territory that the enemy once thought was his. Converts were taught that God not only gave them his Spirit at conversion but also wanted to fill them with his Spirit. The image for this teaching was of a full pan of water (the Holy Spirit given at conversion) that was put onto a hot burner such that the water bubbled over (the filling of the believer with the Holy Spirit).[5]

In a brief news item dated the 25 of December, 1960 in the American *Pentecostal Evangel*, readers found the following update on the Meloding Revival:

> *Revival Continues in Spite of Political Unrest*
> Recently 80 believers were filled with the Holy Spirit in an eight-day Pentecostal outpouring in Virginia, South Africa," reports Missionary Eugene Grams. "Last March about 200 people were saved during tent meetings with Evangelist Philip Molefe . . . .

In June the next year, Eugene Grams again wrote in a newsletter about the Meloding church: "Only a few weeks ago the Power of God fell one evening as I was conducting a Bible Study and again more than twenty were filled with the Holy Spirit for the first time."

---

5. In Assemblies of God teaching, this overflowing of the Spirit was always thought to be evidenced through speaking in tongues, as well as through other possible signs. Not every Pentecostal group holds to the teaching that speaking in tongues is always the initial evidence of being filled with the Holy Spirit. But this is frequently the belief of Pentecostals. Problematic for such a teaching is Paul's question, "Do all have gifts of healing? Do all speak in tongues? Do all interpret?" (1 Cor 12.30). Paul's expected answer is, "No."

The fourth church to be built in one year in the Orange Free State's goldfield towns was in Winburg, to the south of Welkom. The pastor here was David Pinda, who moved to the area in order to start the church. He, and sometimes Gene and Phyllis, would hold outdoor meetings since there was no building and there was no tent campaign in the beginning. A church without a building was soon established, a great illustration that the church is not a building but a community of believers in Christ who are involved in each other's lives in Spirit-gifted ministry. However, a building was eventually built and dedicated on the 1st of April, 1962. Unfortunately, however, the African community was required a few years later to make way in the town's plans for expansion. So they were moved a few miles to the south of Winburg, and the church once again testified to the fact that Christians are the church, with or without a building. The new believers of Winburg were, as Paul wrote about Christians in general, no longer

> strangers and foreigners but . . . fellow citizens with the saints and people who dwell in God's home, . . . [because they had] been built upon the foundation of the apostles and prophets, its cornerstone being Christ Jesus, in whom the whole dwelling is brought into unity and grows into a holy people in the Lord, in which also [they themselves were] being built together into God's dwelling place in the Spirit (Eph 2.19–22).

With the establishment of these churches and the construction of four buildings for them, a second term of mission work in South Africa came to its conclusion. The Grams had observed God's grace outpoured in the townships and villages of the northern Transvaal and in the Orange Free State goldfields and towns as people came to Christ. They had rejoiced to see lives dramatically transformed. And they had helped form believers into churches that were related to the growing number of God's people and nurtured in the faith. Gene and Phyllis had worked shoulder to shoulder with others in evangelism and church planting. With pastors in place for each of the churches, they knew that the believers' faith in God would grow through their knowledge of the Word of God, that their love for one another would grow in the fellowship they now had in Christ, and that they would abound in hope by the power of the Holy Spirit. They rejoiced over the privilege it had been to work in God's field and to watch as the Lord brought in his abundant harvest.

Afterword

... if indeed you have heard of the stewardship of the grace of
God given me for you .... (Ephesians 3.2)

In May of 1962, the Grams family returned to the United States for
their delayed furlough. They did so by airplane for the first time, travelling from Johannesburg to Entebbe, Uganda to Cairo, Egypt to London,
England to Reykjavik, Iceland to New York to Detroit. Intercontinental
air travel had arrived.

Gene and Phyllis left South Africa with a sense of fulfillment, even
though this was but the beginning of many fruitful years of ministry.
They would return to South Africa a year and a half later in 1964, thinking that their ministry in the Orange Free State would continue. But they
would move again, this time to the Johannesburg area to begin ministry
in places like Soweto. They would continue in evangelistic tent meetings,
Sunday School ministries, and starting churches and building church
buildings until they had seen over fifty churches established. Gene would
travel throughout South Africa, Lesotho, Mozambique, Rhodesia, and
Botswana as one of the missionaries on the International Assemblies of
God's Missionary Field Fellowship's executive board.

After six years in the United States, from 1974–1980, they would
return to South Africa without their children, who were by that time old
enough to fend for themselves in the United States and subject to the
compulsory military draft were they to return to South Africa. By the
mid-1980s, Gene and Phyllis were involved in a new ministry altogether: establishing and teaching in a Bible college in Cape Town—the Cape
College of Theology.[1] Gene would be its first principal. CCT produced
many ministers during those years who pastor today throughout South
Africa and also minister abroad.

From time to time within the years of the 1970s and 1990s, Gene
would minister on the pastoral staffs of Riverside Tabernacle in Flint,

1. Cape College of Theology is now called the Cape Theological Seminary.

197

Michigan and Trinity Assembly of God in Mt. Morris, Michigan—he would finally get that pastoral experience in the United States that many thought he should have before becoming a missionary. At Trinity Assembly, pastored at the time by his old friend Rev. Dave Krist, Gene would begin a church-based college, the Trinity School of Theology, training people in the region in theological studies as they prepared for ministry. Phyllis would essentially bring her days of ministry to a conclusion at this church as she directed a large children's church and taught at Trinity School of Theology. Defying retirement, Gene would yearly return with Phyllis to South Africa to hold seminars in the churches of former students. They would be sent out through support handled by the International Outreach Ministries of Mount Hope Church in Lansing, Michigan that is pastored by Rev. Dave Williams. They also moved back to the Flint, Michigan area in 2009, where Gene serves part time on the pastoral staff of New Life Christian Fellowship in Grand Blanc, planning to return when he can to minister in South Africa. Many in the church, including the pastor, Rev. Bob Roberts, have known the Grams family since the mid-1970s and supported the Grams' ministry through prayer, finances, personal fellowship, and practical assistance.

The story of the lives of Gene and Phyllis runs parallel to the years of apartheid in South Africa and beyond. It covers the greater part of the history of the American Assemblies of God in that country to date. It explores some of the variety of Pentecostalism since the 1930s and into the twenty-first century in the United States of America and South Africa. It illustrates the labors in ministry that went on by numerous other missionaries, evangelists, pastors and teachers, including nationals, in Africa such that missiologists today speak of a shift in Christianity to the so-called "Global South." Their story engages the great missiological questions for Christian missions, and in it we joyfully see that Jesus Christ is indeed building his church, and no power can prevail against it.[2] But most of all, it testifies to the grace that God has poured out on His people in South Africa.

---

2. Many of the stories included in this book testify to this fact: there is no power on earth or under the earth that can stand against the power of Jesus Christ, who has been exalted and seated at God's right hand in the heavenly places, "high above every ruler and authority and power and dominion and every name that is named, not only in this age but also in that to come" (Eph 1.21).

God did this through those who simply and faithfully serve.[3] The God who has planned from the foundations of the earth to show to the world his unfathomable glory has done so by lavishing his grace in Christ Jesus (Eph 1.3–14) on the unworthy (Eph 2.8) through his stewards of grace (Eph 3.2) in order that the church might be holy and without blemish (Eph 5.25–27), sealed by the Holy Spirit (Eph 1.13–14). Such is the mission of God that he accomplishes through his stewards of grace in the church.

3. In Ephesians 3.2, Paul speaks of his ministry as a "stewardship of the grace of God given me for you" (see v. 7). This marvelous understanding of ministry wonderfully eclipses the preferred term for ministry since the mid-1980s: "leadership." Stewards are servants. What they offer is not theirs but their master's. They are not even "servant leaders," as though they can serve others by the strength they themselves have in power, position, or property. Rather, they are "stewards of grace"—God's grace.

Bibliography

Anderson, Allan. *An Introduction to Pentecostalism: Global Charismatic Community.* Cambridge: Cambridge University Press, 2004.

———. "Pentecostals and Apartheid in South Africa During Ninety Years 1908–1998." *Cyberjournal for Pentecostal–Charismatic Research* 9 (February 2001). No pages. Online: http://www.pctii.org/cyberj/cyberj9/anderson.html.

———. "Signs and Blunders: Pentecostal Mission Issues at 'Home and Abroad' in the Twentieth Century." *Henry Martyn Centre* (paper delivered 17 February, 2000). No pages. Online: http://www.martynmission.cam.ac.uk/CSigns.htm. Also published in *JAM* 2/2 (2000) 193–210.

———. "To All Points of the Compass: The Azusa Street Revival and Global Pentecostalism." *Enrichment Journal* (Spring, 2006). No pages. Online: http://enrichment journal.ag.org/200602/200602_164_AllPoints.cfm.

Barnard, Verna. "A Letter from South Africa." *The Pentecost* (July, 1909) 3.

Barwich, Leopold Karl. *Menschen zwischen Welten Heimatbuch Welimirowatz.* Trans. Henry Fischer (1985). Online: http://www.hrastovac.net/slavonia/welemirowatz2.htm.

Bauckham, Richard. *Bible and Mission: Christian Witness in a Postmodern World.* Carlisle: Paternoster and Grand Rapids: Baker, 2003.

"The Black Billy Graham." *Time Magazine* (November 23, 1959). No pages. Online: http://www.time.com/time/magazine/article/0,9171,865071-1,00.html.

Blakeney, Joseph F. "An Encouraging Word From Durban, South Africa." *Weekly Evangel* (February 2, 1918) 5.

———. "Durban, Natal, South Africa." *The Weekly Evangel* (August 18, 1917) 12.

Booysen, G. J. "An Appeal from South Africa." *Weekly Pentecost* (23 December, 1916) 13.

Bosch, David. *Transforming Mission: Paradigm Shifts in Theology of Mission.* Maryknoll, NY: Orbis, 1991.

Brueggemann, Walter, editor. *Hope for the World: Mission in a Global Context.* Louisville: Westminster John Knox, 2001.

Carmichael, Christine. "Progress of Pentecost in South Africa." *Pentecostal Evangel* (May 31, 1964) 7–8.

Chandomba, Lyton. *The History of Apostolic Faith Mission and Other Pentecostal Missions in South Africa.* Keynes, UK: AuthorHouse, 2007.

Clark, Matthew S. "Two Contrasting Models of Missions in South Africa: The Apostolic Faith Mission and the Assemblies of God." *Asia Journal of Pentecostal Studies* 8:1 (2005) 143–161. Online: http://www.apts.edu/aeimages//File/AJPS_PDF/05-1 -MClark.pdf.

Dugmore, W. F. "From Johannesburg, South Africa." *The Weekly Evangel* (July 29, 1916).

———. "A Visit to Zululand." *The Christian Evangel* (November 7, 1914).

Frodsham, Stanley. *With Signs Following.* 3rd edition. Springfield, MO: Gospel Publishing, 1946. Online: http://wesdennison.com/Books/Stanley%20Frodsham/With%20 Signs%20Following/Chapter%2015%20pages%20155-163.htm.

Gohr, Glenn. "Now You Will Know . . . Whatever Happened to Lillian Riggs." *Assemblies of God Heritage,* Vol. 8.1 (Spring, 1988) 7. Online: http://ifphc.org/pdf /Heritage/1988_01.pdf.

Grams, Eugene E. "Revival in Orange Free State." *Pentecostal Evangel* (16 Oct., 1960) 14–15.

——. "Welcome Gift for Welkom." *Pentecostal Evangel* (March 18, 1962) 11.

Grams, Monroe D. "Dad's Faith." *Pentecostal Evangel* (June 15, 1969) 8–9.

Grams, Rollin G. "Transformation Mission Theology: Its History, Theology and Hermeneutics." *Transformation* 2007 (Vol. 24, 4) 193–212.

Rill, Ruth Burke. "Blessings and Hardships: Experiences of the Fred Burke Family in Africa." *Heritage,* Vol. 13.4 (Winter, 1993) 4–5, 25. Online: http://ifphc.org/pdf //Heritage/1993_04.pdf.

Hooper, Ernest. "God's Blessings in the South African Missions." *The Latter Rain Evangel* (April, 1929) 13–14.

Ingham, John J. "Black Diamonds From Darkest Africa." *The Weekly Evangel* (February 16, 1918) 4–5.

Ingram, Mrs. John W. "Glorious Convention at Pretoria, South Africa." *The Weekly Evangel* (July 22, 1916) 7, 9.

Jennings, Charles A. "Life and Ministry of John Alexander Dowie." No pages. Online: http://www.truthinhistory.org/life-ministry-of-john-alexander-dowie.html.

Kerr, W. J. "Has Pentecost Come to Johannesburg?" *Confidence* II.2 (February, 1909) 27–31. Online: http://ifphc.org/pdf/Confidence/02-1909.pdf#Page3.

Kirk, Andrew. *What is Mission? Theological Explorations.* London: Dartman, Longman, and Todd, 1999.

Lake, John G. "A Call for Helpers." *The Pentecost* (December, 1908) 7.

——. "Asleep in Jesus." *The Pentecost* (January–February, 1909) 4.

"Latest News from Africa," *The Pentecost* (September 1908) 2.

Lehman, J. O. "Apostolic Revival in South Africa: People Being Saved, Healed, Sanctified, and Baptized in the Holy Ghost in Great Numbers." *The Pentecost* (December, 1908) 1–2.

——. "Missionary Work Amongst the Natives in the Mines of Johannesburg." *The Pentecost* (June, 1909) 1–2.

Lindsay, Gordon. *John Alexander Dowie: A Life Story of Trials, Tragedies and Triumphs.* Christ for the Nations, Inc., 1951. No pages. Online: http://sites.google.com/site /leavesofhealing/leavesofhealingpartone%3Athelife (accessed 26 February, 2010).

——. *John G. Lake: Apostle to Africa.* Christ for the Nations, 1981.

Lovelace, Richard. *Dynamics of Spiritual Life: An Evangelical Theology of Renewal.* Downers Grove, IL: InterVarsity, 1979.

Luther, Martin. "Letter no. 99 to Melanchthon on 1 August, 1521." *Saemmtliche Schriften,* Vol. 15, col. 2590. Edited by Johannes Georg Walch. St. Louis: Concordia, n.d.

McGee, Gary. "Three Notable Women in Pentecostal Ministry." In "Women in Ministry." *A/G Heritage,* special edition. (Spring 1985–6) 3–5. Online: http://ifphc.org/pdf /Heritage/1986_01.pdf.

Menzies, William W. *Anointed To Serve: The Story of the Assemblies of God.* Springfield, MO: Logion, 1993.

Murray, Stuart. *Biblical Interpretation in the Anabaptist Tradition.* Kitchener, Ontario: Pandora, 2000.

Newberry, Warren Bruce. "Major Missiological Motifs in North American Classical Pentecostal Missions." PhD diss., University of South Africa, 1999.

"Operation Demonstration: CAs Illustrate a Year of Speed–the–Light." *Heritage* (Winter, 1996–97) 18. Also in *Pentecostal Evangel* (30th April, 1967) 24.

"A Pentecostal Revival in Zion City, USA," *Confidence* (April, 1913) 79.

Pettenger, Edgar. "1500 Attend Conference in South Africa." *Pentecostal Evangel* (January 26, 1958) 16.

Pettenger, Vernon. "Before the Sharpeville Massacre." *Pentecostal Evangel* (June 5, 1960) 15.

———. "Missionary Healed in South Africa." *Pentecostal Evangel* (May 22, 1966) 14.

Piper, John. *Let the Nations Be Glad: The Supremacy of God in Missions*. Grand Rapids: Baker, 1993.

"Progress of Pentecost in South Africa." *Pentecostal Evangel* (May 31, 1964) 8.

Reitz, Ada. "South Africa Work Prospering." *Pentecostal Evangel* (August 17, 1940) 9.

"Report of the South African District Council of the Assemblies of God." *Pentecostal Evangel* (May 5, 1928) 11.

Richards, John. "Miraculously Healed for Service in Africa: Fruits of Pioneering in the Northern Transvaal." *Latter Rain Evangel* (August 1, 1932) 20–22.

Schneiderman, Lillie. "A Letter from South Africa." *The Pentecost* (November, 1908) 2.

Schneiderman, Louie. "Called to the Jews." *The Pentecost* (September, 1908) 2–3.

———. "News from Natal." *The Pentecost* (November, 1908) 2–3.

Schoffeleers, Matthew. "Folk Christology in Africa: The Dialectics of the Nganga Paradigm." *Journal of Religion in Africa* 19.2 (June, 1989) 157–83.

Scofield, C. I. "Rightly Dividing the Word of Truth." Originally written in 1885. Online: http://www.biblebelievers.com/scofield/index.html.

Short, Kenneth. "77–A–Minute." *Pentecostal Evangel* (13 Oct., 1957) 14–15, 31.

Spooner, Kenneth E. M. Blessed Outpouring in South Africa." *Pentecostal Evangel* (January 21, 1922) 13.

Synan, Vinson. *The Holiness Pentecostal Tradition: Charismatic Movements in the Twentieth Century*. Grand Rapids, MI: Eerdmans, 1997.

———. "The Origins of the Pentecostal Movement." No pages. Online: http://joyfulministry.com/synanf.htm.

Turney, H. M. "Tests, Triumphs, and Trials in Africa." *The Weekly Evangel* (February 10, 1917) 12.

van der Merwe, Werner. "Alexander A. B. Merensky." In *The Encyclopaedia Africana Dictionary of African Biography*. Vol. Three: *South Africa–Botswana–Lesotho–Swaziland*, edited by Keith Irvine. Algonac, MI: Reference Publications, 1995. Online: http://www.dacb.org/stories/southafrica/merensky_alexander.html.

Vanhoozer, Kevin. *First Theology: God, Scripture and Hermeneutics*. Leicester, UK: Apollos, 2002.

Wacker, Grant. *Heaven Below: Early Pentecostals and American Culture*. Cambridge, MA: Harvard University Press, 2003.

Watt, C. P. *The Assemblies of God: A Missiological Evaluation*. MTh diss. University of South Africa, 1991.

Watt, Peter. *From Africa's Soil: The Story of the Assemblies of God in Southern Africa*. Cape Town: CTP, 1992.

Weaver, C. Douglas. *William Marion Branham: A Study of the Prophetic in American Pentecostalism*. Macon, GA: Mercer, 2000.

Wilson, Lewis. "Odendaalsrus." In "South Africa Digest." *Pentecostal Evangel* (Nov., 1962) 24–25. Online: http://ifphc.org/pdf/PentecostalEvangel/1960-1969/1962/1962_11_18.pdf.